INTERCULTURAL MUSIC STUDIES
12

INTERCULTURAL MUSIC STUDIES
12

Edited by Karl Reichl and Linda Fujie
A Series of the Department of Ethnomusicology
Otto-Friedrich University of Bamberg

ISSN 1435-5590

Karl Reichl (Ed.)

The Oral Epic:
Performance and Music

VWB – Verlag für Wissenschaft und Bildung

Die Deutsche Bibliothek CIP – Cataloguing-in-Publication Data

The **oral epic** : performance and music / Karl Reichl (ed.). - Berlin :
VWB, Verlag für Wiss. und Bildung, 2000

(Intercultural music studies ; 12)
ISBN 3-86135-643-0

By Promotion of the Deutsche Forschungsgemeinschaft (DFG)

Max Peter Baumann
Department of Ethnomusicology
Otto-Friedrich University of Bamberg
Feldkirchstraße 21, D-96045 Bamberg / Germany
http://www.uni-bamberg.de/~ba2fm3/home.html

© Copyright 2000 by
VWB – Verlag für Wissenschaft und Bildung
Amand Aglaster
Besselstr. 13 • D-10969 Berlin / Germany
Phone: +49-30-251 04 15 • Fax: +49-30-251 11 36
E-mail: 100615.1565@compuserve.com
Web Site: http://www.vwb-verlag.com

music

CONTENTS

Preface   vii

1 Introduction: The Music and Performance of Oral Epics   1
   Karl Reichl

2 Epic as Music: Rhapsodic Models of Homer in Plato's *Timaeus*
   and *Critias*   41
   Gregory Nagy

3 Music of South Slavic Epics   69
   Stephen Erdely

4 The Singing of Albanian Heroic Poetry   83
   Wolf Dietrich

5 Creativity in Performance: Words and Music in Balkan
   and Old French Epic   95
   Margaret H. Beissinger

6 The Singing Traditions of Turkmen Epic Poetry   115
   Dzhamilya Kurbanova

7 The Performance of the Karakalpak *Zhyrau*   129
   Karl Reichl

8 *Dudak değmez*: A Form of Poetry Competition among
   the *Aşıks* of Anatolia   151
   Emine Gürsoy-Naskali

9 The Musical Curtain: Music as a Structural Marker in Epic Performance 159
   Hiromi Lorraine Sakata

10 The Power of Performance: West Mongolian Heroic Epics   171
   Carole Pegg

11 Singing Epics among the Palawan Highlanders (Philippines):
   Musical and Vocal Styles   191
   Nicole Revel

12 Word and Music: The Epic Genre of the *Fulbe* of Massina (Mali)   211
   Christiane Seydou

13 The Performance of Old Norse Eddic Poetry: A Retrospective   225
   Joseph Harris

14 Reflections on the Music of Medieval Narrative Poetry   233
   John Stevens

PREFACE

There is plenty of evidence that both in ancient Greece and in medieval Europe orally performed epics were sung rather than spoken, often to the accompaniment of a musical instrument. Although scholars studying epics such as the *Iliad*, the *Odyssey* or the *Chanson de Roland* have commented on this fact, little progress has been made in incorporating the musical and more generally the performative aspect of oral epic into their interpretations. This is partly explained by the scarcity of musical documents that have come down to us. There is, however, a wealth of comparative material from living traditions of oral epic. The analysis of at least some of these traditions and the implications of their study for traditional medieval epics (and possibly also the Homeric poems) forms the subject of this book.

The chapters of this book are based on the papers given at an international colloquium on the performance and music of oral epic poetry, which took place at the University of Bonn from 7 to 10 September 1997. It was organized to inaugurate my "Forschungsstelle für mündliche Epik und mittelalterliche Oralität" at the English Department of the University of Bonn. I am grateful to the "Deutsche Forschungsgemeinschaft" for a generous grant, which allowed me also to invite two bards from Central Asia to take part in the colloquium and perform for the participants. The singer Zhumabay-zhyrau Bazarov was born in 1927 and lives in Shomanay, Karakalpakistan (Aral Sea region of Uzbekistan). He is the last Karakalpak *zhyrau* (singer of epics) who learned his repertoire in the traditional manner. In the 1940s, he spent three years with a famous Karakalpak bard, from whom he acquired his repertoire in a purely oral way. Zhumabay-zhyrau knows three lengthy epics (*Edige*, *Qoblan*, *Sharyar*), the performance of which lasts for several nights. The singer accompanies himself on the *qobyz*, a two-stringed fiddle of a fairly archaic type. The singer Allaberdi Ödeev was born in 1972 and comes from the Mary region of Turkmenistan. Although Allaberdi Ödeev is still a young man, he has already mastered a number of oral epics, both of a heroic and a more romance-like nature. He accompanies himself on the *dutar*, a two-stringed lute.

Also present at the symposium were Barbara Thornton and Benjamin Bagy of the early music group *Sequentia*. Benjamin Bagy performed an Old Norse poem from the *Edda* (*Þrymskviða*); Barbara Thornton (together with Benjamin Bagy) sang the musical illustrations to the paper given by John Stevens on the music of medieval narrative. Sadly, it was Barbara Thornton's last appearance in public; the participants of the colloquium will gratefully remember her beautiful contribution.

Finally, I would like to thank Max Peter Bauman for his interest in publishing this book in the series "Intercultural Music Studies" and Linda Fujie for her many valuable suggestions for improvement.

Bonn, September 1999   Karl Reichl

1 INTRODUCTION:
THE MUSIC AND PERFORMANCE OF ORAL EPICS

Karl Reichl

In 1860, the Russian civil servant Pavel Nikolaevich Rybnikov, who had for many years been interested in Russian folklore and searched for survivals of the oral epic of Russia (*bylina*), found himself stranded on an island in Lake Onega. There he made a surprising discovery, which he described as follows:

> I lay down on my bag beside the meagre wood fire, made some tea for myself over the embers, drank it, and ate some of my travelling supply, and then became warmed by the fire and gradually fell asleep. I was awakened by strange sounds. Up to now I had heard many songs and religious poems, but such a sound as this I had not heard. Vivacious, fantastic, and gay, now it grew quicker, now it slowed down, and recalled by its tune something very long ago, forgotten by our generation. For a long time I was unwilling to awaken, and listened to every word of the song — so happy was I to remain totally overpowered by this new sensation.[1]

What Rybnikov was listening to was the performance of a *bylina* by an old man, "with bushy white beard and bright eyes and kindly expression of face." It is interesting to note that Rybnikov first of all talks about the musical aspect of Russian oral epic poetry ("such a sound as this") and only later about the words and their meanings. The *bylina* as an oral phenomenon is indeed poetry which comes to life only when it is performed, when it is sung: it is a composite of words and music, of narrative and melody. This was realized very early in the history of *bylina* collecting in Russia, which goes back to the first half of the eighteenth century, when Kirsha Danilov compiled the first substantial collection of Russian oral epics. Danilov wrote down not only the texts of the *byliny* but also their

---

[1] Rybnikov 1909-10, 1: lxix. I am quoting from N. Kershaw Chadwick's translation (Chadwick 1932, 4). — The word *bylina* (pl. *byliny*) is actually a term invented by scholars (a derivation from *byl* 'was'); the popular term was originally *starina* (pl. *stariny*), 'song of long ago.' For a concise survey of Russian *byliny*, see Oinas 1978; Russian oral (epic) poetry is treated extensively in vol. 2 of H. Munro and N. Kershaw Chadwick's *Growth of Literature* (1932-40).

melodies. These melodies are invaluable for an understanding of the *bylina* as sung poetry.[2]

What is true of the *bylina* is also true of other forms of oral epic poetry: these narratives are generally performed in singing, often accompanied by a musical instrument, and it is as sung poetry that these epics are appreciated by their native audience. The musical nature of oral epic poetry is attested from very early times. In a well-known scene in the *Odyssey*, the performance of oral narrative poetry is vividly described: when Odysseus is entertained at the court of Alcinoos, Demodocos, the blind singer (*aoidos*) of the Phaeacian king, sings narrative poetry to the accompaniment of the phormynx. One of these poems, on Achilles' quarrel with Odysseus, is clearly an epic (or part of an epic: VIII. 62ff.). It emerges also from Plato's dialogue *Ion* (as well as from other Greek writings) that rhapsodes performed the Homeric epics as song. Similarly, the Old Germanic heroic lays and epics must have been sung or chanted, as is shown in the Old English epic of *Beowulf*: during a feast, a singer gets up to recite the heroic lay of Finnsburh, a tragic tale about a feud between Danes and Frisians. The performance of the oral singer (Old English *scop*) is unambiguously characterized as singing (*swutol song scopes*, "the clear song of the singer"), and references to the lyre (Old English *hearp*, 'harp') allow us to infer that the *scop* accompanied his singing with a musical instrument.

Despite these clear indications of the "poetico-musical" character of oral epic, scholars generally consider the Homeric poems and Old Germanic epic poetry, as well as the Russian *byliny*, as poetry only. This is understandable in the case of past traditions from which no melodic material has survived — as with Ancient Greek or Old Germanic epics — but it is problematic in the case of traditions for which musical evidence is in existence — as with the Russian oral epic. The neglect of the musical side of epic raises a fundamental question of aesthetics: is the interpretation of epic as poetry, as words only, justifiable? Or are we missing an essential part of the nature of oral epic when music is ignored? Parallels like folksongs, ballads or *lieder* come to mind.

In the case of poems set to music, the poem as text and the *lied* as the union of words and music are two different things, each to be interpreted on its own. No one will maintain that Eichendorff's poem "Mondnacht" can only be appreciated in Schumann's setting. We might feel that Schumann's setting significantly deepens the aesthetic appeal of Eichendorff's poem, but there is no doubt that the poem as poetry is completely independent of any musical setting. Folksongs and ballads, on the other hand, are quite different in this respect. Could any American read

---

[2]Danilov's collection was not published until 1804, and then only partially. For a full edition, see Danilov 1977; for a detailed musical analysis of his transcriptions, see Belyaev 1969.

On top of old Smokey
On the mountain so high
Where the wild birds and turtledoves
Can hear my sad cry

and not immediately sing the melody? For many Americans — and not only Americans — this poem only exists as the text of a folksong, and if they recognize the poem they will presumably only know it as a folksong. Of course, one can try to read the poem without thinking of its melody, but this is probably only possible if the folksong is unfamiliar to the reader. While it is surely possible to appreciate folksongs and ballads as texts only, one could argue that their interpretation solely as texts is partial and fragmentary, that something is in fact missing when music is not taken into consideration. The ballad scholar Bertrand Bronson has emphatically affirmed the necessity of studying the ballad as a whole, as an entity which consists of both text and music:

> Yet, I insist, if the student of the ballad is not prepared to give equal attention to the musical, as to the verbal, side of his subject, his knowledge of it will in the end be only half-knowledge. If he lacks the necessary acquaintance with musical rudiments, or is indisposed or unable to enlist the active and continual collaboration of others properly equipped, he had better turn to other fields. For he dismisses the ballad music at his peril.[3]

Does the same apply to epic? Whether the restriction of our attention to the words alone seriously distorts our understanding is a difficult question whose answer depends on whether the music is seen as only accidental and ornamental or as an essential and integral component of the poetico-musical form. The relationship between words and music can take different forms in different traditions as well as for different subgenres of the epic; there is hence no simple solution to this problem.

Before an answer can be given, a descriptive and taxonomic framework for the discussion of the relationship between words and music must be established. In order to do so, I will return to the *bylina*. The importance of the musical aspect of the *bylina* is underlined in the subtitle of the most comprehensive and detailed edition and study of Russian *byliny* as sung narratives, that by B. M. Dobrovol'skiy and V. V. Korguzalov (1981): "*Byliny*: The Russian Musical Epic" (*Byliny: Russkiy muzykal'nyi epos*). On the basis of the music and performance of the *byliny*, Dobrovol'skiy and Korguzalov provide a characterization and typology of epic traditions

---

[3]Bronson 1969, 38.

in Russia which is of interest not only for the Russian oral epic but also for other traditions, as will be seen further in this introductory essay as well as in the contributions to this volume. It is for their more general relevance that I will briefly sketch the distinctions made by Dobrovol'skiy and Korguzalov.

The various regional traditions can be divided into two main areas: a northern tradition, on the shores of the White Sea, covering an area that stretches roughly from the Onega district via Arkhangelsk to Mezen', and a southern tradition, among the Cossacks of the Don region. The northern tradition is the more archaic of the two; here the home of Russian *bylina*-singing is found. The melodies are monophonic and generally unaccompanied, while the melodies of the southern tradition have undergone the influence of choral singing and are generally polyphonic. As a rule, the melodies of the northern tradition are stichic, that is, the same melody (or nearly the same melody) is used for every line of verse, while the southern tradition prefers strophic melodies, melodies consisting of melodic phrases which extend over more than one verse line. Stichic melodies are more restricted in their tonal ambitus and often closer to a recitative-type melody; strophic melodies, on the other hand, tend to be more varied and song-like.

Although this is basically the taxonomy which emerges from Dobrovol'skiy's and Korguzalov's discussion, the picture they paint is far more complex. First, they distinguish a third tradition, a central or mixed area (along the Volga, but found also among the Russian population of Siberia), which shows characteristics of both the northern and the southern tradition. Second, they stress that within each tradition there is a multiplicity of forms, which leads to further subdivisions and distinctions.

In order to illustrate at least some traits of the singing of *byliny*, I will briefly discuss an example from the northern tradition. This is the beginning of a *bylina* which was taken down in 1955 from the then seventy-year-old singer Nikita Fedorovich Yermolin in the Ust'-Tsilemskiy district in northern Russia (in the northern part of the Komi Republic).[4] The *bylina* is a variant of a well-known Russian epic song, the narrative of Il'ya Muromets and Solovey the Robber. In this epic song, of which more than sixty variants are known, Il'ya of Murom rides out to pay a visit to Prince Vladimir in Kiev. On his way, he frees the town of Byketovets (according to Yermolin's version) from the besieging Lithuanians and then overcomes the mighty robber Solovey, a monster-like being with both human and animal traits (*solovey* means "nightingale"). When

---

[4]The text is found in Astakhova et al. 1961, 124-26; the melody is found *ibid.*, 501. For the music of the *byliny* of this tradition, see Sokolov 1961. — In this book Russian is transliterated according to the "English" (rather than the "linguistic") system of transliteration as illustrated in the *Chicago Manual of Style*.

Vladimir asks Il'ya why he has arrived so late, the latter answers that he had to fight first the Lithuanians and then Solovey-Razboynik ("Nightingale the Robber"). Il'ya then leads Prince Vladimir to his horse and shows him Solovey, whom he has bound to the stirrups. Solovey-Razboynik insults Prince Vladimir and is killed by Il'ya in the end.[5] This *bylina* may well date back to the fourteenth century; in Yermolin's version it comprises 76 lines. The first five lines read:

> Sobiralse staróy da v put'-dorozhochku,
> A vo tu on subbotu da vo khristovskuyu,
> A k zautrenni pospet' vo stol'nëy Kiev-grad.
> Akh vsë pryamym-to putem tuda pyat'sot tut vérst,
> Akh okol'niim putem dak vosem'sot tut vérst.

> The old hero set out on his way and journey,
> He set out on a Christian Saturday,
> To get in time to the morning mass in the town of Kiev.
> If you went there the direct way it was five-hundred verst,
> If you went there a roundabout way it was eight-hundred verst.

If we look at the music (see Ex. 1) it is immediately obvious that every line of the text is sung to the same melody. Variations are found, but they are on the whole minimal. Before discussing the few variations that are found in the melody, I would first like to characterize the melody as a whole. This can only be a rough characterization and not a detailed stylistic analysis. It has to be noted also that any transcription is only an approximate reflection of the actual music performed. Transcribing orally performed traditional music is fraught with many difficulties, difficulties that have been discussed extensively in the ethnomusicological literature.[6] In the given case, the transcription must be considered "phonemic" rather than "phonetic." In linguistics, a phonemic transcription symbolizes only those sound elements which are structurally necessary to differentiate meanings, while a phonetic transcription marks all the nuances of sound. In English, for instance, the initial sound of *pin* is phonetically an aspirated voiceless bilabial plosive, symbolized in the International Phonetic Alphabet as [pʰ]. The initial sound of *bin*, on the other hand, is an unaspirated voiced bilabial plosive, symbolized as [b]. Phonetically, *pin* and *bin* are differentiated by both voicing and aspiration, but only voicing is necessary to distinguish *pin* and *bin* as words with different meanings. If the initial sound of *pin* is unaspirated (as pronounced by a Frenchman),

---

[5] For an English translation of a fuller version, see Chadwick 1932, 66-73; compare also Trautmann 1935, 292-300; and for an interpretation, see Propp 1955, 227-47. For the mythological figure of Solovey-Razboynik, see Tokarev et al. 1980-82, 2: 460.

[6] For a survey, see Ellingson 1992.

the semantic difference between *pin* and *bin* is preserved; if, however, the initial sound of *pin* is voiced, the two words cannot be distinguished any more. Phonemically, voicing is all that counts. We can hence replace [pʰ] in a phonemic transcription by /p/. Analogously, a "phonemic" musical transcription represents structurally important elements but neglects nuances of actual performance.[7]

The performance of the *bylina* in the northern tradition is without accompaniment. There is furthermore, as in many traditions of epic poetry (but not all), only one singer performing the epic; the music is hence monophonic. As every line is basically sung to the same melody, the music of the *bylina* can be termed stichic. The relationship between words and melody is predominantly syllabic, i.e. with one note per syllable. Two notes per syllable are also found, and there are two segments of the melody with four notes per syllable. The rhythm and (musical) metre is clear and regular; according to the transcription provided we have a combination of two metres, an upbeat of three quavers is followed by an 11/8 bar (with a caesura after the fifth quaver) and a 9/8 bar (five quavers plus rest). In other words, the melody consists metrically of groups of three, five and six quavers. Rhythmically, these metres are realized by combinations of crotchets, quavers and semiquavers.

Ex. 1

In its outline, the melodic contour can be described as "flowing" and "song-like." This is to say that there is a succession of ascending and descending melodic phrases, which keep generally within the range of a fifth (e^1–b^1), but also occasionally exceed the fifth by going a whole tone lower (d^1 in lines 2 and 3, leading up to e^1) and a minor third higher (d^2 in line 4). The intervals between the various notes of the melody are mostly seconds (i.e. the notes are conjunct), a feature most prominent in the two descending phrases of four semiquavers (b–a–g–f♯, a–g–f♯–e). Apart from seconds, there are various upward leaps — minor third (f♯–a), fourth (f♯–b), fifth (e–b), and sixth (f♯–d) — and the occasional downward leap (minor third a–f♯, fourth g–d). The basic contour of the melody could be described as a threefold rise from e to b with a subsequent descent to f♯ or e. There are three downward runs, an initial and medial run (b–a–g–f♯) and a final run one tone lower (a–g–f♯–e). The melody has e as final tone; the scale (as transcribed) resembles modern E minor (Aeolian mode).

From this very sketchy description it emerges that various parameters for the description of epic melodies can be set up. Some of these are:[8]

> unaccompanied vs. accompanied (one instrument vs. several instruments)
> monophonic vs. polyphonic[9]
> stichic vs. non-stichic (strophic, through-composed)
> syllabic vs. non-syllabic (melismatic)
> regular metre/rhythm vs. irregular (free) metre/rhythm
> "flat" melodic contour vs. "varied" melodic contour
> small range vs. wide range
> small intervallic steps vs. wide intervallic steps
> one-phrase melody vs. multi-phrase melody
> pentatonic vs. diatonic vs. chromatic scale
> Western scales (Church modes etc.) vs. non-Western scales (*sléndro* etc.)

To these should be added further indications concerning stylistic characteristics such as dynamic features and vocal qualities:

---

[8]Specifically on the analysis and classification of folksong melodies, see the taxonomy proposed by Vetterl and Gelnár 1969, who distinguish between (I) melodies without strophic structure (including stichic melodies) and (II) strophic melodies (melodies of two, three or more lines); among the latter they differentiate between (A) melodies with a fixed rhythm and (B) melodies with a free rhythm, both with further subdivisions (p. 82). The classification of the melodies of Slovak folksongs by Galko and Poloczek 1969 runs along similar lines. They group strophic melodies into those with a bound movement (giusto) and those with a free movement (rubato); the former employ either a regular (musical) metre or an irregular metre (mixed measures) (p. 61). For a classification of melodic types with examples, see also Bose 1953, 164-92.

[9]Strictly speaking, monophonic should, of course, be differentiated from homophonic, and polyphonic from heterophonic.

slow tempo vs. fast tempo
low volume vs. high volume
low vocal pitch vs. high pitch
smooth singing vs. non-smooth singing (rubato, rasping sound etc.)
natural voice quality vs. non-natural voice quality (glottalized voice, na-
   salized voice etc.)

There is a large body of writings on the stylistic analysis of folk music
and non-Western music which reveals the complexity and problematic
character of ethnomusicological analysis. On the basis of this literature,
the parameters listed above could easily be supplemented by a finer and
more sophisticated grid. In the context of the present discussion this
rough guide must, however, suffice; some elaborations will be made later
in this introduction as well as in the various chapters of this book.[10]

Before pursuing the analysis of epic melodies, I will have a closer look
at the variations encountered in the melody. Although the variations are
slight and at first sight easy to tabulate, they present a problem insofar as
their analysis concerns the relationship between music and (poetic) metre.
In the printed text the five lines of our example comprise 13 syllables
each. If one takes into account the relationship between stressed and
unstressed syllables (some of the stressed syllables are indicated in the
edited text), the following picture emerges:

Sobiralse staróy da v put'-dorozhochku,
A vo tu on subbotu da vo khristovskuyu,
A k zautrenni pospet' vo stol'nëy Kiev-grad.
Akh vsë pryamym-to putem tuda pyat'sot tut vérst,
Akh okol'niim putem dak vosem'sot tut vérst.

x x	á x x x	á x x á x	á x x
x x	(á) x x	á x x x x	á x x
x x	á x x x	á x x á	á x x
x x x	á x x	á x x x	á x á
x x	á x x x	á x x x	á x á

This schema can be interpreted as follows. The first ictus is preceded by
two or three unstressed syllables; line 2 is exceptional in that there is no

[10]For an informative survey, see Blum 1992. A comparatively full set of parameters for the
analysis of musical style is proposed in Lomax 1968, 22-23; for a critical discussion of
classificatory terms, see Suppan 1969. For an interpretative description of melodic possibilities in folksong, see Wiora 1966, 8-9. Also taking the singers' attitudes and voice characteristics into account, Wiora proposes twelve parameters (e.g., "10. The voice moves in round,
flexible and supple curves or in square, brittle, sudden lines... 11. It can sing expressively,
warmly, with meaning, and even dramatically ... or more coolly and with reserve...." [my
translation]).

"natural" first ictus: *tu* is not generally stressed but must (for metrical reasons) be stressed here. There follow another two or three unstressed syllables before the next stressed syllable. This ictus begins a fairly varied sequence of unstressed and stressed syllabes; it ranges from a group of unstressed syllables (three or four) to a combination of unstressed plus stressed syllables. The line concludes with a stressed syllable followed either by two unstressed syllables or an unstressed plus stressed syllable. This somewhat irregular configuration of stressed and unstressed syllables becomes regular if we assume the following schema (where unstressed syllables in brackets are optional):

$$x \; x \; (x) \quad \acute{a} \; x \; x \; (x) \quad \acute{a} \; x \; x \quad \acute{a} \; x \; (x) \quad \acute{a} \; x \; x \; [\text{or: à}]$$

That is, we have an anacrusis of two to three syllables and then a sequence of four metrical feet, which in their most regular form are dactyls.

I have dwelt on the metrical problems of these lines because there is no agreement on the metre of Russian *byliny*. The difficulty of their metrical analysis is notorious. The least one can say about their metre is to affirm its existence, or as the Chadwicks put it: "Although the character of metre cannot be said to be established, it is impossible to doubt that metre in some form exists."[11] A somewhat more positive general statement is, however, possible; in the words of Felix Oinas: "The byliny have several types of meters, but the most common of them has three stresses per line and a varying number (one to three) of unstressed syllables between stresses. Usually the ending is dactylic and may receive a secondary stress on the last syllable."[12] As the work on Slavic epic verse by Roman Jakobson has shown, the metrical analysis of the *bylina* can become fairly involved; there is no space here for further elaborations.[13] (For a discussion of Slavic metrics, more specifically of the South Slavic epic metre, the decasyllabic verse line or *deseterac*, see also the contribution by Stephen Erdely, Ch. 3) But there is one point which is of importance here, and that is the relationship between metre and music.

Aleksandr Fedorovich Gil'ferding (Hilferding), who collected *byliny* in the Onega region in the summer of 1871, remarked that there were three types of singers:

   (1) singers who accurately observe a regular metre in every bylina;
   (2) singers who observe metre, but not always accurately;

---

[11]Chadwick and Chadwick 1932-40, 2: 20.
[12]Oinas 1978, 250.
[13]See in particular Jakobson 1966; for the place of Slavic metre within the Indo-European system (and an evaluation of Jakobson's thesis), see West 1973, 170-73.

(3) singers who in general do not observe metre.[14]

As emerges from Gil'ferding's discussion, the singers who performed the *byliny* in singing were generally the ones who preserved the metre intact, while singers who recited only the text of the *byliny* generally belonged to the third type. Metrical structure and musical structure are hence intimately related. H. Munro and Nora Kershaw Chadwick have expressed this in the following terms:

> A certain amount of variation appears to exist between the metres of the *byliny* according as they are sung or recited. In the latter case it was noted by Gilferding that the metre almost entirely disappeared. It has also been observed that I. T. Ryabinin, in reciting *byliny*, frequently abandoned the metrical form for several lines consecutively, reciting in pure prose. He appears to have done this more especially in reciting the speeches of his characters. It may be noted that I. T. Ryabinin recited a generation later than Gilferding's minstrels, and probably represents a more advanced stage in the metrical disintegration.[15]

Looking back at the music of the extract given, we can now note that the variations between the melodies concern on the whole metrical matters and help the singer to perform the verse in a regular way. In a number of cases extra notes are inserted to add an extra syllable: line 1 *So-bi-ral-se* > *So-bi-ra-ly-se*, line 2 *khris-tov-sku-yu* > *khy-ris-tov-sku-yu* etc. Apart from changes due to metre, there are also slight variations in the melody. The e towards the end of the second descending phrase is generally reached by a descending scale (g–f♯–e), but also occasionally, as in line 2, via the d below (g–d–e); a similar variation is found at the end of the phrase in line 3 (f♯–d–e). Furthermore, in line 4, the figure a–f♯, leading into the second descending phrase, is replaced by d–c (*pu-*). When the music is taken into consideration, the scansion of these lines becomes completely regular and conforms to the "dactylic" pattern suggested above. These findings confirm what Betrand Bronson has shown in regard to ballads: their metre is only partially intelligible if the text only is taken into consideration.[16]

While it is undeniable that the musical aspect is of importance, at least when it comes to properly understanding the metrical structure of an orally performed poem such as the Russian *bylina*, the precise nature of

---

[14]Balandin 1983, 50 [originally published in 1873]; the translation is taken from Chadwick and Chadwick 1932-40, 2: 20.

[15]Chadwick and Chadwick 1932-40, 2: 20. On the metrical theory Gil'ferding evolved, see Balandin 1983, 50ff.; for a modern appraisal of his theory, see Fedotov 1995.

[16]Bronson 1969, 38-39. Compare also the discussion of *bylina* metre in Costello and Foote 1967, 72ff.

this importance depends very much on the tradition under discussion. I want to show briefly by looking at a second example how difficult it is to generalize, even about one tradition. This is a strophic melody, sung to a *bylina* on Dobrynya and Alësha. The narrative nucleus of this *bylina* is the widely diffused folklore motif of the husband returning in disguise from a long absence, just in time before his wife (or bride) is (re-)married to someone else. The best-known representative of this motif in world literature is, of course, the return of Odysseus.[17] In the *bylina*, Dobrynya Nikitich rides out to exact tribute for Prince Vladimir. On his departure he bids his wife Nastasya to wait for him for twelve years, after that she will be free to marry again — anyone other than Alësha Popovich. When twelve years have past, Alësha treacherously reports Dobrynya dead and persuades Nastasya to marry him. Dobrynya, however, returns just in time and punishes the traitor.[18] I will restrict the example to the first four lines:

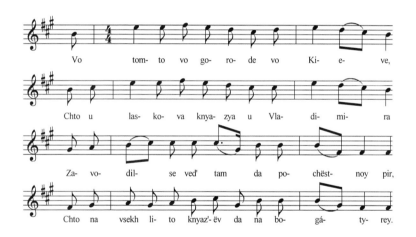

Ex. 2

[17]It is also found in other epics, most notably in the epic *Alpamish*, which is popular among various Turkic peoples; see further Zhirmunsky 1966.

[18]This version of the *bylina*, comprising 309 lines, is found in Dobrovol'skiy and Korguzalov 1981, 123-27 (with the melody of the first eleven lines on pp. 123-24). The *bylina* was taken down from the singer A. F. Orgina in the Lake Onega region in 1932 (see Dobrovol'skiy and Korguzalov 1981, 531). This is a well-known *bylina*, of which according to Propp more than 160 variants have been recorded; for the English translation of one of these versions (one recorded by Rybnikov), see Chadwick 1932, 80-90; compare also Trautmann 1935, 280-91 (German translation); on the *bylina*, see Propp 1955, 265-74.

Vo tom-to vo gorode vo Kieve,
Chto u laskova knyazya u Vladimira
Zavodilse ved' tam da pochëtnoy pir,
Chto na vsekh li-to knyaz'ëv da na bogátyrey.

It was in the well-known town of Kiev
That at the court of dear Prince Vladimir
A glorious banquet was held
For all princes and heroes.

In comparison with the first example, this melody is more purely syllabic. The verse lines comprise between eleven and thirteen syllables, which are sung to a fairly regular 4-beat measure (with upbeat). The melody consists of two repeated melodic lines (A A' B B'), which correspond to four lines of text. This four-line strophe is repeated (with variations) throughout the poem. Melodic line A rises from b^1 to e^2 and $f\sharp^2$ and descends again to b^1 (i.e. ranges over a fifth); melodic line B rises from g^1 to c^2 and descends to $f\sharp^1$ (i.e. ranges also over a fifth); in its totality the melodic range comprises an octave; the final tone is $f\sharp$. Dobrovol'skiy and Korguzalov comment that this type of strophic melody is unusual for the Onega tradition. They term the melody "strophic, of a declamatory character" (*stroficheskiy, deklamatsionnogo kharaktera*, 531). By "declamatory" they mean that the melody is syllabic and lacks melismas. As this is not the usual meaning of the term "declamatory," it might be appropriate at this point to briefly discuss terminology.

When it comes to describing the vocal side of an epic performance, various terms are used, such as "reciting/recitation," "declaiming/declamation," "chanting," "singing," and "recitative." According to the *Oxford English Dictionary* (*OED*), "to recite" means in modern usage "to repeat or utter aloud (something previously composed, heard, or learned by heart); now *spec.* to repeat to an audience (a piece of verse or other composition) from memory and in an appropriate manner" (sense 1.a). In the following I will employ this term in the more general sense of "uttering aloud to an audience a piece of verse or other composition," leaving out the specification that what is recited is "something previously composed, heard, or learned by heart" for the simple reason that in many traditions epics are "composed in performance" in such ways as described by Milman Parry and Albert Lord for South Slavic epics. I will furthermore use the term neutrally as to the precise nature of uttering: it could be speaking, but it could also be singing. Hence the expressions "to recite an epic" and "to perform an epic" are used synonymously in the present chapter. "Recitative," of course, is a technical musical term and I will use it in this sense, as for instance defined in the *New Harvard Dictionary of Music* (*NHDM*): "A style of text setting that imitates and emphasizes the natural inflections, rhythms, and syntax of speech. Such a setting avoids extremes of pitch and intensity and repetition of words, allowing the music to be primarily a vehicle for the words." "Chanting," too, is a technical term of music, and it is in this sense that the word is used here. The *NHDM* defines "chanting" as "to sing plainsong or in the style of plainsong; to sing a simple pitch or a limited range of pitches repetitively." "Declaiming," finally, is defined in the *OED* as "To speak aloud with studied rhetorical force and expression" (senses 1 and 5). In this sense "declaiming" could be used to refer to the speaking rather than the singing of poetry. There is, however, also a musical use of the term "declamation," defined in the *NHDM* as "That aspect of the musical setting of a text that corresponds to the purely sonorous quality of the text itself." The borderline between speaking and singing seems to be blurred. In so-called tone languages (like Chinese or many African languages) pitch and pitch movement are distinguishing features of speech, acoustic qualities closely associated with music. Furthermore, there is a way of singing, generally termed "parlando," which is even closer to speech than recitative; as Willi Apel put it, while recitative might be called "musical speech," parlando is "spoken music."[19] Despite these theoretical and practical complications, the difference between speaking and singing is nevertheless clear in most traditions. What has to be borne in mind, however, is that singing styles can be very different, ranging from forms of singing very close to the sound of speaking ("parlando," "chanting," "recitative") to styles more easily recognizable as musical performance.

Going back to the melodies of these two examples, we can see that although they are different, structurally as well as in their relationship to the text, they also have a number of characteristics in common. They are both unaccompanied and monophonic; they are both quite regular as to rhythm and metre; their melodic phrases are built on repetition and variation; they are predominantly syllabic; and they are firmly grounded in (Western-type) tonality. A systematic study of the music of the *byliny* would, however, significantly enlarge this picture: apart from unaccompanied melodies, we would find accompanied melodies, apart from monophonic melodies, we would find polyphonic melodies, apart from metrically and rhythmically regular melodies, we would find melodies in a freely flowing rhythm.[20] Does this mean that in theory all the parameters listed above can be combined? While one tradition might have a preferred combination, it is conceivable that the more traditions we study, the more possibilities for the musical performance of epic we will find.

---

[19]Apel 1969, 643 (s.v. *Parlando, parlante*). The (sometimes blurred) distinction between speech and song is discussed by Feld and Fox 1994, with extensive references.
[20]In addition to the discussion in Dobrovol'skiy and Korguzalov 1981, see also Korguzalov 1978 and 1995, and Vasil'eva 1989 on the music of the Russian *byliny*.

Or is there a typical way of performing epic poetry, which — despite variation and multiformity — is found in all traditions?

The latter seems natural when we reflect on the nature of epic poetry: it is narrative poetry, a tale to be told; it is rhythmically structured (i.e. poetry rather than prose); it is often of great length (such as the Homeric epics; but even longer oral epics are known); it is an archaic form of literature, in many cases reaching back into the distant past. True, there are many qualifications necessary for a fuller characterization of the oral epic. According to C. M. Bowra the genre term "epic" can be defined on the basis of a few salient features:

> In the disputable and usually futile task of classifying the forms of poetry there is no great quarrel about the epic. An epic poem is by common consent a narrative of some length and deals with events which have a certain grandeur and importance and come from a life of action, especially of violent action such as war. It gives a special pleasure because its events and persons enhance our belief in the worth of human achievement and in the dignity and nobility of man.[21]

Bowra goes on to make a distinction between "authentic" epics such as the *Iliad* or the *Chanson de Roland* and "literary" epics such as Virgil's *Aeneid* or Milton's *Paradise Lost*, or, as he prefers to call these two types, between "oral" and "written" epics. It has become customary to replace "oral" by "oral-derived" or "traditional" when speaking of epics such as the *Iliad* or the *Chanson de Roland*, for the simple reason that these poems have only survived in a written form, which shows the influence of writing and literacy. Besides, scholars are divided on the question of their orality, though practically unanimous in according them the status of traditional poems, ultimately derived from oral poetry. It might be comparatively easy (though by no means uncontroversial) to identify epics (or traditional epics) in Western literature, where our models for the epic poem are generally the *Iliad* or the *Odyssey*.[22] But it is far from easy to draw the line between "epics" and other forms of narrative poetry in oral traditions. While "some length" is necessary for a narrative poem to be called an epic, there are traditions with shorter heroic poems which, although not epics, should be considered on a par with heroic epics proper. This is true of the *byliny* discussed above: many of them are quite short, at any rate when compared to epics like the *Iliad* (of ca. 15,000 lines) or even the *Chanson de Roland* (of ca. 4,000 lines), but they are

---

[21]Bowra 1945, 1.

[22]Medievalists, for instance, are not in agreement on the generic nature of poems like *Beowulf* or the *Chanson de Roland*, which Bowra calls "epics," although they do agree that if we do not consider these works *sui generis*, "epic" is a closer term than "romance" or "saga." For a discussion of the "idea of epic," see Hainsworth 1991.

undeniably representatives of a genre which in spirit, narrative technique and manner of performance has strong affinities with what in other traditions would be termed epics/heroic epics. Another problem is the verse form which is generally associated with the genre of epic. There are narratives in a mixture of verse and prose which from the point of view of genre are definitely epics, although not consistently composed in verse.[23] Furthermore, while the archaic nature of the oral epic, in particular the heroic epic, is incontestable, there are degrees of archaicness, and not all epics belong to the oldest stratum of oral poetry. But despite these and other qualifications, some fixed points seem to emerge. As narratives, epics tell a story, i.e. the emphasis is on words and their meaning and not (primarily) on music. If in the light of our discussion of (poetic) metre, music fulfils a quasi-metrical function, i.e. that of helping to group the words into rhythmical, repetitive units, then music plays primarily a structural role. And it follows from these assumptions that this type of melody will be fairly simple, modelled on the inflections of speech rather than developing into full-fledged song. This is certainly the impression a rapid survey of epic melodies conveys, as is witnessed by the characterization Curt Sachs gives in his *The Wellsprings of Music*, when he speaks of the "unbelievably simple recitation of national epics":[24]

> How strict this domination of poetry over music can be — and here we return to our primitive ground — appears in the unbelievably simple recitation of national epics. We think of the Georgian *mestwirebi* and their recitations of myth and of history:

> of the Finnish *kalevala*, the Balkan epics of the *guslari*, or the Arabian Abu Said romances, with their wearisome, hardly varied melody patterns as a vehicle for many thousands of lines; of the archaic cantillation of

---

[23]Prosimetric epics are typical of many oral traditions of the Turkic-speaking peoples; see below the contributions by Dzhamilya Kurbanova on Turkmen oral epics (Ch. 6) and by myself on Karakalpak oral epics (Ch. 7). On the mixture of verse and prose in world literature, in particular narrative and traditional literature, see Harris and Reichl 1997.

[24]Sachs 1962, 78. I have omitted Sachs's footnotes; instead of *lais* it should read *laisse(s)*. On the Georgian minstrel mentioned by Sachs, compare the remarks by Grigol Chkhikvadze in the *New Grove* article on Georgia (Sarkisian et al. 1980, 19: 363): "The repertory of *mestvire* is varied. They compose songs about historical figures, national heroes and the hard lot of people enslaved by feudal lords; topical and humorous songs are also important items in their repertory. Their wit, resourcefulness and special talent for improvisation as well as their important function as social commentators attract wide sections of the population, and they are welcome guests everywhere." See also Korganow 1899-1900.

Persian and Yemenite Jews; and of the medieval French *chansons de geste* whose sections or *lais* [sic], up to fifty verses long, obeyed each the same melody before the last broke loose to form the cadence. And we may assume that the Homeric epics were no exception. Such melodic scraps can be repeated for hours and hours without annoying a listener exclusively interested in the narrative.

What Sachs states about epic melodies is echoed by a number of writers. Walter Wiora, in his survey of European folksong melodies, divides his material on a scale of increasing complexity into non-strophic melodies, strophic melodies, and part-singing. It is probably no coincidence that melodies from epics are predominantly found among the group of stichic tunes within his category of non-strophic melodies.[25] Although variety is not denied, the stichic epic melody is often seen as the epic melody *par excellence*, which belongs to the most archaic phase of melodic development. Robert Lach's appraisal of the music of Finnish epic songs or *runos* is typical of this view:[26]

> The oldest musical traditions of the Finns, the so-called runo melodies (runolaulua), have all the symptoms of an archaic melodic structure in the highest degree: they are characterized by the greatest monotony, uniformity and obstinate repetition of the same motif, as for example:

While general remarks on the music of epic confirm this picture, more specialized studies of individual traditions emphasize their variety, thus apparently contradicting the widely held opinion that epic is performed to comparatively simple, stichic melodies. One type of variation concerns rhythm and "measure." The melodies exemplified so far (with one exception) are all characterized by a regular division into recurring groups of beats, which in transcription is expressed by bar lines and indications of measure (as in Ex. 1). The one exception is the illustration Sachs gives. He compares the melodies used for the performance of epic with liturgi-

---

[25]See Wiora 1966, 18-20; among his examples are several melodies from Russian *byliny*, one of the few extant melodies of the Old French *chanson de geste*, a Vogul heroic song and an Icelandic heroic song.

[26]Lach 1913, 228-29 (my translation); I omit Lach's footnote and give only the first line of his musical example; the translation is mine. For musical transcriptions of four Finnish *runos* from Karelia, see also Kondrat'eva 1977, 87-96 (no. 42-45). Sound recordings are available on a CD produced by the Finnish Literature Society, *The Kalevala Heritage* (Helsinki, Ondine ODE 849-2, 1995). Elias Lönnrot based his epic *Kalevala* on *runos* from oral tradition.

cal chant. In fact, medievalists often invoke the analogy of plainchant, in particular the chanting of liturgical readings (epistle, gospel) and of the psalms, when they speculate on the musical performance of oral epics. This type of melodic and rhythmic structure is generally referred to as "recitative-like."[27] A deviation from regularity (in the sense of "measure-music")[28] is also provided by highly melismatic, freely flowing melodies. James Notopoulos, who in the early fifties carried out extensive recordings of Greek heroic oral poetry, has many examples of stichic melodies that fit the picture sketched above, but his collection also includes florid, highly melismatic melodies, in particular among the so-called klephtic songs. These songs go back to the activities of the klephts (lit. 'thieves'), mostly in the eighteenth and early nineteenth centuries, guerilla warriors who fought against the Ottoman dominion of Greece. The *kléphtika tragoúdia* can be characterized as heroic songs which are generically closer to ballads than to epics. In this they are not unlike the shorter South Slavic heroic songs. One of the klephtic songs in the Notopoulos collection, entitled "Tis Elénis Bótsari" (Of Eléni, the wife of Bótsaris), is particularly noticeable in its melismatic floridity; the word *kapetánisses* ('commander's wives') in the first line of the poem, for instance, which consists of five syllables, is sung to no less than fifty notes, not counting the occasional "grace note."[29]

I have mentioned this type of "epic melody" not only because it contrasts with what one might call the paradigmatic case, but also because it is an example of the way the singing of epic and narrative poetry changes in the course of time, under the influence of other styles of musical performance and of other genres of musical folklore. Notopoulos gives a succinct description of this transformation:

> The klephtic ballad emerged from the older tradition of the Akritan ballads from which it borrowed its metre, formulaic typology and many of its stock themes. Yet we find significant changes. The Akritan poem is a narrative sung to a regular basic melody which is content to accompany the words. Such is the case with the Cretan and the Serbo-Croatian he-

---

[27]For an attempt to re-imagine the melody of the Old English *Beowulf* on the basis of liturgical chant, see Cable 1974. For a further discussion of this type of melody in relation to medieval narrative, see the contribution by John Stevens (Ch. 14).

[28]By "measure-music" I mean music which has one or several musical measures; on the definition of "measure" as "a unit of musical time consisting of a fixed number of note-values of a given type, as determined by the prevailing meter, and delimited in musical notation by two bar lines," see *NHDM*, 478 (s.v. *Measure*).

[29]On Modern Greek oral poetry, see Beaton 1980; on the klephtic songs, see *ibid.*, 102-11. Extracts from the Notopoulos collection (housed in the Parry Collection of Harvard University) are found on the Folkways record FE 4468, which contains a highly informative booklet with detailed description and transcription (also musical) of the songs (Notopoulos 1959). This particular song is found on p. 24 in the booklet.

roic poems. Both in the text and melody the klephtic ballad partakes of
the epic and the lyric. In it we have a heightening of emotional effect
through the more lyrical character of the music which is filled with ornamentation, repetition of syllables, heaping up of vocalisations, factors
which often tend to obscure the text. Yet it is this musical character of
the ballads that makes them popular and gives them a more interesting
character in the repertory of Greek heroic songs.[30]

If an oral tradition is alive, changes and transformations cannot be ruled
out, even in such highly traditional genres as the epic. Similar develop-
ments towards the incorporation of lyric songs can also be found in other
traditions, as for instance among some Turkic peoples or in the southern
style of *bylina* singing, typical of the Cossacks of the Don region, which
was mentioned above.

The southern style of *bylina* singing is also characterized by polyphony,
a musical form not usually associated with the performance of epic.
Bruno Nettl and Roman Rosdolsky pointed this out in a note to the *Journal of American Folklore* in 1955: "In view of the fact that Russian epic
songs, *byliny*, have in the past been thought to be strictly monophonic
(melodic), it is of interest to find that in the recent large collection of Don
Cossack folk songs by A. Listopadov (*Pesni donskikh Kazakov* [Moscow,
1949], I, pt. 1) is included a group of about seventy polyphonic *byliny*.
These are usually sung by three separate voices and are in a style similar
in nature and complexity to the Russian polyphonic folk songs at large."[31]
In Dobrovol'skiy's and Korguzalov's study and edition of Russian *byliny*
and their music, a number of these polyphonic *byliny* from the repertory
of Cossack singers are published, among them also a three-part version of
the *bylina* "Dobrynya and Alësha" illustrated above.[32]

Another area where polyphonic folk music is found is the Caucasus. As
in the case of the singing of epics among the Don Cossacks, the musical
styles typical of the region as a whole have had a profound influence on
the performance of epic poetry. The Caucasus is rich in languages and in
epic traditions. One of the epics, or rather epic cycles, which is widely
diffused among speakers of different languages in the northern and central
Caucasus — comprising Caucasian languages (like Adyge or Abkhaz),
Indo-European languages (like Ossete), and Turkic languages (like Karachay and Balkar) — is the cycle of narratives about the Narts, mythological and heroic figures from the distant past.[33] It is generally assumed that

---

[30]Notopoulos 1959, 9 (booklet). For a detailed study of the music of klephtic songs, see Baud-
Bovy 1958; see also Themelis 1994.

[31]Nettl and Rosdolsky 1955, 34.

[32]Dobrovol'skiy and Korguzalov 1981, 382-84 (No. 82).

[33]Although it would be wrong to call the Nart narratives epics, these very archaic legends
have in style, content and manner of performance (in particular when performed by profes-

these narratives (sometimes in prose, sometimes in verse, sometimes in a mixture of prose and verse) have their origin among the Ossetes, from whom they spread to other Caucasian peoples. The Ossetes have two different types of performer, a narrator, who only tells the tale, and a singer, who accompanies himself on a two-stringed bowed instrument (called *khisyn-fœndyr*). The melodies can be classified into two groups, stichic melodies (sometimes elaborated into strophic melodies) of regular rhythm and metrical structure ("measured"), and recitative-like melodies, rhythmically freer and "unmeasured." In addition to the singing of epic to the *khisyn-fœndyr*, a two-part performance by a soloist and a choir is also current. The latter is the more modern style, also found in other traditions of the Caucasus.[34] Among the Karachay and Balkars, the Nart epics can be performed (1) solo, (2) solo with the accompaniment of a kind of rattle (*khars*) or the clapping of hands, (3) interspersed with musical refrains on the *sybyzgy* (a type of flute), (4) antiphonally with a soloist singing the melody and a choir singing a simple harmonic accompaniment (see Ex. 3), or finally (5) antiphonally with the soloist and the choir singing in the stretto manner.[35] The fourth performance style can be illustrated by the beginning of a poem on the Nart Karashavay; it is this style which is also typical of other Caucasian traditions:

Ba-ra, dzhor-ta ket-di Sha-vay,   ert-den-lik-de zhet-di Sha-vay.

Oy, o - - - - - - - - - - Oy, o !

Ex. 3

The following chapters will show that these examples are far from exhausting the variety encountered in the performance of oral epic poetry. But some preliminary conclusions can nevertheless be drawn. A survey of the performance of epic seems to confirm the general impression that

sional singers) many affinities with what in other traditions would be epics. It is for this reason that these narratives are generally called "epics" in Russian and have been included in the series "Epics of the Peoples of the USSR (or Eurasia)." The best translation of the Ossete Nart cycle into a Western language is by Georges Dumézil (1965).

[34]On the question of the metre of the Ossete Nart narratives, see Abaev 1990, 72-74; on the music of the Ossete Nart cycle, see Tskhurbaeva 1969.

[35]On the music of the Nart cycle of the Karachay and Balkars, see Rakhaev 1994; the musical example is found *ibid.*, 614. For a survey of the folklore of these Turkic peoples of the northern Caucasus, see also Reichl 1993.

"epic melodies" are characterized by simplicity and repetitiveness, that they are subservient to the words of the epic and fulfil an important function as rhythmical and metrical moulds. By the same token, epics — like other forms of oral poetry — develop and change in the course of time, incorporating — or coalescing with, or adapting to — other styles and genres of folklore. As there is, on the literary side, a continuum ranging from long epics and epic cycles via short epics and heroic songs to heroic ballads and finally reflections of heroic action in lyric poetry (as in the klephtic songs), so we find on the musical side a comparable scale, which has at one end a type of melody which is stichic, unaccompanied, unadorned, and consists of one phrase of only a few notes, and at the other a strophic type of melody which is song-like, elaborate, musically sophisticated, perhaps even polyphonic, and accompanied by a number of instruments. Although it is difficult to put these performance styles and melodic types into a chronological perspective, it can be shown that in a number of traditions deviations from the more simple manner of performing the epic are innovations and that hence the "paradigmatic case" as described by Curt Sachs and others can be considered the more archaic musical form.[36] There is a further point which can be made in regard to the examples discussed so far. Both the southern tradition of *bylina* singing and the Caucasian traditions show that the performance of epic adapts itself to the musical styles current in a particular region. We might, in analogy to folktales that are found in a specific area and share a common style, speak of *oicotypes*.[37] It can be observed that traditions have, so to speak, a centripetal force which assimilates various genres of folklore (including the epic) to a regional style.

Few will doubt that in traditions where the music of an epic performance is highly elaborate and predominates over the textual side, the study of the words alone would be one-sided, if not inadequate. Here, as with folksongs, music is an integral element of the whole event and cannot be ignored in interpretation and appreciation. This is particularly obvious in those cases where the words have almost receded into the background. This can be seen, for instance, in prosimetric traditions like those found among a number of Turkic peoples. In Khorezm in Uzbekistan (in the oasis of Khiva on the Amu-Darya), to give just one example, oral epics — both heroic epics and romances — have a prosimetric form, i.e. a mixture of verse and prose. As a rule, the prose parts are narrated and

---

[36]This question of the possibility of a "historical typology" of epic melodies is discussed in detail by Kondrat'eva 1975. She concludes that for the oldest strata of musical folklore two opposing tendencies can be discerned in epic melodies, the adherence to a fixed rhythm (metre) and the predominance of rhythmic fluctuation (p. 158).

[37]The term "oicotype" was coined by C. W. von Sydow to designate folktales found in and typical of a region, where they were passed down over the ages without substantial influence from the outside. See von Sydow 1948.

the verse parts are sung. These verse-portions are often song-like and have come under the influence of folksongs as well as native classical music; furthermore the singer not only accompanies himself on a plucked instrument (generally the *dutâr* or the *târ*) but is also accompanied by a small ensemble of three to six people. It might consist of players of bowed and plucked instruments, percussion instruments and wind instruments as well as perhaps an accordionist.[38] Even more extreme is the predominance of music in the klephtic songs, admittedly the genre furthest removed from the epic proper. Samuel Baud-Bovy has contrasted the relationship between words and music in the klephtic songs with that of the South Slavic epics, a contrast which leads him to emphasize the closeness of the Greek songs to lyrics:

> Alors que les mélodies des guzlars sont une simple récitation cadencée, où chaque strophe correspond à un vers et où le texte est continuellement au premier plan, ce qui caractérise la chanson cleftique, c'est le fait que la répétition des syllabes, l'insertion des refrains, la non-concordance des cadences du texte et de la mélodie, le foisonnement enfin des vocalises, tendent à rendre le texte de moins en moins intelligible. En particulier, tout enchaînement logique, tout développement chronologique échappent nécessairement à l'auditeur. Seules s'imposent quelques images, celles-là même qui frappent le chanteur, qui provoquent son émotion.[39]

But what about cases like those evoked by Curt Sachs where monotony, simplicity and repetitiveness prevail and music seems to play a predominantly functional role? Musical structure and poetic metre are closely related and the latter is, as Bronson has pointed out with reference to the English ballad, not always correctly analysable without the former. It has often been observed that since the musical form provides the singers with a metrical/rhythmic mould into which they can pour their verse-lines, singers who are able to perform fluently have difficulty in dictating their texts without the help of music. There is, of course, also a merely practical side to the singing, rather than speaking, of epic poetry: the singer's voice carries further and thus increases the audibility of his tale. Singers can even be famous for their mighty voice; it is reported (somewhat apocryphally) of the Uzbek singer Dzhumanbulbul that his voice could be heard within a radius of one *tâsh*, which is no less than five miles![40] On the other hand, even in the case of stichic melodies which on account of their relative simplicity we might term "archaic," there is no denying that in their most repetitive and monotonous form they are music and not the

---

[38]On Turkic traditions see further Chapters 6 and 7.
[39]Baud-Bovy 1958, 13. For critical comments on Baud-Bovy's theories of origin and diffusion, see Beaton 1980, 114-15.
[40]Reichl 1995, 177.

spoken word only, and hence open up an additional dimension for the appreciation of the poetry performed.

As to the relationship between the music and the text in terms of semantics, this is a difficult question which cannot be answered generally.[41] Bronson has noted that the same melody might be used for different ballads, just as the same ballad might be sung to different melodies. This is also true of the klephtic songs. With epics, different singers might perform the "same" epic (which, of course, is never quite the same in an oral tradition, though the degree of variation allowed or even encouraged differs from tradition to tradition) to different melodies, maybe even in different styles. And the same singer might have various melodies for the singing of an epic which he might not always use in the same distribution for every performance. All this suggests that the relationship between words and music is "loose" and in no way comparable to that between words and music in a Romantic *lied*.

This "looseness" and quasi-objective nature of the relationship between words and music does not exclude possibilities of a more intimate link. In some traditions epic tunes are used for particular characters or particular situations, as for instance in the Yakut tradition of northern Siberia.[42] The way these melodies announce a hero of the upper world or some character of the middle world or of the underworld is not unlike the use of leitmotifs in Wagnerian opera. But while these melodies have clear connotations, they are purely conventional and there is nothing in the melodies themselves which links them to what they denote along the lines of onomatopoeia or programme music. But imitative elements can also be found in the music of epic. The plucked instrument used to accompany Uzbek and Kazakh singers (*dombira*) is sometimes played in such a way as to suggest the gallop of horses, in particular in type-scenes like that of the hero riding through the steppe. Also, different forms of music might be incorporated into an epic to mark particular events in the story. Thus at the end of the Uzbek epic *Alpâmish*, when the hero returns in disguise at his wife's enforced wedding feast (as in the Russian *bylina* illustrated above), he engages in a song contest with his wife and her (evil) mother-in-law-to-be. These songs are sung in the style of wedding songs (called *yâr-yâr*), and the wicked mother-in-law's songs are sometimes sung in

---

[41]This is not the place to enter into a theoretical discussion of musical semantics; of interest is Susanne Langer's discussion of music in her influential book *Philosophy in a New Key* (1957, 204ff.); see also Davies 1994.

[42]On the music of Yakut epics, see below, pp. 141-42 (with bibliographical and discographic references). A very interesting case, of a similar kind, is the use of melodies in the performance of the Tibetan Gesar epic; for a full and illuminating study of these melodies, see Helffer 1977.

imitation of a toothless crone's singing.[43] Even stichic melodies of a comparatively simple structure can be made to express dramatic effects. Kirghiz singers increase the speed and intensity of singing at moments of climax. The transition from singing to reciting on a high note, found in a number of Turkic traditions, is a similar technique used to underline emotional tension or dramatic narrative situations. But despite such exceptions, it is probably correct to say that the relationship between words and music is in general "loose" in the sense that there is no semantic relationship between them. The music does not "express" the meaning of the words in the way an Italian madrigal by Monteverdi or his contemporaries does. This statement is, however, in need of qualification when particular traditions are discussed; it should only be taken as provisional, to be revised in the chapters that follow. In particular the idea of a musical motto, as found in the Fulɓe tradition of Western Africa, discussed by Christiane Seydou, raises doubts as to the non-symbolic nature of music in epic.

There is a final point to be made in this preliminary discussion. As the title of this book indicates, the various contributions to this volume concern not only the music but also more generally the performance of the oral epic. Classicists and medievalists tend to see traditional epics like the *Iliad* or the *Chanson de Roland* as texts only. This is natural as these oral-derived epics have come down to us only in written form. But as oral epics — which they, or rather their predecessors, presumably once were — they are not primarily texts but rather speech events. The disciplines of ethnolinguistics (ethnography of communication) and ethnopoetics have in the course of the last decades elaborated a sophisticated terminological grid to describe and analyse speech events (or communicative events) such as a court-session in an oral society, the exchange of insults among black urban youths in America — or the performance of epic poetry. Various components of such an event can be distinguished, such as the setting of the event (time, place, occasion etc.), its participants (their number, ages, social status, sex etc.), its function and type (e.g., arbitration in court, negotiating a marriage, reciting an epic etc.), its act sequence or sequential structure (what comes first, what comes next), the rules of interaction valid for the participants (who says or does what?) and the cultural norms according to which the event is to be interpreted.[44] The recitation of epic poetry is generally part of a structured social event

---

[43]This is also found in other Turkic traditions, as for instance in the Kazakh version of the epic; compare the version sung by Muqash Baybatyrov, published as a set of records under the title *Alpamys* (Tashkent, Melodiya D-026293-96). For further comments on the Turkic traditions, see Chapters 6 and 7.

[44]For a general introduction, see Saville-Troike 1989, 107ff.; for an application of ethnopoetics to Turkic oral epics, see Reichl 1995; for a discussion of South Slavic, Homeric and Old English poetry from an ethnopoetic point of view, see Foley 1995.

such as a secular or religious feast. In Islamic societies, for instance, the long evenings of the fasting month often provide such a framework. Albert Lord, in his seminal book on the *Singer of Tales*, has described the performance of epics during the month of Ramazan in Bosnia; similar accounts are also known from other traditions.[45] Often the singing of epics follows a strict act sequence. A particularly vivid account is given by Viktor Zhirmunskiy and Hadi Zarifov in their study of Uzbek epics (called *dastan* in native terminology). As their description is typical of a number of Turkic traditions, and as many features of the Uzbek case also apply to the performance of epic in other geographical and ethnic/linguistic contexts, I will quote the passage in question in full:[46]

> When the singer (*bakhshi*) came to a village he stayed with his friends or with a person who had invited him specially and in whose house the performance was arranged. By the evening all the neighbours had gathered in the house. The singer was put in the seat of honour. Around him, along the walls, but also in the middle of the room if there were many guests, the men would sit. In the old days women and children did not take part in these gatherings and would listen through the windows and the doors. The evening began with light refreshments. Then the singer sang the so-called *terma* (literally "selection") as a prelude to the performance of the main part of his repertoire: short lyric pieces of his own composition, excerpts from *dastans*, sometimes songs from classical literature — all of these songs works of small dimensions (approximately up to 150 lines), forming a unity by their function as a prelude, attuning the singer himself and his audience to the more serious epic theme. There are *termas* in which the singer enumerates the *dastans* of his repertory, turning to his audience with the question: "What shall I sing?" (*Nima aytay?*). A special group in this genre is formed by songs in which the singer addresses his *dombira*, the unfailing companion of his poetic inspiration ("My dombira," *Dombiram*). Such songs, which are interesting for their autobiographic elements, have been written down from a number of singers (Fâzil Yoldâsh-oghli, Polkan, Abdullâ-shâir and others).
>
> Then the performance of the *dastan* itself begins, which lasts from sunset to sunrise, with an interval at midnight. Gradually the singer enters into a state of inspiration; he "boils" (*qaynadi*); the word 'boil' (*qaynamâq*) is used in this context in the sense of 'get excited, sing with enthusiasm'. The *bakhshi* himself uses at this point the expression: *Bedawni minib haydadim* ("Mounting the steed I rode it hard"); his *dombira* is the *bedaw*, the good steed galloping along. Physical signs of the

---

[45]Lord 1960, 15; for the performance of Turkish minstrels during Ramazan, see Boratav 1973, 63 (translated in Reichl 1992, 96).

[46]Zhirmunskiy and Zarifov 1947, 29-31. The translation is mine and has been published in Reichl 1992, 97-99.

singer's inspired state are the sharp, rhythmic jerks of his head with which he accompanies the "throwing out" of each verse-line. He is covered in perspiration and takes off one after the other of the *khalats* (robes) he is wearing. Nonetheless, a good singer, a master of his art, preserves the ability to listen attentively and sensitively during the performance of a *dastan* to the reactions of the audience to his playing. Depending on the degree of interest and participation shown by the listeners, he enlarges or shortens the text of the poem. Even the choice of the plot and the more detailed elaboration of single episodes take their cue from the composition of the audience and its taste, as it is known to the singer: among old people or elderly listeners he will sing differently than among young people, etc.

At midnight there is an interval. The singer interrupts the performance at a particularly interesting moment; on leaving the room he leaves his top *khalat* and his belt-scarf, in which he puts his *dombira* face down (*dombira tonkarmâq*), behind in his seat. During his absence someone in the audience spreads his belt-scarf in the middle of the room and everyone of those present puts whatever he has got ready as payment into it, payment in kind or in money. This remuneration had been prepared by the guests earlier, but depending on the quality of the performance the size of the gifts gets larger or smaller. In addition to these presents, which they brought along, in the old days the rich gave the singer they had invited also more valuable gifts at his departure: a new *khalat*, a horse, or livestock; among these gifts a horse was held a particularly honourable present.

These performances of a singer continued for several nights, from three or four nights to a whole week and longer, sometimes in different houses in turn, by mutual agreement with the host at whose house the singer was staying. At that time the singer performed one or several *dastans*, depending on the speed of the performance, which was in turn determined by the interest of the listeners. An epic poem like *Alpâmish*, which in Fâzil's version runs to about 6,000 verse-lines in print, with a corresponding amount of prose, needed for its performance usually two nights (each part took up one sitting). If there was, however, a keen interest on the part of the audience, the singer was able to lengthen the performance by several times. The *bakhshi* left the selection of the *dastan* always to his audience, but the listeners themselves could ask him to sing according to his judgement.

Zhirmunskiy and Zarifov point out that the performance of epic is a dynamic process which depends not only on the singer but also on the audience. If the listeners show sufficient interest, the *bakhshi* is motivated to go on with his recitation and strives to give his best. Riveting the attention of an audience demands many talents on the part of the singer. He has to have a good, audible voice; he has to be an accomplished narrator (in particular if parts of the narrative are in prose) and a skilled musician.

In some traditions the singer sings solo without the accompaniment of a musical instrument, as for instance among the Kirghiz. It is said that the singer cannot play an instrument because he needs his hands for gestures. Despite the fact that the Kirghiz national epic *Manas* is performed to a stichic melody of the simple type, there is enough variation in the musical and gestural performance to make the singer's performance a dramatic and captivating event. This is brilliantly illustrated in a short film on the famous Kirghiz singer Sayaqbay Qaralaev (1894–1970) by the filmmaker Bolot Shamshiev (first shown at an international film festival in Germany in 1965), when the listeners, gathered on a plain, continue to follow entranced the singer's words and gestures, without seeming to notice that it has meanwhile started to rain and that they are getting soaked in the downpour.

As part of the living performance of epic, music is no mere ornament but an essential element of the communicative event. Without the singer's voice, an epic cannot be recited. And it is furthermore not performed without music, be it singing, chanting or recitative. It is on account of this performative aspect that a transcription of melodies (however sophisticated) is not enough to capture the role of music. Ethnomusicologists have realized this and adapted the insights of ethnolinguistics and ethnopoetics to musical analysis. In the course of her study of Sufi music in India and Pakistan (*qawwali*), Regula Burckhardt Qureshi has developed a performance-oriented model for musical analysis which recommends itself also for the description of the oral epic as a communicative (and musical) event. Apart from the musical analysis in the strict sense, she proposes to study background dimensions of the event such as the socio-economic setting or the performer's identity, audience interaction and the relationship between performance context and musical structure.[47] In some of the following contributions performance aspects will be further in the foreground than in others; although they do not explicitly use Qureshi's model, they discuss much the same elements highlighted by Qureshi as important contextual features of the music.[48]

*****

While the texts of oral epic poetry have been collected and studied intensively, the music and performance of oral epics is still a largely uncharted territory. Comparative works like the Chadwicks' *Growth of Literature* in three volumes (1932-1940) or C. M. Bowra's *Heroic Poetry* (1952) have helped to bring oral epics to the attention of a wider public.

---

[47]See Qureshi 1987.
[48]See in particular the contributions by Hiromi Lorraine Sakata (Ch. 9), Carole Pegg (Ch. 10), and Nicole Revel (Ch. 11).

Collaborative surveys like the two-volume *Traditions of Heroic and Epic Poetry*, published by the Modern Humanity Research Association under the general editorship of A. T. Hatto (1980-89), underline the vastness and multiplicity of epic traditions still (or until recently) alive in many parts of the world. Yet most literature on the subject of the oral epic is curiously silent about music (and performance in general) and editions only rarely give an indication of the sound of epic. Notable exceptions can be found, however. The French series "Classiques Africains" adds to text and translation a small record which illustrates the performance of the epic. In the former Soviet Union a great number of epics from many different traditions have been taken down in the course of this century, and the archives of the various Academies of Sciences often also contain musical transcriptions of text extracts. Audio-recordings were also made, in particular in the last decades; video-recordings, on the other hand, are rare (with the exception of some film material, such as the film "Manaschy" mentioned above). It is to be noted, however, that the scholarly series of "Epics of the Peoples of the USSR" (*Epos narodov SSSR*), now called "Epics of the Peoples of Eurasia" (*Epos narodov Evrazii*), almost always contains an appendix with musical transcriptions. The impressive series "Monuments of the Folklore of the Peoples of Siberia and the Far East" (*Pamyatniki fol'klora narodov Sibiri i Dal'nego Vostoka*), published in Novosibirsk, even includes a record.[49] Ethnomusicologists dealing with the music of a particular area or linguistic/ethnic group often include information on the music and performance of epic. Viktor Belyaev's studies on the music of the peoples of the former Soviet Union, partially available in English translation (1975), contain a number of observations on the music of oral epics in the various traditions found in this vast area. Similarly, the articles on the folk music of various regions and peoples in the *New Grove* also touch on the performance and music of epic poetry where appropriate.[50] While a number of studies on the music of individual epics or epic traditions can be found (in particular in Russian), there are only very few comparative studies and almost no monographs or collaborative works on this topic.[51] The fullest treatment of the music of epic is, to my knowledge, a collection of articles (in Russian) edited by I. I. Zemtsovskiy in 1989; it contains contributions on the music of various traditions found in the former Soviet Union

---

[49]In this series, there is also a volume on Russian *byliny* as sung in Siberia and the Far East (Smirnov 1991), with musical transcriptions and a small record.
[50]This applies only to a limited extent to the articles in *Die Musik in Geschichte und Gegenwart* (*MGG*); see Kuckertz 1980. But see the article on epic by Wolfgang Suppan in the second supplementary volume to *MGG* (1979; with an excursus on Icelandic *rímur* by Hallgrímur Helgasson).
[51]A useful comparative analysis is the article by Kondrat'eva 1975 quoted above; for an earlier attempt, see Hoerburger 1952.

(Russian, Kazakh, Uzbek, Turkmen, Azeri, Armenian, Kalmuck, Buryat, Yakut, and Mari) as well as general comparative articles.[52] A recent issue of the journal *Asian Music* (volume 26, 1994/95) is devoted to musical narrative traditions of Asia; among the contributions, the article by Dwight F. Reynolds on the performance and music of oral epics in Egypt is of particular relevance to our topic.[53]

Given the wide diffusion of oral epics even today, the articles gathered in this volume can only represent a small portion of epic traditions. The book begins with Ancient Greece, place of origin of the most accomplished "authentic epics" of the Western world. Although Greek music has been studied in detail, the performance and music of epics is of only marginal interest to most Homerists and musicologists.[54] One of the reasons for this is clearly the nature of the transmitted musical material, which is heavily weighted on the theoretical side. Evidence for the actual performance of Greek epic is only indirect as no music has survived. One of the items from which we can try to piece together a picture of epic performance is Plato's dialogue *Ion*, in which the protagonist, the rhapsodist Ion, confesses his trance-like state of empathy when performing an epic:

> SOCRATES: Then go on and tell me something more, my dear Ion; don't hide it, just answer my question. When you speak your verses well, and astound the audience most — you know when you sing how Odysseus leaps onto the threshold, and reveals himself to the wooers, and spreads out the arrows before his feet, or how Achilles rushes on Hector, or one of those touching scenes about Andromache or Hecuba or Priam — are you in your right mind then, or do you get beside yourself, does your soul feel itself inspired and present in the action which you describe, somewhere in Ithaca or at Troy or wherever the epic scene is?
>
> ION: Clear as daylight I see your proof, my dear Socrates! I will not hide it, I will tell you frankly. Why, whenever I speak of sad and

---

[52]Among the latter are: I. I. Zemtsovkiy and A. B. Kunanbaeva, "Muzykal'nyj epos — fenomen i kategoriya" (The musical epic — phenomenon and category; 6-23), E. Ye. Alekseev, "K postroeniyu tipologii muzykal'nogo eposa" (On constructing a typology of the musical epic, 24-27), S. I. Gritsa, "Dialektika muzykal'no-slovesnogo yedinstva v pesennom epose" (The dialectics of the music-speech unit in the sung epic, 28-33), and A. G. Yusfin, "Nekotorye nereshennye voprosy izucheniya muzyki eposa" (Some unsolved questions in the study of the music of epic, 34-42).

[53]See Reynolds 1994/95; Prof. Reynolds also gave a paper on this topic (with demonstration) at the colloquium which formed the basis for the present collection of articles. See further his study of an Egyptian tradition of oral epics, where special emphasis is laid on the ethnographic analysis of performance (1995).

[54]On Ancient Greek music, see esp. Georgiades 1958, West 1992, and Neubecker 1994; specifically on the singing of Homer, see also West 1981.

touching scenes, my eyes are full of tears; when it is something terrible or awful, my hair stands up straight with fear and my heart leaps![55]

It is therefore fitting that the first contribution is that of a Homerist, Gregory Nagy (Harvard University), who discusses rhapsodic models of Homer in Plato's *Timaeus* and *Critias* (Chapter 2).

It is not only through the work of Parry and Lord that the Balkans have been thought of as the home of the oral epic *par excellence*. Serbian heroic poems had already aroused the interest of Goethe, and scholars like Matthias Murko, Alois Schmaus and Gerhard Gesemann have done much to make South Slavic epics familiar to a wider circle of scholars. In the thirties, Walther Wünsch wrote two short monographs on musical aspects of the South Slavic *guslari*, a book on the oral singer of the Balkans in general, with musical examples (1937), and a study of their playing technique (1934). The first musicologist to study the Parry collection of South Slavic epics in depth was none other than Béla Bartók, who also contributed a musical transcription to the first translation volume of the collection's edition.[56] With the appearance of Stephen Erdely's complete transcriptions of three Bosnian epics from the Parry collection in 1995, musicologists have a solid basis for dealing further with this tradition. Stephen Erdely (Massachussetts Institute of Technology) discusses the results of his study in Chapter 3.

Parry and Lord also recorded bilingual singers such as Salih Ugljanin, a native speaker of Albanian but mostly famous as a performer for Bosnian audiences. Lord collected material in Albania as well (in 1937), and in 1965 the British folklore collector A. L. Lloyd recorded various folk music performers in Albania and subsequently published a record with excerpts from one traditional and one contemporary heroic ballad. Albanian epic singing has, however, only survived in the north into the second half of this century.[57] Wolf Dietrich (Sulzheim), who has been collecting folk music in the Balkans, Greece and Turkey for many years, was able to record an Albanian narrative in 1995, which he discusses and analyses in Chapter 4.

The music of Romanian ballads and heroic songs has also been the subject of musicological analyses, mostly by the collectors and musicologists of Romania (and Moldavia). The authoritative edition of Romanian heroic epic songs (*cîntecul epic eroic*) by Al. I. Amzulescu (1981) is

---

[55]I am quoting from W. H. D. Rouse's translation (1956, 19-20). As a rule the rhapsode recited the epic without accompaniment in the Classical period, while the *aoidos* sang the epic to the accompaniment of the lyre; see West 1981, 113-14; Nagy 1989, 4ff.

[56]In Parry and Lord 1954, 437-67.

[57]A. L. Lloyd's record was released unter the title *Folk Music of Albania* by Topic Records (No. 12T154). For a comparison between the singing of Albanian and South Slavic epics, see Kruta 1985.

particular in giving indications about the music and manner of performance; the study, collection and translation of Romanian epic songs by V.
M. Gatsak of the Institute of World Literature of the Soviet/Russian
Academy of Sciences (1967) also includes an appendix with nineteen
melodies. In her contribution, Margaret Beissinger (University of Wis-
consin) sets the Romanian tradition into the wider context of South Slavic
epic poetry (Chapter 5).

The performance of oral epics has been preserved in many parts of the
Turkic-speaking world. In the nineteenth century, the Turcologist Wilhem
Radloff assembled a huge corpus of texts, many of them epics, from the
various Turkic-speaking peoples of the Russian Empire. Possibly the first
musical example of the performance of a Turkic epic is found in Alexander Chodzko's translation of an Azerbaijanian cycle of epic tales on the
hero Köroghlu (or Göroghli), published in 1842. These are prosimetric
tales, with the verse portions (called "improvisations" by Chodzko) sung.
Chodzko states that most of these "improvisations" are sung to the tune
he prints in an appendix (arranged for the pianoforte as typical of that
period); it is quite clearly a stichic melody.[58] Two traditions not represented in Radloff's volumes are that of the Turkmens (or Turcomans) and
that of the Karakalpaks. Hermann Vámbéry, a Hungarian orientalist who
travelled to Central Asia in the disguise of a dervish in 1863, gives a
rather negative impression of the musical art of Turkmen epic when he
comments on the performance of a singer or *bakhshy* he has heard: "His
song consisted of certain hoarse guttural sounds, which we might consider
more a rattling noise than singing and which he accompanied at first by a
soft, and later, when he became agitated, by a wild strumming of his
dutar."[59] What Vámbéry is referring to is the Turkmen manner of ornamental vocalisation, a series of glottal trills, generally on a descending
scale, termed "dzhuk-dzhuk" in Turkmen.[60] As Dzhamilya Kurbanova
(Ashkhabad Conservatory) shows in her contribution, there are various
styles of Turkmen epic singing, with influences both from folksongs and
from classical music (Chapter 6).

The Karakalpaks live on the southern shores of the Aral Sea and on the
lower reaches of the Amu-Darya in present-day Uzbekistan. They have
two types of epic singers, the *baqsy* and the *zhyrau*. The *baqsy*'s manner
of performance (as well as his repertoire) is reminiscent of that of the
Turkmen *bagshy*, in particular of northern Turkmenistan and Khorezm in

---

[58]See Chodzko 1842, 583-84. The music of the Azeri version of the epic cycle on Köroghlu is
the subject of a book by Tariel' Mamedov (1984), in which detailed musical analyses and
transcriptions of a number of *dastans* (as these epics are called in Azeri and other Turkic
languages) are found. On this cycle of prosimetric epics, see also Reichl 1992, 318-33.
[59]Vámbéry 1865, 258.
[60]For a description of Turkmen singing (including "dzhuk-dzhuk"), see also Uspenskiy and
Belyaev 1979, 106-11.

Uzbekistan. The *zhyrau*, on the other hand, is the representative of a fairly archaic singer type; his performance style is analysed in a comparative Turkic context in Chapter 7.

As we have seen, in Greece the epic genre has been transformed into short songs, some narrative, some predominantly lyric. Similar transformations can be found in Turkey, where the traditional singer of tales, the *aşık* (lit. 'lover'), whose repertoire has, in addition to epic poetry, always comprised songs and instrumental pieces, is today mostly an instrumentalist and singer (as well as composer) of lyrics.[61] But the agonistic tradition has survived; Emine Gürsoy-Naskali (Marmara Üniversitesi) describes these poetic competitions and interprets the *aşıks*' poems in Chapter 8.

The epic cycle on Göroghli, as performed by speakers of an Iranian language in northern Afghanistan, is the topic of Hiromi Lorraine Sakata's (University of California at Los Angeles) contribution, in which she pays particular attention to performance-oriented aspects of musical structure (Chapter 9). While there is a symbiosis of Turkic and Iranian speakers in some parts of Central Asia (Uzbekistan, Tajikistan, Afghanistan), in others contacts are very intimate between speakers of Turkic and speakers of Mongolian languages. Their epic traditions, too, have many traits in common, in particular as regards the epics of the Turkic peoples of the Altai and of the Mongolians of Mongolia and Sinkiang. The texts of many of these epics have become available to non-Mongolists, mainly through the efforts of Walther Heissig, editor of the monumental series "Mongolische Epen."[62] Their music has fared less well. Carole Pegg (University of Cambridge and *New Grove*, London), one of the few ethnomusicologists working on the music of Mongolian epics, offers an interpretation of bardic performance with special emphasis on ethnographic and sociological data (Chapter 10).

The vast area of Asia is rich in epic traditions, many of which are only imperfectly known while doubtless many more exist than are known to epic scholars. It is true that many forms of sung narrative are fairly remote from the canonical form of an epic as represented by the *Iliad* or the *Odyssey*, nor are many of these narratives heroic. C. M. Bowra points out that much of this poetry is shamanistic rather than heroic, and he decided for this reason to exclude the epics of some Central Asian peoples — such as the Tibetans and the Mongols — as well as of Southeast-Asian peoples such as the Sea Dyaks of Borneo.[63] Bowra was not

---

[61]In eastern Anatolia orally transmitted prosimetric narratives could still be heard in the sixties and seventies; the edition of the version of Köroghlu collected by the folklorist Ferruh Arsunar is notable for its numerous musical transcriptions (Arsunar 1963).

[62]Thirteen volumes of the series "Mongolische Epen," published by Harrassowitz in Wiesbaden since 1975, have appeared to date. Professor Heissig kindly chaired one of the sessions of the colloquium on which this book is based.

[63]Bowra 1952, 5-8.

familiar with the multiplicity of epic traditions in the Philippines, but he might have disregarded many of them on the same grounds; as Nicole Revel (C.N.R.S., Paris) shows in her discussion of Palawan epics, these narratives are closely related to shamanism and shamanistic practices (Chapter 11).[64] Bowra was, however, aware of India, but because of the dominant position accorded to the *Mahâbhârata* and the *Râmâyana* apparently thought of Indian epics only in terms of a written tradition. As research carried out in the last decades has revealed, there is a large body of living epic traditions on the subcontinent. One of them is that of the Tulu, a Dravidian language people of southern Karnataka and northern Kerala. Their *Siri* epic was introduced at the colloquium by Lauri and Anneli Honko, who have meanwhile completed an edition and translation of this epic.[65] Epic scholars have also become familiar with the epic of Pâbûjî of Rajasthan through the work of John D. Smith. Smith stresses the intimate connection between music and metre, confirming the observations made above: "The epic of Pâbûjî is sung, and any account of it which failed to give some description of its music would be incomplete. What is more, textual form is here largely determined by musical form, so that it is literally impossible to study the words in isolation from the music."[66] Although from a musicological point of view, Indian music is well explored (in particular the *râgâ* system), there is certainly room for more studies on the music and performance of Indian epics.[67]

In her book on oral literature in Africa, Ruth Finnegan gave a systematic survey of the major genres, with however only a "Note on 'epic'."[68] Her dismissal of this genre (and indeed questioning of its existence in sub-Saharan Africa) has been much criticized, and a number of studies on African epic traditions have subsequently appeared.[69] While it is, of course, debatable whether the term "epic" as defined by reference to Western literature is applicable to all of the narrative poetry subsumed under this term in comparative studies, there can be little doubt that the oral narratives recorded in West Africa, in particular from the Mande and Ful populations, conform to the general idea of epic. Various versions of the epic of Sunjata (also known outside scholarly circles through Alex Haley's *Roots* of 1976 and its televised version) have been recorded,

---

[64]For a summary survey of Philippine epic traditions, see Manuel 1963.

[65]In collaboration with Chinnappa Gowda and Viveka Rai; see Honko 1998 and Honko et al. 1998.

[66]Smith 1991, 30; see further his description of the music on pp. 30-38 and the musical examples on pp. 46-53.

[67]It is to be regretted that the present volume does not contain a contribution on the music and performance of an Indian epic tradition. For a useful survey of these traditions, see Blackburn, Claus, Flueckiger, and Wadley 1989.

[68]Finnegan 1970, 108-10.

[69]To mention just two: Isidore Okpewho's monograph of 1979 and Daniel Biebuyck's 1978 study of Banyanga epics (following his earlier edition of the *Mwindo* epic).

edited and translated.[70] Gordon Innes, in his edition, distinguishes three modes in the performance of the epic, a speech mode, a recitation mode, and a song mode. The choice of these modes is dependent on content: for predominantly narrative portions of the epic the speech mode is chosen, for passages in which a character or action is praised or general observations on life are made, the recitation mode is used, while the song mode is reserved for songs associated with Sunjata.[71] In any mode, the recitation is accompanied by musical instruments, generally the *kora* (a harp-lute with twenty-one strings) and/or the *balo* (a xylophone). This accompaniment "is almost always built on a two, four or eight bar phrase (more rarely six) characterised by a distinctive melodic, tonal or rhythmic structure. It is normally homophonic in character, though sometimes heterophonic and more rarely monophonic. In passages of vocalisation it is subdued and subordinate to the voice. In many of the more extensive breath pauses it increases in elaboration as it does in dynamic level, and at such points may show considerable fioritura" (18). In the speech mode the singer's voice is generally raised; in the recitation mode the voice is raised almost to the limits; as Anthony King (who wrote the respective sections in Innes' edition) points out: "Vocalisation in this mode occurs as a variety of song, though common misconceptions have in the past led observers to mistakenly classify this kind of performance elsewhere in Africa as chant" (18). He adds that "the use of stable pitch values, measured rhythm and phrases of balanced length distinguishes performance in this mode from the freer intonation and rhythm, and contrasted phrase lengths of the Speech mode" (19). The song mode, finally, is comparable to singing in the usual sense of the word: "The pitch, intensity and resonance of the voice are at levels similar to those of the Recitation mode. The Song mode is however distinguished from the Recitation mode by its much slower syllabic rate, by the rhythmic variety brought to the realisation of its text, by the occurrence of long held syllables especially in line final position, and by the use of contrasted melodic phrases and motion, ascending and descending" (19). Similar performance modes are found in other West African traditions, to judge from descriptions and audio-material available on records and compact disks. Christiane Seydou (C.N.R.S., Paris), a specialist in the epic traditions of the Ful people,[72] supplements this picture by a detailed analysis of the musical motto, a

---

[70]See, *inter alia*, Innes 1974 and Johnson 1986.

[71]For a summary of the three modes, see Innes 1974, 15-20; for comments on the musical instruments and musical transcriptions, see pp. 20-24.

[72]The name of this people and their language appears in different forms (Ful, Fulani, Peul, Fulfulde) due to the difference between singular and plural: sg. Pulo (hence French Peul), pl. Fulɓe; their language is called (in some regions) Fulfulde.

device comparable to the leitmotifs of Yakut (and other Asian) epics (Chapter 12).

In view of such overwhelming evidence as to the musical performance of epic it seems strange that medievalists continue to be sceptic about the singing (in its various senses) of medieval epics for which an oral background can be assumed. "Scandinavia non cantat" was Andreas Heusler's apodictic statement. Joseph Harris (Harvard University), Anglo-Saxonist, Nordist and folklorist, sifts the documentary and scholarly evidence on the performance of Old Norse oral narrative and poetry in order to provide a basis for a fuller understanding of the performance of oral poetry in the older Germanic tongues (Chapter 13). John Stevens (University of Cambridge), who has written widely on music and poetry in the Middle Ages, sums up the present state of our knowledge of the singing of medieval narrative poetry, thus linking the ethnomusicological study of live oral performances to the musicological analysis and interpretation of what has survived in medieval manuscripts (Chapter 14). It is to be hoped that the following chapters, while showing diversity and variation, will help to provide a basis for comparison (also with epics no longer accessible in live performance) and will enhance an awareness of the oral epic as a poetico-musical form which is only incompletely appreciated when music (and more generally performance) is ignored.

References

Abaev, V. I. 1990. "Nartovskiy epos Osetin." *Narty: Osetinskiy geroicheskiy epos.* Epos narodov SSSR. 2 vols. Moscow: Nauka. 1: 7-76.

Amzulescu, Al. I., ed. 1981. *Cîntecul epic eroic: Tipologie şi corpus de texte poetice.* Bucarest: Editura Academiei Republicii Socialiste România.

Apel, Willi. 1969. *Harvard Dictionary of Music.* 2nd ed., rev. and enl. Cambridge, MA: Harvard UP.

Arsunar, Ferruh, ed. 1963. *Köroğlu.* Ankara: Türkiye İş Bankası.

Astakhova, A. M., et al., eds. 1961. *Byliny Pechory i Zimnego Berega (Novye zapisi).* Pamyatniki russkogo fol'klora. Moscow: Nauka.

Balandin, A. I., ed. 1983. *Onezhskie byliny zapisannye A. F. Gil'ferdingom letom 1871 goda.* Arkhangel'sk: Severo-Zapadnoe Knizhnoe Izd.

Baud-Bovy, Samuel. 1958. *Études sur la chanson cleftique.* Collection de l'Institut Français d'Athènes 53. Athens: Institut Français d'Athènes.

Beaton, Roderick. 1980. *Folk Poetry of Modern Greece.* Cambridge: Cambridge UP.

Belyaev, V. 1969. *Sbornik Kirshi Danilova: Opyt restavratsii pesen.* Moscow: Sovetskiy kompozitor.

Beliaev [=Belyaev], Viktor M. 1975. *Central Asian Music: Essays in the History of the Music of the Peoples of the U. S. S. R.* Ed. and trans. Mark and Greta Slobin. Middletown, CT: Wesleyan UP.

Biebuyck, Daniel. 1978. *Hero and Chief: Epic Literature from the Banyanga (Zaire Republic).* Berkeley: U of California P.

Blackburn, S. H., P. J. Claus, J. B. Flueckiger, and S. S. Wadley, eds. 1989. *Oral Epics in India.* Berkeley: U of California P.

Blum, Stephen. 1992. "Analysis of Musical Style." *Ethnomusicology: An Introduction.* Ed. Helen Myers. New York: Norton. 165-218.

Boratav, Pertev Naili. 1973. *100 Soruda Türk Halk Edebiyatı.* 2nd ed. Istanbul: Gerçek.

Bose, Fritz. 1953. *Musikalische Völkerkunde.* Freiburg i. Br.: Atlantis.

Bowra, C. M. 1945. *From Virgil to Milton.* London: Macmillan.

——. 1952. *Heroic Poetry.* London: Macmillan.

Bronson, Bertrand Harris. 1969. "The Interdependence of Ballad Tunes and Texts." *The Ballad as Song.* Berkeley: U of California P. 37-63. [Or. publ. in 1944.]

Cable, Thomas. 1974. *The Meter and Melody of 'Beowulf'.* Illinois Studies in Language and Literature 64. Urbana, IL: U of Illinois P.

Chadwick, N. Kershaw, trans. 1932. *Russian Heroic Poetry.* Cambridge: Cambridge UP.

Chadwick, H. Munro, and N. Kershaw Chadwick. 1932-40. *The Growth of Literature.* 3 vols. Cambridge: Cambridge UP.

Chodzko, Alexander, trans. 1842. *Specimens of the Popular Poetry of Persia, as Found in the Adventures and Improvisations of Kurroglou, the Ban-*

dit-Minstrel of Northern Persia; and in the Songs of the People Inhabiting the Shores of the Caspian Sea. London.

Costello, D. P., and I. P. Foote, eds. 1967. *Russian Folk Literature: Skazki, Liricheskie pesin, Byliny, Istoricheskie pesni, Dukhovnye stikhi.* Oxford: Clarendon.

Danilov, Kirsha, ed. 1977. *Drevnie rossiyskie stikhotvoreniya.* Ed. A. P. Evgen'eva and P. N. Putilov. Literaturnye pamyatniki. 2nd ed. Moscow: Nauka.

Davies, Stephen. 1994. *Musical Meaning and Expression.* Ithaca, NY: Cornell UP.

Dobrovol'sksiy, B. M., and V. V. Korguzalov, eds. 1981. *Byliny: Russkiy muzykal'nyi epos.* Moscow: Sovetskiy kompozitor.

Dumézil, Georges, trans. 1965. *Le Livre des Héros: Légendes sur les Nartes.* Caucase. Paris: Gallimard.

Ellingson, Ter. 1992. "Transcription." *Ethnomusicology: An Introduction.* Ed. Helen Myers. New York: Norton. 110-52.

Erdely, Stephen. 1995. *Music of Southslavic Epics from the Bihać Region of Bosnia.* New York: Garland.

Fedotov, O. I. 1995. "A. F. Hil'ferding o narodnom stikhe." *Russkiy Fol'klor. XXVIII. Epicheskie traditsii. Materialy i issledovaniya.* Sankt Petersburg: Nauka. 206-16.

Feld, Steven, and Aaron A. Fox. 1994. "Music and Language." *Annual Review of Anthropology* 23: 25-53.

Finnegan, Ruth. 1970. *Oral Literature in Africa.* Oxford: Clarendon.

Foley, John Miles. 1995. *The Singer of Tales in Performance.* Bloomington, IN: Indiana UP.

Galko, Ladislav, and František Poloczek. 1969. "Systematik der formbildenden Elemente der slowakischen Volkslieder." *Methoden der Klassifikation von Volksliedweisen.* Slowakische Akademie der Wissenschaften, Institut für Musikwissenschaft, Simposia 2. Bratislava: Slowakische Akademie der Wissenschaften. 57-72.

Gatsak, V. M. 1967. *Vostochno-romanskiy geroicheskiy epos: Issledovanie i teksty.* Moscow: Nauka.

Georgiades, Thrasybulos. 1958. *Musik und Rhythmus bei den Griechen: Zum Ursprung der abendländischen Musik.* Hamburg: Rowohlt.

Hainsworth, J. B. 1991. *The Idea of Epic.* Berkeley, CA: U of California P.

Harris, Joseph, and Karl Reichl, eds. 1997. *Prosimetrum: Crosscultural Perspectives in Prose and Verse.* Cambridge: Brewer.

Hatto, A. T., gen. ed. 1980-89. *Traditions of Heroic and Epic Poetry. I. The Traditions. II. Characteristics and Techniques.* 2 vols., vol. 2 ed. by J. B. Hainsworth. London: The Modern Humanities Research Association.

Helffer, Mireille. 1977. *Les Chants dans l'épopée tibétaine de Ge-sar d'après le Livre de la course de cheval: Version chantée de Blo-bzah bstan-'jin.* Hautes Études Orientales 9. Geneva, Paris: Droz.

Hoerburger, Felix. 1952. "Westöstliche Entsprechungen im Volksepos." *Die Musikforschung* 5: 354-61.

Honko, Lauri. 1998. *Textualising the Siri Epic.* FF Communications 264. Helsinki: Suomalainen Tiedeakatemia.

Honko, Lauri, in collaboration with Chinnappa Gowda, Anneli Honko, and Viveka Rai, eds. and trans. 1998. *The Siri Epic As Performed by Gopala Naika.* 2 vols. FF Communications 265, 266. Helsinki: Suomalainen Tiedeakatemia.

Innes, Gordon, ed. and trans. 1974. *Sunjata: Three Mandinka Versions.* London: School of Oriental and African Studies, University of London.

Jakobson, Roman. 1966. "Slavic Epic Verse: Studies in Comparative Metrics." *Selected Writings. IV. Slavic Epic Studies.* The Hague, Paris: Mouton. 414-63.

Johnson, John William, ed. and trans. 1986. *The Epic of Son-Jara: A West African Tradition.* Text by Fa-Digi Sisòkò. Bloomington, IN: Indiana UP.

Kondrat'eva, S. N. 1975. "K istoricheskoy tipologii epicheskikh napevov." *Tipologiya narodnogo eposa.* Ed. V. M. Gatsak. Moscow: Nauka. 152-62.

———. 1977. *Karel'skaya narodnaya pesnya.* Moscow: Sovetskiy Kompozitor.

Korganow, Basil. 1899-1900. "Mestwirebi, die Troubadoure des Kaukasus." *Sammelbände der internationalen Musikgesellschaft* 1: 627-29.

Korguzalov, V. V. 1978. "Napevy bylin novgorodskogo tsikla." *Novgorodskie byliny.* Ed. Yu. I. Smirnov and V. G. Smolitskiy. AN SSSR, Literaturnye pamyatniki. Moscow: Nauka. 336-61.

———. 1995. "Dvizhenie epicheskoy traditsii na russkom severe." *Russkiy fol'klor. XXVIII. Epicheskie traditsii. Materialy i issledovaniya.* Rossiyskaya AN, Inst. Russkoy literatury. Sankt-Peterburg: Nauka. 133-45.

Kruta, Beniamin. 1985. "Éléments musicaux convergents et divergents entre l'épopée albanaise et celle sud-slave." *Culture Populaire Albanaise* 5: 103-21.

Kuckertz, Josef, ed. 1980. *Außereuropäische Musik in Einzeldarstellungen.* Mit weiterführender Literatur und Diskographie von Rüdiger Schumacher. München: dtv/ Kassel: Bärenreiter.

Lach, Robert. 1913. *Studien zur Entwicklungsgeschichte der ornamentalen Melopöie.* Leipzig: Kahnt.

Langer, Susanne K. 1957. *Philosophy in a New Key: A Study in the Symbolism of Reason, Rite, and Art.* 3rd ed. Cambridge, MA: Harvard UP.

Lomax, Alan. 1968. *Folk Song Style and Culture.* Washington, DC: American Association for the Advancement of Science. [Rpt. New Brunswick, NJ: Transaction, 1978.]

Lord, Albert B. 1960. *The Singer of Tales.* Harvard Studies in Comparative Literature 24. Cambridge, MA: Harvard UP.

Mamedov, Tariel'. 1984. *Pesni Këroglu.* Baku: Gyandzhlik.

Manuel, E. Arsenio. 1963. "A Survey of Philippine Folk Epics." *Asian Folklore Studies* 22: 1-76.

Nagy, Gregory. 1989. "Early Greek Views of Poets and Poetry." *The Cambridge History of Literary Criticism. I. Classical Criticism.* Ed. George A. Kennedy. Cambridge: Cambridge UP.

Nettl, Bruno. 1964. *Theory and Method in Ethnomusicology.* New York: Schirmer.

Nettl, Bruno, and Roman Rosdolsky. 1958. "Russian Polyphonic Epics." *Journal of American Folklore* 68: 34.

Neubecker, Annemarie J. 1994. *Altgriechische Musik: Eine Einführung.* 2nd ed. Darmstadt: Wissenschaftliche Buchgesellschaft.

NHDM: see Randel 1986.

Notopoulos, James, ed. 1959. *Modern Greek Heroic Oral Poetry.* Ethnic Folkways Library Album FE 4468. New York: Folkways Records. [Record and booklet.]

OED: *The Oxford English Dictionary.* 1989. Ed. J. A. H. Murray et al. 2nd ed. J. A. Simpson and E. S. C. Weiner. Oxford: Clarendon.

Oinas, Felix J. 1978. "Russian Byliny." *Heroic Epic and Saga: An Introduction to the World's Great Folk Epics.* Ed. Felix J. Oinas. Bloomington, IN: Indiana UP.

Okpewho, Isidore. 1979. *The Epic in Africa: Toward a Poetics of the Oral Performance.* New York: Columbia UP.

Parry, Milman, coll., Albert B. Lord, ed. and trans. 1954. *Serbocroatian Heroic Songs. I. Novi Pazar: English Translations.* Cambridge, MA: Harvard UP/ Belgrade: Serbian Academy of Sciences.

Propp, V. Ya. 1955. *Russkiy geroicheskiy epos.* Leningrad: Izd. Leningradskogo Universiteta.

Qureshi, Regula Burckhardt. 1987. "Musical Sound and Contextual Input: A Performance Model For Musical Analysis." *Ethnomusicology* 31: 56-86.

Rakhaev, A. I. 1994. "O muzyke nartskogo eposa Balkarii i Karachaya." *Narty: Geroicheskiy epos Balkartsev i Karachaevtsev.* Eds. A. I. Alieva, R. A.-K. Ortabaeva, T. M. Khadzhieva, A. Z. Kholaev. Epos narodov Evrazii. Moscow: Nauka. 605-14.

Randel, Don Michael, ed. 1986. *The New Harvard Dictionary of Music.* Cambridge, MA: Harvard UP.

Reichl, Karl. 1992. *Turkic Oral Epic Poetry: Traditions, Forms, Poetic Structure.* The Albert Bates Lord Studies in Oral Tradition 7. New York: Garland.

——. 1993. "Karatschaier und Balkaren." *Enzyklopädie des Märchens.* Vol. 7: col. 960-62.

——. 1995. "Epos als Ereignis: Bemerkungen zum Vortrag der zentralasiatischen Turkepen." *Formen und Funktion mündlicher Tradition.* Ed. Walther Heissig. Nordrhein-Westfälische Akademie der Wissenschaften, Abh. 95. Opladen: Westdeutscher Verlag. 156-82.

Reynolds, Dwight F. 1994/95. "Musical Dimensions of an Arabic Oral Epic Tradition (Egypt)." *Asian Music* 26: 53-94.

——. 1995. *Heroic Poets, Poetic Heroes: The Ethnography of Performance in an Arabic Oral Epic Tradition.* Myth and Poetics. Ithaca, NY: Cornell UP.

Rouse, W. H. D., trans. 1956. *Great Dialogues of Plato.* Ed. Eric H. Warmington and Philip G. Rouse. New York: New American Library of World Literature.

Rybnikov, P. N., ed. 1909-10. *Pesni.* 3 vols. 2nd ed. by A. E. Gruzinskiy. Moscow: Sotrudnik shkol. [First ed. in 4 vols. Moscow, 1861-67.]

Sachs, Curt. 1962. *The Wellsprings of Music.* Ed. Jaap Kunst. The Hague: Nijhoff.

Sarkisian, Svetlana, et al. 1980. "Union of Soviet Socialist Republics." *The New Grove Dictionary of Music and Musicians.* Ed. Stanley Sadie. 20 vols. London: Macmillan. 19: 334-424.

Saville-Troike, Muriel. 1989. *The Ethnography of Communication: An Introduction.* 2nd ed. Oxford: Blackwell.

Sokolov, F. V. 1961. "O napevakh pechorskikh bylin." *Byliny Pechory i Zimnego Berega (Novye Zapisi).* Ed. A. M. Astakhova et al. Pamyatniki russkogo fol'klora. Moscow: Nauka. 497-524.

Smirnov, Yu. I., ed. 1991. *Russkaya epicheskaya poeziya Sibiri i Dal'nego Vostoka.* Pamyatniki fol'klora narodov Sibiri i Dal'nego Vostoka. Novosibirsk: Nauka.

Smith, John D., ed. and trans. 1991. *The Epic of Pābūjī: A Study, Transcription and Translation.* Cambridge: Cambridge UP.

Suppan, Wolfgang. 1969. "Zur Verwendung der Begriffe Gestalt, Struktur, Modell und Typus in der Musikethnologie." *Analyse und Klassifikation von Volksmelodien: Bericht über die 3. Arbeitstagung der Study Group of Folk Music Systematization beim International Folk Music Council vom 24. bis 28. Oktober 1967 in Radziejowice.* Ed. Doris Stockmann and Jan Stęszewski. Cracow: Polskie Wydwnictwo Muzyczne. 41-52.

——. 1979. "Epos." *Die Musik in Geschichte und Gegenwart. 16. Supplement: Earsden – Zweibrücken.* Basel: Bärenreiter. Col. 101-14.

Sydow, C. W. von. 1948. "Geography and Folk-Tale Oicotypes." *Selected Papers on Folklore, Published on the Occasion of his 70th Birthday.* Ed. Laurits Bødker. Copenhagen: Rosenkilde and Bagger. 44-59. [Or. publ. 1934 in *Béaloideas* 8.]

Themelis, Dimitris. 1994. "Bemerkungen zur Struktur der griechischen Klephtenlieder." *Historische Volksmusikforschung.* Ed. Doris Stockmann and Annette Erler. Orbis musicarum 10. Göttingen: Edition Re. 147-55.

Tokarev, S. A., gen. ed. 1980-82. *Mify narodov mira.* 2 vols. Moscow: Izd. Sovetskaya Entsiklopediya.

Trautmann, Reinhold. 1935. *Die Volksdichtung der Großrussen. I. Das Heldenlied (Die Byline).* Sammlung slavischer Lehr- und Handbücher, III.7. Heidelberg: Winter.

Tskhurbaeva, K. G. 1969. "O napevakh osetinskikh nartovskikh skazaniy." *Skazaniya o Nartakh — Epos narodov Kavkaza.* Ed. A. A. Petrosyan,

A. I. Alieva, V. M. Gatsak, and U. B. Dalgat. Moscow: Nauka. 469-83.

Uspenskiy, V., and V. Belyaev. 1979. *Turkmenskaya muzyka.* 2nd ed. Ashkhabad: Turkmenistan. [Rpt. of 1st ed. 1928.]

Vámbéry, Hermann. 1865. *Reise in Mittelasien von Teheran durch die Turkmanische Wüste an der Ostküste des Kaspischen Meeres nach Chiwa, Bochara und Samarkand, ausgeführt im Jahr 1863.* Leipzig.

Vasil'eva, E. E. 1989. "Etnomuzykovedecheskaya problematika russkogo eposa (v svyazi s vykhodom pervoy muzykal'noy antologii bylin)." *Muzyka eposa. Stat'i i materialy.* Ed. I. I. Zemtsovskiy. Yoshkar-Ola: Komissiya muzykovedeniya i fol'klora Soyuza kompozitorov RSFSR. 44-68.

Vetterl, Karel, and Jaromír Gelnár. 1969. "Die Melodienordnung auf der Basis der metrorhythmischen Formgestaltung." *Methoden der Klassifikation von Volksliedweisen.* Slowakische Akademie der Wissenschaften, Institut für Musikwissenschaft, Simposia 2. Bratislava: Slowakische Akademie der Wissenschaften. 81-90.

West, M. L. 1973. "Indo-European Metre." *Glotta* 51: 161-87.

——. 1981. The Singing of Homer and the Modes of Early Greek Music." *Journal of Hellenic Studies* 101: 113-29.

——. 1992. *Ancient Greek Music.* Oxford: Clarendon.

Wiora, Walter, ed. 1966. *European Folk Song: Common Forms in Characteristic Modifications.* Cologne: Arno Volk/ London: Oxford UP.

Wünsch, Walther. 1934. *Die Geigentechnik der südslawischen Guslaren.* Veröffentlichungen des Musikwissenschaftlichen Instituts der Deutschen Universität in Prag 5. Brünn: Rohrer.

——. 1937. *Heldensänger in Südosteuropa.* Arbeiten aus dem Institut für Lautforschung an der Universität Berlin 4. Leipzig: Harrassowitz.

Zemtsovskiy, I. I., ed. 1989. *Muzyka eposa: Stat'i i materialy.* Yoshkar-Ola: Komissiya muzykovedeniya i fol'klora Soyuza kompozitorov RSFSR.

Zhirmunskiy, V. M., and H. T. Zarifov. 1947. *Uzbekskiy narodnyi geroicheskiy epos.* Moscow: OGIZ.

Zhirmunsky [=Zhirmunskiy], Victor. 1966. "The Epic of 'Alpamysh' and the Return of Odysseus." *Proceedings of the British Academy* 52: 267-86.

2 EPIC AS MUSIC: RHAPSODIC MODELS OF HOMER IN PLATO'S *TIMAEUS* AND *CRITIAS*

Gregory Nagy

Plato's *Timaeus* and *Critias* contain valuable references to the performative techniques of *rhapsôidoi* or "rhapsodes" and to the compositional techniques of Homeric poetry. These techniques belong to the *tekhnê* 'art' known to Plato and his contemporaries as *mousikê*.[1] The word's meaning is self-evident: *mousikê* is the art of the Muses. As we will see from the testimony of inscriptions and other evidence, this term *mousikê* included the "music" of (1) rhapsodes, (2) citharodes = cithara-singers = singers self-accompanied by the cithara or "lyre," (3) aulodes = aulos-singers = singers accompanied by the aulos or "pipe," (4) cithara-players, and (5) aulos-players. In Plato's time, the high point of this kind of *mousikê* in the civic calendar of Athens was the Festival of the Panathenaia.[2] Primarily by way of the *Timaeus* and the *Critias* of Plato, in addition to his definitive work concerning rhapsodes, the *Ion*, we can make considerable progress in reconstructing a central event in the *agônes* or 'contests' of *mousikê* at the Panathenaic Festival of Athens, that is, rhapsodic competitions in the performance of Homer. Also, the *Timaeus* and the *Critias* reveal details about the "musical" techniques of rhapsodes and of "Homer" himself. These details provide a basis for understanding the

---

[1]See especially Plato *Laws* VI 764c-765d, to be discussed below.

[2]For Plato, the term *mousikê* also included the "music" of *khorôidia*, the singing and dancing of a *khoros* 'chorus': see Plato *Laws* 764e (in this passage, *khorôidia* is explicitly connected with *orkhêsis* 'dancing' as well as singing). By default, Plato (*ibid.*) designates as *monôidia* all forms of *mousikê* that are not *khorôidia* (such a designation is problematic, because *monôidia* does not account for the "music" of such categories as solo cithara-playing and solo aulos-playing). A primary form of *khorôidia* was the choral ode of tragedy and comedy. In Plato's time and earlier, the high point of this kind of *mousikê* in the civic calendar of Athens was the Festival of the Dionysia (also, secondarily, the Festival of the Lenaia). From the standpoint of the Classical period of the fifth century, tragedy and comedy *per se* are not "music." For Plato, *mousikê* applies to *khorôidia* only, which is just one aspect of tragedy and comedy. In the Classical period, the "music" of tragedy and comedy *per se* is not officially inspired by the Muses: hence it is not technically *mousikê*, which is the "art" or *tekhnê* of the Muses. In later periods, however, such distinctions are blurred by the growing professionalization of theatrical performances, as we see from the evolution of such institutions as the *Dionusou tekhnitai* in the early third century (cf. PP 174n74 and 177n89). — For bibliographical abbreviations, see the References at the end of this chapter.

nature of the *Timaeus* and the *Critias* as artistic — even "rhapsodic" — productions in their own right.

It is important to start by stressing that the rhapsodic performances of Homer at the Panathenaic Festival were based on the principle of competition. The key word is *agôn* 'competition, contest, ordeal', as evoked in the striking expression of Friedrich Nietzsche, "der agonale Geist."[3] The agonistic principle underlying the rhapsodic performances of Homer at the Panathenaia is evident in Plato's *Ion*. This dialogue is named after a rhapsode from Ephesus who comes to Athens to compete for first prize at the Panathenaia (καὶ τὰ Παναθήναια νικήσομεν, *Ion* 530b2). Plato's wording makes it explicit that the occasion for the performing of Homer by rhapsodes at the Panathenaia is in effect a competition or contest among rhapsodes, an *agôn* (ἀγῶνα at *Ion* 530a5, picked up by ἠγωνίζου and ἠγωνίσω at a8), and that the agonistic art of the *rhapsôidoi* 'rhapsodes' falls under the general category of *mousikê* (μουσικῆς at a7). These words *agôn* and *mousikê* are essential for understanding the traditional art or *tekhnê* of the rhapsodes.[4]

Let us start with *mousikê*, as mentioned in the passage just cited, Plato *Ion* 530a7. To repeat, the word's meaning should be self-evident: *mousikê* is the art or *tekhnê* of the Muses. And yet, as we shall see, *mousikê* is subject to misunderstandings. Accordingly, it is essential to stress right away what our passage in Plato *Ion* 530a7 indicates clearly: that the art of *mousikê* includes the art of the rhapsode.[5] The art or *tekhnê* of *mousikê* is an agonistic art: those who practice this *tekhnê* must compete with each other in formal and institutionalized competitions called *agônes*.

At the Panathenaia, there are *agônes* of *mousikê* not only for rhapsodes but also for *kitharôidoi* 'citharodes' [= cithara-singers], *aulôidoi* 'aulodes' [= aulos-singers], cithara-players, and aulos-players, as we learn directly from an Athenian inscription dated at around 380 BC, IG II² 2311, which records the winners of Panathenaic prizes.[6] We also learn about these categories of "musical" competition from Plato *Laws* VI 764d-e (mention of rhapsodes, cithara-singers, and aulos-players), where

---

[3]Cf. Berve 1966.

[4]The principle of *agôn* is common to the "music" of epic and the "music" of tragedy/ comedy. Like the Festival of the Panathenaia, the Festivals of the Dionysia and the Lenaia were a setting for *agôn* 'competition' among composers of what we would call "music": see especially Plato *Laws* VIII 835a. See also PH 386-387 and 401-403, especially with reference to Euripides *Bacchae* 975 and Aristophanes *Wasps* 1439. Still, tragedy and comedy are not *mousikê*: only the *khorôidia* of tragedy and comedy is *mousikê*. See above.

[5]Conversely, to repeat, the art of *mousikê* does not technically include the overall art of the dramatist of tragedy or comedy.

[6]For an introduction to this inscription, see Parke 1977, 35.

the wording makes it clear that the point of reference is the Panathenaia.[7] The wording also makes it clear that competition is involved: this kind of *mousikê* is described as "agonistic," *agônistikê* (*Laws* VI 764d). In fact, the only aspect of *mousikê* that is not overtly competitive is the educational: *mousikê* is subdivided into two aspects, *agônistikê* and *paideia* (*Laws* VI 764c6-7).

As we take a closer look at the Panathenaic inscription dated at around 380 BC, we may notice straight off that the winning competitors received prizes of high monetary value: for example, the first prize in the competitions of citharodes was a crown of gold worth 1000 drachmas in addition to 500 silver drachmas. This same inscription must have mentioned the prize-winning rhapsodes at the beginning of the document, lines 1-3, where the stone is broken off. It is unfortunate that the break happens at exactly the point where we would expect the victorious rhapsodes to be listed.[8] The author of a most influential work on the Panathenaia, J. A. Davison, has expressed doubt that this 4th-century BC inscription had mentioned the prize-winning rhapsodes at lines 1-3,[9] adding: "rhapsodic competitions are known only to the literary tradition."[10]

But there is in fact a very important piece of direct epigraphical evidence about rhapsodic competitions. The document in question comes from a city other than Athens. It is IG XII ix 189, an inscription from the city of Eretria in Euboea (ca. 341/40 BC) concerning a festival of Artemis.[11] Right at the beginning, the program of the Artemisia is explicitly formulated:[12]

τιθεῖν τὴμ πόλιν ἀγῶνα μουσικῆς

that the city is to organize a competition [*agôn*] of *mousikê*.
(IG XII ix 189.5)

As we read on, we find more details:

τὴν δὲ μουσικὴν τιθεῖν ῥαψωιδοῖς, | αὐλωιδοῖς, κιθαρισταῖς, κιθαρωιδοῖς, παρωιδοῖς, | τοὺς δὲ τὴν μουσικὴν ἀγωνιζομένους

---

[7]In Plato *Laws* VI 764e and VIII 835a, the officials in charge of these *agônes* 'competitions' in *mousikê* are specified as *athlothetai*. As we will see from what follows, these officials are specific to the Panathenaia.
[8]Parke 1977, 35.
[9]Davison [1968], 56. The IG II[2] 2311 edition conjectures "citharists" rather than "rhapsodes" for the lacuna.
[10]Davison [1968], 56n2.
[11]PP 111n24. For more on this inscription, see Nilsson 1906, 239.
[12]I alert the reader, in advance, to the "culture shock" of the Euboean dialect (e.g. shortening of η to ει, rhotacism of sigma, etc.).

πάντα[ς] | ἀγωνίζεσθαι προσόδιον τεῖ θυσίει ἐν τεῖ αὐλεῖ ἔ|[χο]ντας
τὴν σκευὴν ἥμπερ ἐν τοῖ ἀγῶνι ἔχουρ[ι]

. . . and that [the city] is to organize the *mousikê* for rhapsodes, aulodes
[= aulos-singers], cithara-players, *citharodes* [cithara-singers], and par-
ody-singers; further, that those who compete [*agônizomai*] in the
mousikê should all compete [*agônizomai*] in the *prosodion* [= processional song] for the sacrifice [*thusia*][13] in the *aulê*, having the same costume that they have in the competition proper.   (IG XII ix 189.10-15)

This inscription from Eretria contains valuable comparative evidence
for helping us understand the *agônes* of *mousikê* at the Panathenaia in
Athens. These Athenian competitions seem to be the historical basis for
the theoretical models discussed in Plato *Laws* VI 764d-e, where we read
of competition (*agônistikê* d5) in *mousikê* (d6) for rhapsodes, citharodes,
auletes [= pipe-players], and so on (other categories are not specified).[14]
Such theoretical references in the *Laws*, as I argue, are based on the
specific historical realities of the Panathenaia.

Moving beyond Plato, we may turn to Aristotle for a less theoretical
and more historical perspective on the Panathenaia. Aristotle gives a brief
outline of the main features of the Panathenaia at Athens in his *Constitution of the Athenians* 60.1-3:

1. *agôn* 'competition' in *mousikê* (τὸν ἀγῶνα τῆς μουσικῆς); prizes
awarded: gold and silver.
2. *agôn* 'competition' in athletics (τὸν γυμνικὸν ἀγῶνα), including
equestrian events (horse-racing and chariot-racing: ἱπποδρομίαν);
prizes awarded: Panathenaic amphoras containing olive oil.
3. *peplos* 'robe' = the ceremonial robe, Peplos (τὸν πέπλον);
woven for the goddess Athena, it was formally presented to her at
the Panathenaia.
4. *pompê* 'procession' = the Panathenaic Procession (τήν τε πομ-
πὴν τῶν Παναθηναίων); at the climax of this procession, the Peplos
was formally presented to Athena. Aristotle does not say it explicitly, but the occasion of this climactic moment is a *thusia*
'sacrifice', more on which later.
5. *athlothetai* = a board of ten magistrates, with one from each
phulê appointed (by lot) every four years for a term of four years;
their function was to organize and supervise all the events of no. 1,

---

[13]More on the implications of the *thusia* 'sacrifice' in the discussion below.
[14]Extended discussion of the parallelisms linking rhapsodes, citharodes, aulodes: PH 54, 85-
104.

no. 2, no. 3, no. 4, including the arranging and awarding of prizes in the case of no. 1 and no. 2.

For the moment, I have kept this outline at a minimum, recapping as closely as possible the main features as reported by Aristotle (he orders them differently, however: 5, 4, 1, 2, 3).

Aristotle's reference in *Constitution of the Athenians* 60.1 to an *agôn* 'competition' in *mousikê* (τὸν ἀγῶνα τῆς μουσικῆς) which he says was held at the Panathenaia does not make explicit the correlation of rhapsodic competitions with the citharodic, the aulodic, and so on. Aristotle's elliptic reference has led to some confusion about the "musical contests" of the Panathenaia, and the conventional but anachronistic translation "musical" confuses the matter even further, since the English word seems to suggest, misleadingly, an exclusion of *rhapsôidoi* 'rhapsodes' and the inclusion only of *kitharôidoi* 'citharodes', *aulôidoi* 'aulodes', and so on.[15] Still, what I infer to be implicit in Aristotle's statement is made explicit in a corresponding mention of the Panathenaia by Isocrates, *Panegyricus* 159, whose words specify that Homeric performances were taking place "in *athla* [contests] of *mousikê*," ἐν τοῖς μουσικοῖς ἄθλοις.[16] Other sources too provide explicit evidence about the institution of rhapsodic contests at the Panathenaia, and many of these specify the correlation of contests in athletics with contests in *mousikê*.[17]

The rhapsodes at the Panathenaia not only competed with each other in performing the poetry of Homer: they also had to take turns following the narrative sequence of that poetry in the process of competition. In the *Hipparkhos* of "pseudo-Plato," there is a story that purports to explain an Athenian law requiring that the *Iliad* and *Odyssey* be performed *in sequence* by the *rhapsôidoi* 'rhapsodes' at the Panathenaia:

---

[15]The term "musical" is used by Davison [1968], 56. As we have seen, Davison even expresses doubt that the 4th-century BC inscription of Panathenaic prizes, IG II² 2311, had mentioned the prize-winning rhapsodes at the beginning of the list, where the inscription is broken off. In his commentary on Aristotle *Constitution of the Athenians* 60.1, Rhodes 1981, 670-71 does not mention rhapsodic contests, speaking only generally of "musical contests." For evidence in the visual arts on rhapsodic competitions at the Panathenaia, see Shapiro 1993, who disputes some commonly-held assumptions about representations of competing rhapsodes (for example, he argues convincingly that the performer represented on Side A of the red-figure neck amphora [London, British Museum E270], ca. 500-490 BC, is an aulode, not a rhapsode).

[16]See PP 111n24.

[17]There is a collection of testimonia assembled by Kotsidu 1991, 243-92. In Plato *Laws* VIII 828b-c, we see a collocation of the noun *agônes* with the adjectives *mousikoi* and *gumnikoi*, mentioned in the context of *athlothetai*. The latter term makes clear a Panathenaic context, as we know from Aristotle's reference to these officials, mentioned above. Cf. Plato *Laws* VIII 834e-835a: again *mousikê*, again specifically including rhapsodes, mentioned again in the context of *athlothetai*. Cf. also Plato *Laws* VI 764d-e: *agôn* of *mousikê*, specifically including rhapsodes as well as citharodes, etc.

Ἱππάρχῳ . . . ὃς ἄλλα τε πολλὰ καὶ καλὰ ἔργα <u>σοφίας</u> ἀπεδείξατο, καὶ <u>τὰ Ὁμήρου</u> <u>ἔπη</u> πρῶτος <u>ἐκόμισεν</u> εἰς τὴν γῆν ταυτηνί, <u>καὶ ἠνάγκασε τοὺς ῥαψῳδοὺς</u> Παναθηναίοις <u>ἐξ ὑπολήψεως ἐφεξῆς</u> αὐτὰ <u>διιέναι</u>, <u>ὥσπερ νῦν ἔτι οἶδε ποιοῦσιν</u>

Hipparkhos, . . . who made a public demonstration of many and beautiful accomplishments to manifest his <u>expertise</u> [<u>*sophia*</u>], especially by being the first to <u>bring over</u> [<u>*komizô*</u>] to this land [= Athens] <u>the poetic utterances</u> [<u>*epê*</u>] of <u>Homer</u>, and he forced the <u>rhapsodes</u> [<u>*rhapsôidoi*</u>] at the Panathenaia <u>to go through</u> [<u>*diienai*</u>] these utterances <u>in sequence</u> [<u>*ephexês*</u>], by relay [<u>*hupolêpsis*</u>], <u>just as they</u> [= the rhapsodes] <u>do even nowadays</u>.[18]

("Plato" *Hipparkhos* 228b-c.)

In this extract, I have highlighted two words with special rhapsodic implications: *ephexês* 'in sequence' and *hupolêpsis*, which I translate as 'relay'. In dramatized dialogue, the corresponding verb of *hupolêpsis*, *hupolambanô*, marks the response of one speaker to the previous speaker: *ephê hupolabôn* 'he said in response' (e.g. Plato *Republic* I 331d, etc.; cf. Herodotus 1.11.5, 1.27.4, etc.). In Aristotle *Politics* V 1310a10, *hupolambanô* is correlated with *hupokrinomai* 'reply, make answer'.[19] As for *ephexês auta diienai* 'go through them [= the *epê* 'poetic utterances' of Homer] in sequence', we may compare the contexts of Plato *Timaeus* 23d3-4 / 24a1-2: *panta . . . hexês dielthein / ephexês diienai* 'go through everything in sequence' / 'go through in sequence'. We will return at a later point to these contexts in the *Timaeus*.

If we supplement the passage from the *Hipparkhos* with a passage taken from a speech delivered by the Athenian statesman Lycurgus (330 BC), we may infer that the Homeric *epê* 'poetic utterances' performed at the Panathenaia were the *Iliad* and *Odyssey*:

βούλομαι δ' ὑμῖν καὶ τὸν Ὅμηρον παρασχέσθαι <u>ἐπαινῶν</u>. οὕτω γὰρ ὑπέλαβον ὑμῶν οἱ πατέρες σπουδαῖον εἶναι ποιητήν, ὥστε νόμον ἔθεντο καθ' ἑκάστην πενταετηρίδα τῶν Παναθηναίων μόνου τῶν ἄλλων ποιητῶν <u>ῥαψῳδεῖσθαι</u> <u>τὰ ἔπη</u>, <u>ἐπίδειξιν</u> ποιούμενοι πρὸς τοὺς Ἕλληνας ὅτι τὰ κάλλιστα τῶν ἔργων προῃροῦντο.

---

[18]General commentary on the whole passage in HQ 80-81.
[19]In LSJ, meaning II of *hupokrinomai* is given as "speak in dialogue, hence play a part on the stage," as in Demosthenes 19.246, where the part played is in the accusative: τὴν Ἀντιγόνην Σοφοκλέους . . . ὑποκέκριται 'has played the part of Sophocles' Antigone'.

I wish to adduce[20] for you Homer, quoting [*epaineô*] him,[21] since the reception[22] that he had from your ancestors made him so important a poet that there was a law enacted by them that requires, every fourth year of the Panathenaia, the rhapsodic performing [*rhapsôideô*] of his poetic utterances [*epê*] — his alone and no other poet's. In this way they [= your ancestors] made a demonstration [*epideixis*],[23] intended for all Hellenes to see,[24] that they made a conscious choice of the most noble of accomplishments.[25]

(Lycurgus Against Leokrates 102[26])

According to the story in "Plato" *Hipparkhos*, quoted earlier, we see that there existed in Athens a custom of maintaining a fixed narrative sequence of Homeric performance at the Panathenaia, with each performing rhapsode taking up the narration where the previous rhapsode left off. Classicists conventionally refer to this custom as the "Panathenaic Rule."[27]

The author of the *Hipparkhos* says that this custom was initiated by Hipparkhos, son of Peisistratos, in the era of the tyrants. There are those who view this story as the reflex of a historical event, estimating the date at around 530 BC.[28]

---

[20]The orator, by "adducing" the classical authors (I mean "classical" from his synchronic point of view), assumes the role of statesman.

[21]To make his arguments here in *Against Leokrates* 102, the orator Lycurgus is about to adduce a "quotation" from Homer, the equivalent of what we know as *Iliad* Book XV verses 494-499. Adducing a Homeric "quotation" is presented here as if it were a matter of adducing Homer himself.

[22]I deliberately translate *hupolambanô* 'receive' here in terms of "reception theory." As a rhapsodic term, as we saw above in "Plato" *Hipparkhos* 228b-c, *hupolêpsis* is not just 'reception' but also 'continuation' in the sense of reception by way of relay.

[23]Cf. the context of *epideigma* 'display, demonstration' in "Plato" *Hipparkhos* 228d, as discussed in PH 161; cf. also PH 217 and following on *apodeixis* 'presentation, demonstration'. The basic idea behind what is being "demonstrated" is a model for performance.

[24]By implication, the pan-Hellenic impulse of the "ancestors" of the Athenians in making Homer a "Classic" is mirrored by the impulse of Lycurgus, statesman that he is, to "quote" extensively from such "Classics" as Homer.

[25]I infer that the *erga* 'accomplishments' include poetic accomplishments: on the mentality of seeing a reciprocity between noble deeds and noble poetry that becomes a deed in celebrating the deed itself, see PH 70, 219.

[26]Further discussion of this passage: PH 21-24.

[27]Davison 1955, 7. Cf. HQ 75, 81-82, 101.

[28]Davison [1968], 60. Cf. Shapiro 1992, 72-75. (See also Kotsidu 1991, 41-44.) Even if the Panathenaic Rule were to be viewed in terms of a single historical moment centering on the political initiatives of Hipparkhos, it is a given that the institution of rhapsodic competitions at the Panathenaia predates such a theoretical moment. Note the formulation of Shapiro 1993, 101-3: "performances by rhapsodes at the Panathenaia did take place before Hipparkhos introduced the so-called Panathenaic Rule." He cites as evidence the depiction of a rhapsode on a black-figure Liverpool amphora of Panathenaic shape, dated to ca. 540 BC (figures 26 and 27).

My own analysis does not rule out the possibility that such a reported event was a historical fact — to the extent that an important political figure like Hipparkhos may well have reformed the custom of epic performances at the Panathenaia.[29] But I insist that there are two far more basic historical facts to be inferred from the story: (1) the author of the *Hipparkhos* says that this custom of relay performances of Homer by rhapsodes at the Panathenaia was still in effect during his own lifetime and (2) the custom is described in terms of a customary law, instituted by Hipparkhos in the role of a "lawgiver."[30]

As we saw earlier, the Panathenaic event of Homeric performances by rhapsodes is designated by ancient sources in terms of an *agôn* or an *athlon*, both words meaning 'competition' or 'contest'. Thus there are really two aspects of the Panathenaic Rule: not only must the rhapsodes take turns as they perform the *Iliad* and *Odyssey* in sequence: they must also compete with each other in the process.[31]

These two aspects of the Panathenaic Rule, sequencing and competition, are neatly reflected in two different mythologized versions of the concept of the rhapsode, as reported in the scholia to Pindar *Nemean* 2.1:

> οἱ δέ φασι τῆς Ὁμήρου ποιήσεως μὴ <u>ὑφ'</u> <u>ἕν</u> συνηγμένης. σποράδην δὲ ἄλλως καὶ κατὰ μέρη διῃρημένης, ὁπότε <u>ῥαψῳδοῖεν</u> αὐτήν, <u>εἱρμῷ</u> τινι καὶ <u>ῥαφῇ</u> παραπλήσιον ποιεῖν, <u>εἰς</u> <u>ἕν</u> αὐτὴν ἄγοντας

And some say that — since the poetry of Homer had been in a state of not being brought together <u>under</u> the <u>heading</u> <u>of</u> <u>one</u> <u>thing</u>,[32] but instead, in a negative sense [=ἄλλως], had been in the state of being scattered and divided into parts — whenever they would <u>perform</u> it <u>rhapsodically</u> they would be doing something that is similar to <u>sequencing</u> or <u>sewing</u>, as they brought it together <u>into</u> <u>one</u> <u>thing</u>.

[version 1 at 2.1c]

***

> οἱ δέ, ὅτι <u>κατὰ</u> <u>μέρος</u> πρότερον τῆς ποιήσεως διαδεδομένης τῶν <u>ἀγωνιστῶν</u> ἕκαστος ὅ τι βούλοιτο <u>μέρος</u> <u>ᾖδε</u>, τοῦ δὲ ἄθλου τοῖς νικῶσιν ἀρνὸς ἀποδεδειγμένου προσαγορευθῆναι τότε μὲν ἀρνῳδούς, αὖθις δὲ <u>ἑκατέρας</u> <u>τῆς</u> <u>ποιήσεως</u> εἰσενεχθείσης τοὺς <u>ἀγωνιστὰς</u> οἷον ἀκουμένους πρὸς ἄλληλα τὰ <u>μέρη</u> καὶ <u>τὴν</u> <u>σύμπασαν</u> <u>ποίησιν</u> ἐπιόντας, <u>ῥαψῳδοὺς</u> προσαγορευθῆναι, ταῦτά φησι Διονύσιος ὁ Ἀργεῖος

---

[29]HQ 74, 80-81.

[30]On myths about lawgivers as founders of customary laws, see the discussion in GM 21, 71-75, 81, 102, 105.

[31]I confront for the first time this competitive aspect of rhapsodic performance in PH 23-24n28.

[32]My translation here is attempting to capture the metaphorical implications of *hupo* in the sense of 'under'.

Others say that previously — since the poetry had been divided <u>into</u> <u>parts</u>, with each of the <u>competitors</u> [*agônistai*] <u>singing</u> whichever <u>part</u> he wanted, and since the designated prize for the winners had been a lamb — [those competitors] were in those days called *arnôidoi* [= lamb-singers], but then, later on — since the <u>competitors</u> [*agônistai*], whenever <u>each</u> <u>of</u> <u>the</u> <u>two</u> <u>poems</u> was introduced, were mending the parts to each other, as it were, and moving toward the whole poem — they were called *rhapsôidoi*. These things are said by Dionysius of Argos [between 4th and 3rd centuries BC; FGH 308 F 2]

[version 2 at 2.1d]

The myth in version 2, which restates the principle of sequencing as stated in the myth of version 1, adds the principle of competition. According to version 2, the principle of competition was there all along, and the principle of sequencing was added to it only later. So we have here a myth that narrates an "evolution" of sorts, from an unsequenced competition for the prize of an *arên* 'lamb' to a sequenced competition for a prize that is no longer that of a lamb.[33] The rhapsodes no longer compete for the prize of a lamb, but they still compete with each other even as they "sew together" the parts of the two poems. The two aspects of the Panathenaic Rule are hereby both aetiologized. That the myth refers to the Panathenaic Rule is indicated by the explicit reference to two poems: when we combine this detail with the testimony of Lycurgus, we can see that the Rule applies to the *Iliad* and the *Odyssey*.

The myth in version 2 motivates the principle of rhapsodic competition in terms of the institution of sacrifice, specifically the sacrifice of an *arên* 'lamb'. In this connection, let us return to the inscription from Eretria that we have just considered, concerning *agônes* 'competitions' of *mousikê*. We find here a remarkable analogy with the myth in version 2, since these Eretrian competitions of *mousikê* are motivated, again, in terms of the institution of sacrifice, specifically the sacrifice of *arnes* 'lambs'. In this case, however, the motivation is formulated explicitly from the synchronic viewpoint of the organizers of the festival themselves. At the very beginning of the Eretrian inscription we read:

[θ]εο[ί]. | Ἐξήκεστος Διοδώρου εἶπεν· ὅπωρ ἂν τὰ Ἀρ-|τεμίρια ὡς κάλλισα ἄγωμεν καὶ θύω[ριν ὡς π-|λε]ῖστοι, ἔδοξεν τεῖ βουλεῖ καὶ τοῖ δήμοι | [..] <u>τιθεῖν τὴμ πόλιν</u> <u>ἀγῶνα</u> <u>μουσικῆς</u> ἀπὸ χιλίων | δραχμῶν τεῖ Μεταξὺ καὶ τεῖ Φυλακεῖ καὶ παρέχει-|ν ἄρνας τεῖ πρὸ τῶν Ἀρτεμιρίων πέντε ἡμέρας, τ-|ούτων δὲ δύο ἐγκρίτους εἶναι

---

[33]In light of e.g. *Iliad* III 103, we may re-translate *arên* as 'sheep' (of either sex) instead of 'lamb'.

(Invocation to the gods.) Exekestos son of Diodoros spoke: in order that the Artemisia [= Festival of Artemis] be conducted by us in the most beautiful way possible and in order that as many people as possible may make sacrifice [= *thuô*], it was decided by the Boule and the Demos that the city is to organize a competition [*agôn*] of *mousikê*, at the expense of 1000 drachmas, on the days Metaxu and Phulakê, [34] and that (the city) is to provide lambs [= *arnes*] on the day that is five days before the Artemisia, and, of these [lambs], two are to be *enkritoi* [specially selected (for sacrifice)].[35]

(IG XII ix 189.1-8)

The inscription goes on to specify that the *mousikê* should begin on the fourth day before the end of the month of Anthesterion (lines 8-10: ἄρχειν δὲ τῆς μο-|υσικῆς τετράδα φθίνοντος τοῦ Ἀνθεστηρι-|ῶνος μηνός). Then the inscription lists the categories of competition in *mousikê* (lines 10-14), and I repeat here my translation of the wording: "and that [the city] is to organize the *mousikê* for rhapsodes, aulodes, citharists, citharodes, and parody-singers; further, that those who compete [*agônizomai*] in the *mousikê* should all compete [*agônizomai*] in the *prosodion* [= processional song] for the sacrifice [*thusia*] in the *aulê*, having the same costume that they have in the competition proper." As at the beginning of the inscription, we see here again the highlighting of *thusia* 'sacrifice' (line 13) as the central theme of the institution of competitions in *mousikê*.

The climactic sacrifice at the place called the *aulê* is marked by a *prosodion* 'processional song' (line 13) in which all the competitors in the individual competitions of *mousikê* are to "compete" in a preliminary way. I infer that this merged "competition" is a sort of preview of the individual competitions, after which the *athla* 'competitive prizes' (line 15) are to be awarded (lines 15-20):[36]

category	prizes	drachmas
rhapsodes	1st prize:	120
	2nd:	30
	3rd:	20
aulodes (boys' category)	1st:	50
	2nd:	30

---

[34]My interpretation here is not certain.

[35]On the semantics of *enkrisis* in the sense of a "choice selection" in a competitive context, see LSJ 473-74.

[36]I infer that these prize-allotments correspond to the actual winners on the first occasion of the institution as prescribed by the inscription; on this occasion, I infer further, no aulodes entered the competitions in *mousikê*.

citharists	1st:	110
	2nd:	70
	3rd:	55
citharodes	1st:	200
	2nd:	150
	3rd:	100
parody-singers	1st:	50
	2nd:	10

The inscription goes on to specify the details of per diem payments to be made to the *agônistai* 'contestants' (line 20): one drachma daily, starting no more than three days before what is called the *pro-agôn* at line 22 and extending up to the point where the *agôn* proper takes place (μέ|χρι οὗ ἂν ὁ ἀγὼν γένηται, lines 22-23).[37]

In reality, then, the contestants compete for cash prizes. Notionally, however, the prizes are sacrificial, in that they are awarded in the context of a grand *thusia* 'sacrifice' inaugurated by a *prosodion* 'processional song' in which all the contestants notionally "compete" in a preliminary *agôn*, that is, in the *pro-agôn* mentioned at line 22. Moreover, this processional song is the climax of an actual procession, *pompê* (line 39), in which all the *agônistai* 'competitors' of the *mousikê* are required to participate (lines 37-38). The explicit reason given for this required participation of competitors is this:

ὅπως ἂν ὡς καλλίσστη ἡ πομπὴ καὶ ἡ θυσίη γένηται

in order that the procession [*pompê*] and the sacrifice [*thusia*] become the most beautiful possible[38]

(IG XII ix 189.39)

The homology between the *pompê* 'procession' and the *thusia* 'sacrifice' is highlighted by the syntax (ἡ πομπὴ καὶ ἡ θυσίη, line 39). The competitors in *mousikê*, then, participate in and become part of the entire relig-

---

[37] In this context (line 23), it is not clear to me whether *agôn* 'competition' refers to the individual contestant's occasion for competing or to the competition in *mousikê* writ large. The first alternative raises interesting questions: are there different days of *agôn* for different contestants? (The day of the *pro-agôn* must be the same for all.)

[38] A dominant theme in this inscription is the idea conveyed by *kallist-* 'most beautiful': see also lines 1-3 as quoted above: "in order that the Artemisia [= Festival of Artemis] be conducted by us in the most beautiful way possible [*kallista*] and in order that as many people as possible may make sacrifice [= *thuô*]." Perhaps we may connect this theme with the cult-epithet of Artemis, *kallistê* 'most beautiful'.

ious program of the Artemisia, a continuum that extends from the procession to the climactic sacrifice and from the sacrifice to the competitions themselves.

This homology between procession and sacrifice — not even to mention the religious mentality of sequencing that connects one to the other — is strikingly parallel to what we find at the Panathenaia in Athens. On that seasonally-recurring occasion as well, though of course on a vastly larger scale, we see a procession climaxing in a sacrifice: the Panathenaic Procession starts from the Kerameikos and passes through the Agora and ends up on the heights of the Acropolis, reaching its climax in a grand sacrifice within the sacred space of Athena on high. The Parthenon Frieze gives a mythologically synchronic picture of the whole continuum of the Panathenaic Procession as it approaches its climax in the sacrifice to Athena.[39]

From the evidence of such comparisons between the Artemisia of Eretria and the Panathenaia of Athens, I infer that we are dealing here with two institutions that are not only parallel but even cognate. A particularly telling point of comparison, as I have stressed, is the custom of holding *agônes* 'competitions' in *mousikê*. The categories of competition are remarkably parallel, even in the relative rankings of these categories.

There is, granted, a vast difference in scale between the Artemisia of Eretria, as recorded in the inscription IG XII ix 189 from ca. 341/40 BC, and the Panathenaia of Athens, as recorded in the inscription IG II² 2311 from 380 BC. That year at the Panathenaia, as I have already noted, the monetary value of the first prize in the competition of citharodes, a gold crown, was worth 1000 drachmas — and that figure does not even include the additional cash prize of silver worth 500 drachmas. When we compare that sum of 1000 drachmas at the Panathenaia of that time to the sum of 200 drachmas, which was the cash prize for first place in the competition of citharodes at the Artemisia of Eretria just forty-odd years later, we can appreciate all the more the magnitude of the Panathenaia. The monetary value of the gold crown bestowed on the top citharode at the Panathenaia of 380 BC is the equivalent of the entire budget of the Artemisia in 341/40 BC.

Despite the differences in scale, the Eretrian inscription IG XII ix 189 shows enough structural parallelisms with the Panathenaia to encourage extrapolations in areas where we do not have direct information about the Athenian festival. Here I return to the all-important elements of procession and sacrifice. The districts of the city, called *khôroi*, are each to contribute animals (cattle are specified) that are *krita* 'chosen' by state overseers for the sacrifice (lines 25-31). Sacrificial animals can also be

---

[39]Cf. B. Nagy 1992, who also argues that the *athlothetai* are actually represented on the Frieze.

bought, in the sacred precinct, by individual sacrificers from individual sellers (31-34), as also in the agora (35). All those who wish to sacrifice are to march in the procession, which is to be marshaled in the agora by officials called *dêmarkhoi* (34-35); the sacrificial animals are to be led in the procession by their respective sacrificers, in a prescribed sequence determined by the categories of animals: first come the *dêmosia* or victims of the State, including the choicest entry or *kallisteion* 'fairest prize' (35-36); then come the *krita* 'chosen ones', presumably the ones contributed by the *khôroi* (36); and then, finally, all other victims, elliptically indicated by a formula that refers not to the animals but to their sacrificers, and this category includes any private individual who wishes to participate in the procession (*sumpompeuein*: 37).

It is essential to stress here a detail just noted, that the organizers of the procession culminating in the grand sacrifice are officials called the *dêmarkhoi* (34-35). Earlier on in the inscription, these same *dêmarkhoi* are described as the officials in charge of the entire *agôn* of *mousikê* (τὸν δὲ ἀγῶνα τιθόντων οἱ δήμ-|αρχοι, 23-24). By extrapolation, we can say that the *dêmarkhoi* of the Artemisia are analogous to the *athlothetai* of the Panathenaia.

Participation in the grand procession of the Artemisia, then, is an option open to any individual. For the actual competitors in the *mousikê*, however, participation is required. The inscription specifies that all the *agônistai* 'competitors' are to take part in the procession (37-38), and we have already noted the explicit reason given for this required participation: "in order that the procession [*pompê*] and the sacrifice [*thusia*] become the most beautiful possible" (39). Since the other participants in the procession are conducting the various sacrificial animals to the grand sacrifice, can we say the same for the competitors as well? If so, perhaps the sacrificial animals to be conducted by the competitors are the lambs mentioned at the beginning of the inscription, the *enkritoi* of line 8.

The inscription ends by providing for its words to be inscribed on a stele and to be placed in the precinct of Artemis (40-41), with the following express purpose:

ὅπως ἂν κατὰ τοῦτα γί|νηται ἡ θυσίη καὶ ἡ μουσικὴ τεῖ Ἀρτέμιδι εἰς τὸν ἀεὶ χ-|[ρό]νον

so that, according to these specifications, the *thusia* 'sacrifice' and the *mousikê* for Artemis may last forever

(IG XII ix 189.41-42)

One last time we see the all-important factor of sacrifice, and, this time, the homology is between the *thusia* 'sacrifice' and the *mousikê*.

A parallel homology is at work in the *Timaeus* of Plato. The dramatized occasion of this dialogue is "the *thusia* of the goddess" (τῇ ... τῆς
θεοῦ θυσίᾳ 26e3), that is, the Panathenaia.[40] The story of Atlantis and
Athens, about to be narrated by Critias, is described by him metaphorically as a *humnos* to be sung as an encomium of the goddess: to recall the
story, he says, would be a fitting way both to please Socrates "and at the
same time to praise the goddess on the occasion of her Festival in a
righteous and truthful way, just as if we were making her the subject of a
humnos" (καὶ τὴν θεὸν ἅμα ἐν τῇ πανηγύρει δικαίως τε καὶ ἀληθῶς
οἷόνπερ ὑμνοῦντας ἐγκωμιάζειν 21a2-3).[41]

The story of Atlantis and Athens, about to be recalled by Critias, goes
back to his childhood memories — all the way back to a time when he
was only ten years old: his grandfather Critias, whose namesake he is,
had told him the story on a day of initiation, Koureotis Day, during the
Feast of Apatouria (21a-b).[42] As a ten-year-old, however, Critias would
have been too young to be initiated, and this detail about his under-age
status underlines the inherent childishness of the listener.[43] In this specific
context, Plato adds an interesting further detail that reinforces the idea of
childish perceptions: on Koureotis Day, Critias reminisces, he and his
little friends used to engage in a very special game. They played rhapsode, competing for prizes, *athla*, arranged by their fathers (ἆθλα γὰρ
ἡμῖν οἱ πατέρες ἔθεσαν ῥαψῳδίας 21b). In the general context of the
Timaeus, the occasion of which is actually the Panathenaia, this mention
of *rhapsôidia* is suggestive: it evokes the prime occasion of rhapsodic
contests for prizes. This occasion is in fact the Panathenaia. Marcel
Detienne describes Critias' recalled event as a "little theater of the Apatouria,"[44] "une sorte d'antichambre des Panathénées."[45]

On the occasion of this particular Koureotis Day, according to Plato's
dramatized reminiscences of Critias, the boys were competing in rhapsodic performances of "many poets" (πολλῶν μὲν οὖν δὴ καὶ πολλὰ
ἐλέχθη ποιητῶν ποιήματα 21b). Among the "new" poetic compositions of
that era, many of the boys "sang" the poems of Solon (ἅτε δὲ νέα κατ'
ἐκεῖνον τὸν χρόνον ὄντα τὰ Σόλωνος πολλοὶ τῶν παίδων ᾔσαμεν 21b).[46]
Solon's general pertinence to the *Timaeus* is obvious: what this lawmaker

[40]Brisson 1982, 38.

[41]Precisely in this context, *Timaeus* 20e, Plato evokes the first sentence of Herodotus, the so-
called prooemium of the *History*: see PH 226. For the performance of epic, the *humnos* as a
genre is the equivalent of a prooemium, as we see from the reference in Thucydides
(3.104.3-4) to the *Homeric Hymn to Apollo* as a *prooimion* 'prooemium'. Cf. PP 62.

[42]On the identification of this Critias with the leader of the Thirty, see Clay 1997, 52n6.

[43]Brisson 1982, 61.

[44]Detienne 1989, 178.

[45]*Ibid.*

[46]On "singing" as applied to the recitative performances of rhapsodes, see PH 21, 26.

had heard from priests in Egypt is supposedly the source of the grand-father Critias' story about Athens and Atlantis. Solon's specific perti-nence to the Panathenaia, however, is no longer obvious to us. The immediate context of the *Timaeus* helps provide an explanation.

The poetry of Solon, as we know from the surviving fragments, was composed in elegiac and iambic meters; these two meters, along with the dactylic hexameter, are the three basic "non-lyric" media that rhapsodes specialize in performing, while most other meters belong to the "lyric" media performed by citharodes or aulodes.[47] Solon's status as a composer of rhapsodic poetry is pertinent to the *Timaeus* because he is pointedly compared by the grandfather Critias to Homer and Hesiod themselves: if only Solon had not left unfinished his poetic composition about Atlantis and Athens, says the grandfather, this statesman would have surpassed even Homer and Hesiod in poetic fame (21c-d).

We may note a formal parallelism of rhapsodic repertoires in Plato's *Ion*: the rhapsode Ion, who is about to compete in the Panathenaia (530b), is represented as a grand master in performing the poetry of Homer and Hesiod, as also of Archilochus (531a). The rhapsode is a master per-former — without musical accompaniment (533b5-7) — of dactylic hexameter (Homer and Hesiod) as also of elegiac and iambic meters (both these meters were primary compositional media of Archilochus). From such formal parallelisms, we can see that the poetic medium of Solon — elegiac and iambic meters — is appropriate to the performance repertoire of rhapsodes. Solon's poetry is rhapsodic poetry.

Plato's *Timaeus* implies that the rhapsodic poetry of Solon could have replaced the rhapsodic poetry of Homer at the Panathenaia, if only the great Athenian statesman had found the leisure time to finish his unfin-ished poem about Atlantis and Athens (21c-d). By further implication, the rhapsodic tale told by grandfather Critias could have become the poetic centerpiece of the Panathenaia. But Solon did not complete his rhapsodic masterpiece — just as Plato did not complete his trilogy of *Timaeus*, *Critias*, and *Hermocrates*. As I will now go on to argue, this state of incompleteness is expressed by Plato in a nostalgically playful way, and the playfulness cleverly mimics the childish mentality of a ten-year-old boy playing at a game of rhapsodes, where the object of the game is to win celebrity status as the star rhapsode of the Panathenaia.

Critias looks back at those early days when he and the other children playing rhapsode had not yet become eligible to enter the "real" world of grownups. Now, in the *Timaeus* and the *Critias*, we find the adult Critias still at it — playing rhapsode on the occasion of the Panathenaia. Plato's

---

[47]Extended discussion in PH 25-28.

wording of Critias' reminiscences leaves the impression that Critias' game is still in some ways a children's game.[48]

In the *Timaeus*, which features the *dramatis personae* of Socrates, Timaeus, Critias, and Hermocrates, we find references to the subject-matter of an encounter of the same *dramatis personae* that had taken place "yesterday," *khthes* (17c, 26c, etc.). The subject-matter of "yesterday" had concerned an ideal city-state or republic (*politeia*: 17c, etc.), and Socrates had talked about them "yesterday" in the form of a *muthos* (ἐν μύθῳ: 26c, etc.). These references in the *Timaeus* are cross-references, it would seem, to Plato's *Republic*, which begins with a highlighted reference to *khthes* 'yesterday' (κατέβην χθὲς εἰς τὸν Πειραιᾶ : 327a). And yet, the *khthes* 'yesterday' of the *Timaeus* involves the *dramatis personae* of the *Timaeus*, not the *dramatis personae* of the *Republic* (Socrates, Kephalos, Thrasymachus, and so on).[49] So we cannot say that the *Timaeus* cross-refers to the "real" *Republic*.

What we can say, however, is that the *Timaeus* fictionalizes the *Republic*, since we do know for a fact that a "real" *Republic* exists — if indeed we have already read it. Plato's *Timaeus* is marked throughout by the genre of "fiction" — that is, of εἰκὼς λόγος (*eikôs logos*: e.g. 48a, 53d).[50] Since Plato knows that we know fiction when we see it, if indeed we have read the "real" *Republic* carefully, he cannot expect us to take the *khthes* literally.

In the interplay of cross-reference, the fact that the word *khthes* is consistently juxtaposed with *politeia* 'republic' in the *Timaeus* may be viewed, in and of itself, as a reference to the *Republic*, in light of the prominent featuring of *khthes* at the beginning of the *Republic*. For the reference to be a cross-reference, you do not have to reconcile the logic of the immediate context with the logic of the ultimate context, which controls the ultimate purpose of reference.

In terms of the immediate context of the *Timaeus*, its own dramatic moment is the eve of the Panathenaia, which started on the 28th of the month Hekatombaion. By contrast, the dramatic moment of the *Republic* was the feast of the Bendideia, which started on the 19th of the month Thargelion. Recognizing the dramatic moment of the *Republic*, Proclus infers that the dramatic moment of the *Timaeus* must have been the 20th

---

[48]Compare *Timaeus* 22b: the Egyptians tell Solon that he and all the Greeks are mere children, since their myths (as recounted to them by Solon) are so "new" in comparison to the far more ancient myths recovered in the Egyptian records. Thus the story of Atlantis, as recounted to Solon by the Egyptians, has been filtered through the perspective of a "child" when Solon in turn recounts the story to the Greeks.

[49]See Hadot 1983, 122n57.

[50]On *eikôs logos* as a genre (*Gattung*), see Witte 1964, who emphasizes an interesting constraint in Plato's usage: the term *eikôs logos* is avoided in the many references to the central *muthos* about Atlantis.

of Thargelion — that is, the day after the *Republic*. In other words, Proclus is taking the usage of *khthes* 'yesterday' in the *Timaeus* as a historical reference to the setting of the *Republic*. At the same time, he does not want to let go of the immediate context of the *Timaeus*, from which he infers that the feast in question is indeed the Panathenaia.

Proclus attempts to reason his way out of such contradictions by conjecturing that the feast in question is not the Greater Panathenaia, held every four years, but the Lesser Panathenaia, held on each of the other three years. He is guessing that the Lesser Panathenaia in Athens were held in the month of Thargelion, the same time when the Bendideia were held at the Peiraeus. Here he gets caught in a mistake from the standpoint of modern scholars, who have access to more evidence about the scheduling of the Panathenaia in the fifth and fourth centuries BC than did Proclus, who lived almost a millennium later, in the fifth century AD.[51]

Such a mistake is really a mistake only if we follow Proclus in assuming that the dramatic dates of the *Republic* and the *Timaeus* need to be connected historically. For Plato, however, I submit that any intended thematic connection between the *Republic* and the *Timaeus* is purely literary, not historical: the *Republic* of "yesterday" had dealt with the topic of the ideal state, while the *Timaeus* of "today" announces a new topic, that is, a state that must be pure fiction.

That seems as far as we can go in looking for intertextual connections between different works of Plato. It is self-defeating to attempt to go further, as Proclus did, by seeking connections between the internal consistencies of one distinct work of Plato with those of another.[52] Platonic cross-reference cannot be expected to impose an overall sense of order on any single work from the cumulative totality of the outside. Still, my point remains that the usage of *khthes* 'yesterday' in the *Timaeus* is a case of partial intertextuality, that is, where a cross-reference in one given work of Plato to another does not interfere with the individual philosophical and literary agenda of either work.[53]

---

[51]Cf. Hadot 1983, 117, with bibliography. Also Clay 1997, 50-51.

[52]For more on the esoteric outlook of Proclus, see Loraux 1993, 176 and 434n16.

[53]Similarly with the *Timaeus* and the *Critias*. These two works are much more closely connected with each other than the *Republic* is connected with the *Timaeus* (it can be argued, as we will see below, that they are not even separate works), and yet even in this case we may find individual consistencies. For example, the presiding god of the *Timaeus* is Athena, who is also the primary designated subject of the narration, which takes the form of "hymn," *humnos* (21a: τὴν θεὸν . . . ὑμνοῦντας), while the gods of the *Critias* are Apollo/Paeon and the Muses, who are invoked to preside over the next designated subject, "the ancient and noble citizens" of prehistoric Athens, and again the narration takes the form of "hymn," *humnos* (108c: τὸν Παίωνά τε καὶ τὰς Μούσας ἐπικαλούμενον τοὺς παλαιοὺς ἀγαθοὺς ὄντας ἀναφαίνειν τε καὶ ὑμνεῖν). Here too, intertextuality need not prevent individual textuality in *Timaeus/ Critias*.

The intentionality of this kind of intertextuality is reflected, I submit, in Plato's use of the language of rhapsodes. From what I am about to show, it appears that Plato is making a point about individualized rhapsodic style and even individualized rhapsodic content, within the framework of an imposed and previously-agreed-upon sequence of narrative. When it is Critias' turn in the *Critias* to take up where Timaeus in the *Timaeus* had left off, Timaeus says: "I hand over [*paradidomen*] to Critias, as pre-arranged, the continuous discourse [*ephexês logos*]" (*Critias* 106b: παραδίδομεν κατὰ τὰς ὁμολογίας Κριτίᾳ τὸν ἐφεξῆς λόγον). I draw attention here to the expression *ephexês logos* 'continuous discourse'. We may compare the rhapsodic expression *ephexês* in the first literary passage quoted in my essay, in "Plato" *Hipparkhos* 228b-c.

Critias responds by saying that he will now "take up the continuous discourse" at the point where it was handed over to him by Timaeus. I draw attention to the precise wording: *dekhomai* 'I take up', with the direct object *ephexês logos* 'continuous discourse' understood. The whole idea is worded in a noticeably compressed clause marked by the particle *men*, to be followed by an expanded clause, marked by the particle *de*, which expresses the idea that the discourse will now become even more challenging than before, and that the speaker must therefore beg the indulgence of his audience all the more: ἀλλ' ὦ Τίμαιε δέχομαι μέν· ᾧ δὲ καὶ κατ' ἀρχὰς σὺ ἐχρήσω, συγγνώμην αἰτούμενος ὡς περὶ μεγάλων μέλλων λέγειν, ταὐτὸν καὶ νῦν ἐγὼ τοῦτο παραιτοῦμαι . . . 'all right, then, Timaeus, I'm taking it up [*dekhomai*] here [that is, the continuous discourse], on the one hand [*men*]; on the other hand [*de*], I ask for the very same thing that you too made use of at the beginning when you asked for indulgence on the grounds that you were about to speak about great [*megala*] things' (*Critias* 106b-c). Critias goes on to say that his subject matter is surely even greater (106c).

The usage of the verb *dekhomai* 'take up' in this context (106b) is crucial. We may compare the participle of this same verb as applied to Patroklos at *Iliad* IX 191: he sits in a state of anticipation, "waiting" (δέγμενος) for the moment when Achilles will leave off (verb *lêgô*) singing the *klea andrôn* 'glories of heroes'. As I have argued elsewhere, Patroklos is apparently waiting for his own turn to sing, and what we see here in capsule form is "the esthetics of rhapsodic sequencing."[54] The verb *lêgô* 'leave off' is elsewhere attested in explicitly rhapsodic contexts, as in the following passage:

τά τε Ὁμήρου ἐξ ὑποβολῆς γέγραφε ῥαψῳδεῖσθαι, οἷον ὅπου ὁ πρῶτος ἔληξεν, ἐκεῖθεν ἄρχεσθαι τὸν ἐχόμενον

---

[54]PP 73, with further argumentation.

[= Solon the Lawgiver] has written a law that the works of Homer are to be <u>performed</u> rhapsodically [*rhapsôideô*], by <u>relay</u> [*hupobolê*], so that wherever the first person <u>left</u> <u>off</u> [*lêgô*], from that point the next <u>connected</u> person should <u>start</u>.

(Dieuchidas of Megara FGH 485 F 6, via Diogenes Laertius 1.57.)[55]

Critias remarks that his topic, the genesis of humans, is even more difficult than the topic that had just been treated by Timaeus, the genesis of the gods and of the cosmos, since the audience will demand greater verisimilitude about topics that seem closer to their own world of direct experience (107a-b). Socrates jokingly responds that the topic of the next slated speaker, Hermocrates, will surely become even more difficult (108a-b).

Of course, Plato's readers will never get to see even the beginnings of Hermocrates' topic, since the sequence of a would-be trilogy of *Timaeus, Critias,* and *Hermocrates* is cut short well before even the *Critias* can come to a finish. An obvious inference, then, is that Plato never finished his intended trilogy.[56] There is, however, also a less obvious inference that could be drawn: perhaps Plato intended the sequence of *Timaeus/ Critias* to remain unfinished.[57] In support of this inference, we may point to the open-endedness that typifies Plato's dialectic in general.[58]

Critias' speech stops short at exactly the point where he is about to quote the Will of Zeus (δίκην αὐτοῖς ἐπιθεῖναι βουληθείς 121b-c). Plato's wording evokes the epic theme of the *boulê* or 'Will' of Zeus, as announced at the very beginning of the *Iliad*, I 5 (Διὸς δ' ἐτελείετο βουλή) or at the very beginning of the *Cypria* fr. 1.7 Allen (Διὸς δ' ἐτελείετο βουλή). At the point where Critias' speech stops short, Zeus is about to announce that he will now inflict a Flood on the Golden Generation — the last of a doomed race who have finally exhausted their divine genetic destiny (*moira*) because of their habitual interbreeding with ordinary mortals (*Critias* 121c). This point of stopping short, I argue, is analogous

---

[55]Cf. Ford 1992, 115n31, who notes the use of *lêgô* 'stop, leave off' at the point in the narrative where Demodokos leaves off his Trojan narrative (*Odyssey* VIII 87); this verb, Ford argues, "is the technical expression used by a rhapsode to end a performance or a part of one." For parallels, he cites *Homeric Hymn to Dionysus* 17-18, Hesiod fr. 305.4 MW, and *Theogony* 48. He also cites Diogenes Laertius 1.57 and *Iliad* IX 191, the two passages presently under discussion. On the attribution of the "Panathenaic Rule" to Solon, see Nagy 1999b, 135-36.

[56]Cf. Plutarch *Life of Solon* 31.3, 32.1-2.

[57]Cf. Clay 1997. See also Haslam 1976, who argues that *Timaeus + Critias* are really one unfinished dialogue; he makes a similar argument about the *Sophist + Statesman*, discounting the idea that Plato intentionally sets up the expectation of a trilogy comprised of *Sophist + Statesman* (+ *Philosopher*), which would be parallel to *Timaeus + Critias* (+ *Hermocrates*). In what follows, I argue that Plato did indeed intentionally set up the expectation of a sequence *Timaeus + Critias + Hermocrates*.

[58]See especially Dihle 1995.

to a given point in epic narrative where one rhapsode could leave off the narration and another rhapsode could take it up.

In support of this argument, I draw attention to two points in the overall narrative of the *Iliad*: one of them comes at the end of Book VIII and the other, at the end of Book XV. As Bruce Heiden points out, both Books VIII and XV end on a note of asserting the *boulê* or 'Will' of Zeus.[59] Heiden argues that both endings seem to signal major breaks in the performance of the *Iliad*. In stressing the factor of performance, not just composition, he is following the theory of Oliver Taplin, who posits three successive units or "movements" in three successive nights for the actual performing of the *Iliad*: I-IX, X-XVIII 353, XVIII 354-XXIV.[60] Heiden modifies this theory by positing a different set of divisions for the three "movements," which he thinks were performed in three days rather than nights: *Iliad* I-VIII, IX-XV, XVI-XXIV.[61] He argues that these posited divisions in the course of Iliadic performance were meant to achieve points of suspense, not of resolution: at the end of both VIII and XV, the Will of Zeus is being asserted at a moment when the outcome of the overall plot seems as yet undecided.[62]

I agree with Heiden's specific inference that these major divisions at the endings of *Iliad* VIII and XV are compositional as well as performative. I also agree with his general inference that the endings of all Homeric "books" are likewise both compositional and performative.[63] As I have argued in my earlier work, the division of the Homeric *Iliad* and *Odyssey* into twenty-four "books" (a better word would be "scrolls") stems from distinctly rhapsodic traditions of performance, and even the traditional word for designating one of these "books," *rhapsôidia*, reflects the technical language of rhapsodic practice.[64]

I disagree, however, with the position taken by Heiden when he argues that the divisions of the *Iliad* and *Odyssey* into twenty-four books "were

---

[59]Heiden 1996, 19-22.

[60]Taplin 1992, 11-31.

[61]Heiden 1996, 21.

[62]I do not agree with other aspects of Heiden's argumentation, especially the idea that the Will of Zeus is in each of these two cases a "counter-assertion" to the will of Achilles, and that this counter-assertion is expressed programmatically already in *Iliad* I 1-5 (p. 21). Zeus wills the realization of the *mênis* 'anger' of Achilles, not its thwarting, at *Iliad* I 5. See BA 1979 ch.20, where I offer an extended discussion of the synchronization of the Will of Zeus with the plot and the imagery of the *Iliad*. It surprises me to read the claim of Heiden 1997, 222n5 that "Nagy says little about the gods" (also p. 223n9). When he quotes me (p. 223) as saying that "the praise of Homeric poetry is restricted to the heroes of the distant past" (PH 150), he does not note the context of my formulation: I am contrasting these heroes of the past with the audience in the here-and-now of Homeric performance. On the subject of divine models for epic praise, see PH 359-61.

[63]Heiden 1998.

[64]PP 181-83 (68, 79).

designed and textualized by the composer himself."[65] I also disagree with the position taken by Taplin on the other extreme: he argues not only that the book-divisions "do not go back to the formation of the poems" but also that they are relatively recent, probably the work of Alexandrian scholars.[66] The major narrative breaks that Taplin posits for the *Iliad* are more distinct, he contends, than the breaks separating the Books of the *Iliad* as we know them.[67]

As an alternative to these positions, I offer here an intermediate formulation, based on an evolutionary model for the making of Homeric poetry.[68] In terms of such a model, I have argued, "what may be a three-part division in one stage of the tradition, which is what Taplin posits for the *Iliad*, may not necessarily be incompatible with a 24-part division at another stage."[69] These "divisions," I should stress, are not textual in terms of my formulation: rather, they are simultaneously compositional and performative. That is, they are aspects of a process of recomposition, evolving over time in the historical contexts of each reperformance. In short, "I hold open the possibility that the eventual division of the *Iliad* and *Odyssey* each into twenty-four Books results from the cumulative formation of episodes in the process of equalized or even weighting."[70]

Having noted my disagreements with Heiden's formulation of performative breaks in Homeric poetry, I return to a central point of agreement, concerning the suspenseful endings of *Iliad* VIII and XV. So far, we have seen that the effect of suspense is achieved by way of breaking the narrative at a point where the Will of Zeus is not yet fully realized. The choosing of such points for breaking the narrative, I have been arguing, reflects a distinctly rhapsodic practice. Further, I have been comparing these points for breaking the Homeric narrative with the point in Plato's *Critias* where the text breaks off, at the precise moment when the Will of Zeus is about to be quoted directly.

The analogy seems incomplete, however, since the Will of Zeus, as spoken in his own words, is "quoted" in *Iliad* VIII and XV not at the end of these "books" but further back (VIII 470-483 and XV 14-33, 49-77). Still, the actual effects of the words spoken by Zeus are suspensefully held back by the narrative of each of these "books," all the way to the very end of each.

---

[65]Heiden 1998, 82. For a position similar to Heiden's, see Stanley 1993.
[66]Taplin 1992, 285.
[67]Taplin 1992, 285-93.
[68]HQ ch.3-4; PP ch.5-7.
[69]HQ 88n72.
[70]HQ 88; on the concept of "equalized weighting," see HQ 77-82. As I remark in HQ 88, "It is from a diachronic point of view that I emphasize the cumulative formation of episodes in the process of even weighting."

The analogy becomes clearer if we trace the overall metaphorical world of the Will of Zeus in the *Iliad*. From *Iliad* I through *Iliad* XV, as I have argued at length elsewhere, the Will of Zeus is visualized as an archetypal Conflagration inflicted by the thunderbolt of Zeus, and this visualization is applied metaphorically to the fire of Hektor as it threatens to destroy the ships of the Achaeans.[71] In terms of the overall plot of the *Iliad*, if the fire of Hektor had burned down the ships of the Achaeans, these seafaring ancestors of the Hellenes would all have perished, and Hellenic civilization itself would have become extinct.[72] This extinction, had it happened, would have been caused immediately by the fire of Hektor — but ultimately by a Conflagration sent by the Will of Zeus.

Fortunately for the Achaeans, the Will of Zeus stops short of Conflagration: "for Zeus, the *selas* 'flash' of Hektor's fire at XV 600 signals the termination of the Trojan onslaught, which was inaugurated by the *selas* of his own thunderstroke at VIII 76."[73] The Trojans will not be so fortunate: from *Iliad* XV 600 onward, the Will of Zeus will start to turn against them, and the rest of the plot of the *Iliad* will lead inexorably toward their own ultimate extinction by way of Conflagration.

This Homeric theme of ultimate extinction is pertinent to the themes of Plato's *Timaeus* and *Critias*. Already in the *Timaeus*, we see a polar opposition between two kinds of eschatological disaster, that is, Conflagration (Ecpyrosis) and Flood (Cataclysm): the first is exemplified by the myth of Phaethon (22c) and the second, by the myth of Deukalion (22a). At the point where the *Critias* breaks off, the Will of Zeus is about to unleash the second kind of eschatological disaster, the Cataclysm.

In the *Iliad*, the alternative eschatological themes of Ecpyrosis and Cataclysm are in fact both applied: the first threatens both the Trojans and the Achaeans, while the second threatens only the Achaeans.[74] Either way, the essential fact remains: Ecpyrosis and Cataclysm are the visible epic manifestations of the Will of Zeus.

In sum, the *Critias* of Plato breaks off at a point that corresponds to a break in rhapsodic performance. What then, could this correspondence tell us about the narrative sequence of the *Timaeus* and *Critias*?

In the wording of the *Timaeus*, the narrative about Atlantis was told to Solon *hexês* 'in sequence' (23d) by the Egyptian priests, after they had re-read their own written record *ephexês* 'in sequence' (24a). The contexts of these terms *hexês* / *ephexês* are analogous to the context of *ephexês logos* 'continuous discourse' in *Critias* 106b, which I have al-

---

[71]BA 334-47. Cf. also Muellner 1996.

[72]BA 338.

[73]BA 336.

[74]Rousseau 1996, 403-13, 591-92, with special reference to the stylized Cataclysm of *Iliad* XII 17-33 and the Battle of Fire and Water in *Iliad* XXI 211-327 (on which see also HQ 145-46).

ready compared to the overtly rhapsodic context of *ephexês* in "Plato" *Hipparkhos* 228b-c. As we have seen, the context of *Critias* 106b is in fact likewise overtly rhapsodic. When it is Critias' turn in the *Critias* to take up where Timaeus in the *Timaeus* had left off, Timaeus says: "I hand over [*paradidomen*] to Critias, as prearranged, the continuous discourse [*ephexês logos*]" (*Critias* 106b: παραδίδομεν κατὰ τὰς ὁμολογίας Κριτίᾳ τὸν ἐφεξῆς λόγον).

The problem is, Critias can never finish narrating this "continuous discourse," just as Solon never finished turning this narrative into his own poetry in the first place. If only Solon had not left unfinished his poetic composition about Atlantis and Athens, says the grandfather, this states-man would have surpassed even Homer and Hesiod in poetic fame (*Timaeus* 21c-d). If only Solon had finished, his Atlantis would have become the "continuous discourse" of rhapsodes.

The discontinuity of the Atlantis narrative highlights the openendedness of the narrative sequence from the *Timaeus* to the *Critias* to the nonexist-ent *Hermocrates*. The break in continuity happens at a point in the narra-tive when the narration has some time ago shifted from gods to humans: that shift is signaled already at the beginning of the speech of Critias (*Critias* 107a-b). That this speech is seemingly meant to address purely human affairs, not divine, is underlined by Plato's evocative references to the world of history. When Critias describes his whole speech as *parakhrêma legomena* 'things spoken with reference to the present con-tingencies' (107d-e), his wording evokes the passage in Thucydides 1.22.4 where the historian rejects the ephemeral preoccupations of his predecessors (ἀγώνισμα ἐς τὸ παραχρῆμα ἀκούειν 'a competitive occasion meant for hearing in the present [historical] contingencies [*parakhrêma*]'). Later on, when Critias describes the *moira* 'destiny' of golden-age hu-manity as *exitêlos* 'extinct' (*Critias* 121a), his wording evokes the begin-ning of the *History* of Herodotus, where the historian expresses his ulti-mate intent to rescue human affairs from becoming *exitêla* 'extinct' (Herodotus *prooemium*).[75]

It is precisely at this moment in the narrative of the *Critias* that the Will of Zeus is about to reassert itself in the course of human affairs. It is also precisely at this moment that Zeus, just as he begins to speak, is pre-cluded from uttering even one word. How ineffable of Zeus even to try to

---

[75]For a related evocation of the prooemium of Herodotus in *Timaeus* 20e, see PH 226. By implication, Plato's *Timaeus* is a monumental *prooemium* or *humnos* in its own right: see again see n41 above. The genetic implications of *exitêlos* at the end of the *Critias*, 121a, where the *moira* 'destiny' of the golden generation becomes *exitêlos* 'extinct' precisely because of their "mixing" their genes with ordinary mortals, can be compared with the context of *exitêlos* in Herodotus 5.39.2, with reference to the extinction of a genetic line. Cf. PH 225.

speak at this point in the flow of narration, given that the dialogue of
Critias had already started off by shifting from divine to human affairs!

The openendedness of the narrative sequence from the *Timaeus* to the
Critias to the nonexistent *Hermocrates* leaves no chance for Hermocrates,
described as *tritos* (*Critias* 108a6), even to start — let alone finish. If he
had indeed started, Hermocrates would have needed "a second beginning," *hetera arkhê*, in any case (*Critias* 108b). That way, he would not
have had to resort to the same old beginning, *arkhê*.

Before Critias gets to have his own beginning, *arkhê*, Socrates jokingly
prophesies for him the fate that befalls those who compete in the world of
theater, referring to what he calls the "mentality" of that medium
(literally, its *dianoia* 'train of thought': τὴν τοῦ θεάτρου διάνοιαν): the
"previous poet" (ὁ πρότερος . . . ποιητής), he says, will always have a
big advantage (*Critias* 108b).[76]

At this point, Hermocrates responds to Socrates that "we" must bravely
move ahead, that is, that Critias as the second in the sequence of three
speakers must bravely move ahead and start his speech (*Critias* 108c).
Critias responds by expressing his admiration for these brave but doomed
words of Hermocrates, who is "last in line" (τῆς ὑστέρας τεταγμένος)
and, worse, who still "has someone else in front of him," someone who
has not yet even performed for his audience (ἐπίπροσθεν ἔχων ἄλλον
Critias 108c). At this moment, Critias refers to his present audience as
"this theater" (τῷδε τῷ θεάτρῳ 108d).[77]

As I contemplate Hermocrates in his role of the potential *tritos* (108a6),
I see a failed sequence of three would-be rhapsodes: Timaeus, Critias,
Hermocrates. If these three *dramatis personae* had succeeded in putting it
all together, we would have had three rhapsodes performing some kind of
poetic totality for one day.[78] "Yesterday" there was another set of performances, adding up to a fictional equivalent of the *Republic*. "Today,"
the sequence of would-be rhapsodes does not quite add up — unless per-

---

[76]Here I see an explicit merger of the imagery of rhapsodes competing in the festival of the
Panathenaia with the imagery of poets competing in theatrical festivals like the Dionysia.
Plato indulges in such mergers of images, especially in the *Ion*. In a related study, Nagy
1999b, I examine more closely the parallelisms in Plato's references to rhapsodic and
theatrical competitions in light of historical evidence for parallelisms in the evolution of
rhapsôidoi 'rhapsodes' and *hupokritai* 'actors'.

[77]On "theater" as the audience of rhapsodes, see again the previous note. Note that *theatai*
'theater-goers' refers to the audiences of rhapsodes at *Ion* 535d8.

[78]The potential totality of Timaeus/ Critias/ Hermocrates may be the equivalent, in rhapsodic
terms, of one of three "movements" in the performance of the *Iliad*. In terms of the three
performative "movements" of the *Iliad*, as Taplin 1992, 21n20 argues, cross-references in
one given "movement" to the previous "movement" can be worded in terms of "yesterday."
That is, "yesterday" can refer to yesterday's performance, not to an event that happened
yesterday in terms of the narrative per se. In XIII 745, for example, χθιζὸν χρεῖος 'debt of
yesterday' refers to the Trojan victory of Book VIII. See in general Taplin 1992, 21 for other
possible examples.

haps the reader is able take the place of Hermocrates in this ongoing rhapsody.

References

BA = Nagy 1979 [1999a]

Berve, Helmut. 1966. "Vom agonalen Geist der Griechen." *Gestaltende Kräfte der Antike.* 2nd ed. München: Beck. 1-20.

Brisson, Luc. 1982. *Platon. Les mots et les mythes.* Paris: Maspero.

Canto, Monique, trans. and commentary. 1989. Platon. *Ion.* Paris: Flammarion.

Clay, Diskin. 1997. "The Plan of Plato's *Critias.*" *Interpreting the Timaeus-Critias: Proceedings of the IV Symposium Platonicum, Selected Papers.* Ed. T. Calvo and L. Brisson. Sankt Augustin: Academia. 49-54.

Davison, John A. 1955. "Peisistratus and Homer." *Transactions of the American Philological Association* 86: 1-21.

———. 1958. "Notes on the Panathenaia." *Journal of Hellenic Studies* 78: 23-41 = 1968, 28-69.

———. 1968. *From Archilochus to Pindar: Papers on Greek Literature of the Archaic Period.* London: Macmillan.

Detienne, Marcel. 1989. *L'écriture d'Orphée.* Paris: Gallimard.

Dihle, Albrecht. 1995. "Platons Schriftkritik." *Jahrbuch der Akademie der Wissenschaften in Göttingen* 1995: 120-47.

Dougherty, Carol, and Leslie Kurke, eds. 1993. *Cultural Poetics in Archaic Greece: Cult, Performance, Politics.* Cambridge: Cambridge UP.

Ford, Andrew L. 1988. "The Classical Definition of *PAΨΩΔIA.*" *Classical Philology* 83: 300-7.

———. 1992. *Homer: The Poetry of the Past.* Ithaca, NY: Cornell UP.

GM = Nagy 1990b.

Hadot, Pierre. 1983. "Physique et poésie dans le *Timée* de Platon." *Revue de théologie et de philosophie* 115: 113-33.

Haslam, M. W. 1976. "A Note on Plato's Unfinished Dialogues." *American Journal of Philology* 97: 336-39.

Heiden, Bruce. 1996. "The Three Movements of the *Iliad.*" *Greek, Roman and Byzantine Studies* 37: 5-22.

———. 1997. "The Ordeals of Homeric Song." *Arethusa* 30: 221-40.

———. 1998. "The Placement of 'Book Divisions' in the *Iliad.*" *Journal of Hellenic Studies* 118: 69-82.

HQ = Nagy 1996b.

Jensen, Minna Skafte. 1980. *The Homeric Question and the Oral-Formulaic Theory.* Copenhagen: Museum Tusculanum.

Koller, Hermann. 1956. "Das kitharodische Prooimion: Eine formgeschichtliche Untersuchung." *Philologus* 100: 159-206.

Kotsidu, Haritini. 1991. *Die musischen Agone der Panathenäen in archaischer und klassischer Zeit. Eine historisch-archäologische Untersuchung.* Quellen und Forschungen zur antiken Welt 8. München: Tuduv.

Loraux, Patrice. 1993. *Le tempo de la pensée.* Paris: Seuil.

LSJ = Liddell, Henry George, and Robert Scott. 1940. *A Greek-English Lexicon.* 9th ed., rev. H. S. Jones. Oxford: Clarendon.

Martin, Richard P. 1989. *The Language of Heroes: Speech and Performance in the 'Iliad'.* Ithaca, NY: Cornell UP.

Merkelbach, Reinhold. 1952. "Die pisistratische Redaktion der homerischen Gedichte." *Rheinisches Museum* 95: 23-47.

Muellner, Leonard C. 1996. *The Anger of Achilles: Mênis in Early Greek Epic.* Ithaca, NY: Cornell UP.

Murray, Penelope, ed. 1996. *Plato on Poetry: Ion; Republic 376e-398b9; Republic 595-608b10.* Cambridge: Cambridge UP.

Nagy, Blaise. 1992. "Athenian Officials on the Parthenon Frieze." *American Journal of Archaeology* 96: 55-69.

Nagy, Gregory. 1979. *The Best of the Achaeans: Concepts of the Hero in Archaic Greek Poetry.* Baltimore: Johns Hopkins UP.

——. 1990a. *Pindar's Homer: The Lyric Possession of an Epic Past.* Baltimore: The Johns Hopkins UP. Rev. paperback ed. 1994.

——. 1990b. *Greek Mythology and Poetics.* Ithaca, NY: Cornell UP; rev. paperback ed. 1992.

——. 1996a. *Poetry as Performance: Homer and Beyond.* Cambridge: Cambridge UP.

——. 1996b. *Homeric Questions.* Austin: U of Texas P.

——. 1997. "An Inventory of Debatable Assumptions about a Homeric Question." *Bryn Mawr Classical Review* 97: 4.18.

——. 1998a. "The Library of Pergamon as a Classical Model." *Pergamon: Citadel of the Gods.* Ed. H. Koester. Harrisburg, PA: Trinity Press. 185-232.

——. 1998b. "Aristarchean Questions." *Bryn Mawr Classical Review* 98: 7.14.

——. 1999a. 2nd ed. of Nagy 1979.

——. 1999b. "Homer and Plato at the Panathenaia: Synchronic and Diachronic Perspectives." *Contextualizing Classics.* Ed. T. Falkner, D. Konstan, and N. Rubin. Lanham, MD: Rowman and Littlefield. 127-55.

Neils, Jenifer, ed. 1992. *Goddess and Polis: The Panathenaic Festival in Ancient Athens.* Princeton: Princeton UP.

Nilsson, Martin P. 1906. *Griechische Feste.* Leipzig: Teubner.

Parke, Herbert W. 1977. *Festivals of the Athenians.* Ithaca, NY: Cornell UP.

PH = Nagy 1990a.

PP = Nagy 1996a.

Rhodes, Peter J. 1981. *A Commentary on the Aristotelian 'Athenaion Politeia'.* Oxford: Clarendon.

Rousseau, Philippe. 1996. "Διὸς δ' ἐτελείετο βουλή: Destin des héros et dessein de Zeus dans l'intrigue de l'*Iliade.*" Doctorat d'Etat thesis, Université Charles de Gaulle — Lille III.

Saussure, Ferdinand de. 1916. *Cours de linguistique générale.* Critical ed. 1972 by Tullio de Mauro. Paris: Payot.

Schmitt, Rüdiger. 1967. *Dichtung und Dichtersprache in indogermanischer Zeit.* Wiesbaden: Harrassowitz.

Shapiro, H.A. 1992. "Mousikoi Agones: Music and Poetry at the Panathenaia." In Neils 1992, 53-75, plus notes at pp. 199-203.

———. 1993. "Hipparchos and the Rhapsodes." In Dougherty and Kurke 1993, 92-107.

Stanley, Keith. 1993. *The Shield of Homer: Narrative Structure in the Iliad.* Princeton: Princeton UP.

Taplin, Oliver. 1992. *Homeric Soundings: The Shaping of the 'Iliad'.* Oxford: Clarendon.

Witte, Bernd. 1964. "Der ΕΙΚΩΣ ΛΟΓΟΣ in Platons *Timaios.*" *Archiv für Geschichte der Philosophie* 46: 1-16.

3   MUSIC OF SOUTH SLAVIC EPICS

Stephen Erdely

Lecturing on the importance of folk music research, Zoltán Kodály made the following statement: "To questions, on which documents of music history remain non-committal, the study of oral musical folklore will provide answers." And then he added: "But we have to learn how to read from the unwritten pages of musical tradition."

Long narrative poems recited in song are among the oldest literary and musical art forms whose texts have been preserved, but whose music is lost. Their history reaches back into Classical Antiquity and even further, into times unrecorded when narrative poems were part of religious rites, funeral orations, banquets, courts and public ceremonies. Conceived in oral form, the poems were eventually put into writing and became cherished masterpieces of world literature. Their music, however, which imbued the words with magical powers, remained in an oral state and faded into silence.

Musical historians have attempted to reconstruct the performances of medieval epic songs from all available sources but were greatly hampered by the lack of documents; for there are only a handful of fragmentary melodies preserved in the archives that are known to be tunes of the *chansons de geste*, epics of the Middle Ages.

The earliest reference comes from a treatise, titled *De Musica*, written by Johannes de Grocheo, a Parisian musician of the fourteenth century who describes all the musical forms of his times.[1] He states about the *chanson de geste* that it was sung in syllabic fashion to a brief melody, repeated over and over again. He does not say anything about instrumental accompaniments, although the medieval mimes and jongleurs, whose repertories included the epic songs, did use instruments, as we can see them in contemporary illustrations.[2]

Grocheo's description has served as the point of departure for contemporary historians. Some scholars propose that the epics were sung to a litany type of melody.[3] Others believe that the melodies themselves were

---

[1]Wolf 1899, 69. On the music of the *chansons de geste*, see also the chapter by John Stevens in this volume.

[2]Falvy 1986.

[3]Gennrich 1932, 40ff.

taken from liturgical chants,[4] and again others suggest that the epic melodies had several formal types, ranging from lection — or reciting tones
with inflexions corresponding to commas, periods, questions and other
grammatical signs — through *laisse, lai* types of melodies to strophic
forms similar to folk ballads.[5] The lack of written musical sources led
scholars to believe that most of the tunes of long narrative poems were
popularly known liturgical or art songs easy to remember and therefore in
no need to be preserved in writing.

Thanks to the advancements in recording technology, and to the tireless
efforts of fieldworkers there are new discoveries of this ancient minstrelsy
preserved in the oral tradition of people in various parts of the world. The
documentations on records offer renewed hope for insight into the performance of epic songs and into the interrelationship of their music and
poetry.

One of the world's foremost collections of South Slavic epic songs is
housed in the Milman Parry Collection of Oral Literature at Harvard
University. It contains the harvest of Professors Milman Parry's and
Albert Bates Lord's fieldwork recorded in Yugoslavia during the 1930s
and 1950s and 1960s respectively. The linguist Roman Jakobson, known
for his studies of Slavic epic verse, praises the collection for its accuracy
and refinement of methods used. In his words the collection is "unique,
not only in the history of Serbocroatian and of other Slavic epic studies,
but also, without overstatement, in the whole world history of inquiry into
the epic heritage."[6]

Until the end of World War II singing and listening to heroic tales was
one of the favorite forms of entertainment of people in Yugoslavia. The
art was learned from and circulated in oral forms and it could be heard
performed in a variety of styles differing not only from region to region
in the Balkans, but also within the regions from singer to singer.

My study is based on a select number of epic songs in the Milman
Parry Collection which I have transcribed from recordings. I should like
to discuss their music from two points of view: (a) elements of uniformity: that is, the rhythm, melody, tempo, and instrumental accompaniment
of tunes in general, which the singer learned from his traditional environment, and (b) elements that he made his own, developing his personal
style of performance.

The primary unit of South Slavic epic song is the verse; rhythm and
melody, the two fundamental aspects of the song are based on the verse.
There are two ways of viewing the epic verse, by the properties characterizing the archetype, and by the changes affecting its rhythmic and

[4]Gérold 1932, 79-90.
[5]Stevens 1990.
[6]Jakobson 1954, xi.

metric forms. The archetype of the South Slavic narrative poetry is the ten-syllable line. Lines of nine or eleven syllables are also found, but they are the exceptions. The metrical patterns of verses can be iambic or trochaic; whether the iambic meter is borrowed or indigenous in the Slavic tradition has not so far been determined because it also appears to be a widely used meter in the Romance and Germanic poetry. The trochaic meter, on the other hand, is a popular Slavic form. The lines are separated by a breathing break in a length that can vary from one to four or more metric units. Concerning the phonological elements of this verse form, Roman Jakobson states that word stresses fall on uneven syllables and word endings on even ones.[7] A compulsory word boundary marked by the end of a word on the fourth syllable and the beginning of another word on the fifth syllable creates the mid-line caesura which divides the line into two halves of uneven length: four syllables form the first half and six syllables the second half. The ninth syllable receives a quantitative stress which makes it the strongest and longest in the line, whereas the seventh and eighth syllables are the weakest; the tenth syllable can be very short, deformed, even swallowed, or, in some cases, carried over to the beginning of the next line. In normal tempo of recitation a metrical unit is formed of two syllables. Accordingly, the first hemistich comprises two metrical beats and the second hemistich four metrical beats:[8]

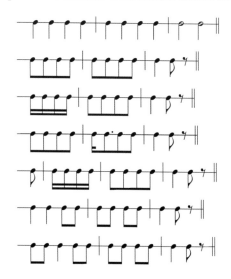

Ex. 1

[7]Jakobson 1966, 58.
[8]For additional rhythmic patterns, see Erdely 1995, 32.

Jakobson observes further that in everyday speech individual words are not distinguished by stress value. Thus, the South Slavic ten-syllable is based on natural pronunciation and recognizes only syntactic stress. He writes (*ibid.*):

> The analysis of the *deseterac* exposes the complete untenability of the frequently heard opinion that this verse is elementary, inferior, monotonous, and a prose type of form. The scheme of word boundary, intentional in the *deseterac*, contains the pronounced phonological characteristics of the entire line, in particular the line endings, the two verse halves, the meter, and finally the syllables. The Rhapsode follows this scheme even without being aware of its features . . . . The scheme has no existence outside the individual verses and the verses rarely embody it completely. The poetry obtains its specific artistic form in the inseparability of the verse and the production of boundaries, or, in the violation of boundaries. The conflict between the metric scheme and the phonological construct of the verse is always present.

Albert Lord, in his classic study *The Singer of Tales*, bases his remarks on his field studies as he probes further into the metrical characteristics of the South Slavic epic line. He directs our attention, in the first place, to the fact that the singer of long narrative songs is different from the folk-singer who is basically involved in a recreative act of the tradition. For the epic bard is the poet, the composer and the performer in one person and at the same time. He composes his lines in performance. To become proficient in his art, the singer of tales puts himself through a long and conscious learning process. He listens to his peers, learns the rhythm and melody of the verse, observes the breaks that separate them, and the speed variation in which the lines are recited. Rhythm and melody will become the vehicle of the story whereas the tempo and spacing of lines will shape the form of the movement. He learns the formulaic expressions for the most common ideas by imitation and repetition, and creates new ones based on their rhythmical patterns for his own thoughts. In Lord's words the formula is the "offspring of thought and sung verse." "Basic patterns of meter, word boundary, melody have become his possession, and in him the tradition begins to reproduce itself."[9]

In the performance, however, language, verse and music do not obey the same principles and the archetype of the line can be affected by many kinds of adjustments. A common occurrence, for instance, is the change of syllable count. Since the South Slavic epic verse begins with a thetic beat, it is almost a psychological necessity to head it with an interjectional word that lends it frontal support in the form of an upbeat. Such nones-

---

[9]Lord 1960, 21.

sential interjections are frequently advanced into the first foot and alter both the rhythm and syllable count of the first half of the line. Conversely, the last syllable of the line is frequently swallowed, taking away an entire metric beat from the second half. If both events take place at the same time, the line divides into 5 + 5 syllables.[10] For an illustration, see lines 9 to 12 from Ibrahim Nuhanović's version of *Robovanje Osmanbeg Omerbegovića*:[11]

9   A ne vi - ju se   vjet͡ri u pla - ni',

10 Da ne tu - či se na g͡ra - ni - ci strar',

11 A ni - je - ku- vet bo - ga ve - li - kog',

12 Da ni - je ku- vet͡ ca - ra stam - bols - kog',

Ex. 2.

Prolonging a syllable, or syllabic groups, or accelerating the pronunciation of words within the metrical half of the line can change the balance between the two hemistichs: their metrical units can be even, or, in some rare cases, the first half of the line can even be longer than the second.

Finally, tempo variations can distort the basic pattern to a degree where it is not recognizable any longer. This happens in the singing of opening lines recited in a "tempo rubato," (Ex. 3, *Sila Osmanbeg i*

---

[10]For further details of performance, see Erdely 1995.
[11]For a transcription of the complete heroic song, see Erdely 1995, 393-609.

Pavišić Luka sung by Murat Žunić, line 1, and Ex. 4, *Robovanje Osmanbeg Omerbegovića*, sung by Ibrahim Nuhanović, line 1) or in the case of run-on lines which, on the other hand, are recited in a very fast tempo and combine two to three verses under one melodic curve (Ex. 5, Nuhanović's *Robovanje*, lines 36-38):

Ex. 3

Ex. 4

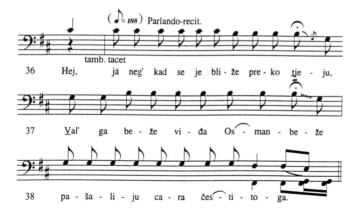

Ex. 5

To turn to the melody, it has been the long held view that epic songs were sung in syllabic fashion to a litany type of tune that hardly rose above articulated speech level, or, if it did, it remained very simple, and that this melody was repeated over and over again.

The music of South Slavic oral epics can hardly support this view. The tunes are narrow in range, three to four notes, rarely reaching the interval of the sixth and hardly ever the octave. Because of this narrow scale range, the tonality of melodies, the cohesive force, which would determine the relation of tones to one another, is frequently ambiguous. The melody is a curve with peaks and ebbs on metrically important syllables. The singer varies the contour notes until he finds the kind of melodic phrase he can be satisfied with. In the process of composition certain notes will be touched with greater or lesser frequency. Cadential notes, after stabilizing, may impart the feeling of a perfect ending, while others, one or two degrees above, or below this note, will be felt as imperfect endings. There is also a third kind of final note reached with a vocal slide down several scale degrees from the cadential note. Such line ending slides have no tonal, or melodic significance; they seem to be imitations of the bagpipe emitting its reserved air, and are mannerisms in South Slavic vocal music (compare Ex. 5, line 38).

Many singers have their own musical formulas which they apply to their epic verses. There can therefore be no further generalization of the musical motive. But one particular melody line is known to and used by many singers of the South Slavic tradition: it is an invocatory type of melody which begins with a shout and is followed by the text verse recited on a gradually descending melody. The formula is used as an epic opener and at times at the head of new sections. The shout and its primitive curve suggest that the formula survived from times when the epics were still associated with rituals and magic (see Ex. 3 and 4).

There are many ways a singer may vary his melodies. In addition to the rhythmical changes mentioned above, embellishments, replacements of scale notes can alter the melodic phrase. Sometimes variations affect only the first metrical half while the second metrical half remains relatively stable; at other times the process is just the opposite. The most interesting aspect of the compositional process is when the scale notes and the mode of the melody undergo gradual transformation; see Ex. 6, lines 63-81 of Mujo Velić's version of *Ženidba Ograšović Ale*.

Some singers adhere to one melody, varying the rhythm, meter and notes only slightly (as, for example, Murat Žunić in his version of *Sila Osmanbeg i Pavišić Luka*); others arrive at different melodic patterns through the process of variation; and again others introduce different melodic types with varying functions, like "introductory line," "special line," "main melodic formula," "second, third formula" etc. and combine them in stanzaic forms (as, for example, Ibrahim Nuhanović in his version of *Robovanje Osmanbeg Omerbegovića*).

During the course of his singing the epic bard may change the tempo of his lines several times. Little attention has been given to this phenomenon although it has its own musical consequences. At the beginning of an epic song the lines are recited slowly with a great deal of deliberation; breathing space separating them can consist of four or more metrical beats. Coming to a more familiar, more practiced part in the story, the singer accelerates the recitation; the breathing breaks become shorter, and the lines form paragraphs. Such blocks of lines remind scholars of the *laisses* in medieval *chansons de geste*. The resemblance, however, is only in appearance, for the *laisses* round up a unit in the story, whereas the blocks in South Slavic oral epics do not.

There are two kinds of tempos (a) a free, and slower than speech type of *parlando rubato* and (b) a normal, or slightly faster speech, tempo, or *tempo giusto*. In *parlando rubato* tempo the time allotted to a syllable becomes too long for a single note and it is broken up by "heavy" ornamental notes added to the main note. The metrical feature of this type of melodic lines is obscured by the tempo.

As the singing gradually accelerates the ornamental notes are left off and the verses are sung in syllabic fashion with clearly audible metrical articulation. Reaching the normal speech controlled *tempo giusto*, the rhythm and melody become stable over a number of lines. It is in this tempo range that we find the epic melody in its clearest form. Any further acceleration leads to run-on lines wherein twenty, or even thirty syllables — that is, two or three epic verses — are sung in one breath without syntactic break.

66   O - me-re bra - te,   da s'o-že-nim š njo-me."

67   O - ho, ja kad ču - o   nal - ba - te O - me - re,

68   Oh, nje - mu 'va - ko   nal - bat be - si - di - jo:

69   "Oh, ne bu - da - li,   bo-gom po - bra - ti - me.

70   Nis - ko je, bra - te,   na Ko - ta - re si - ći.

71   O - ho, ta - mo se - dam   i - ma po - gla - vi - ca,

72   Pa po - bra - ti - me,   O - gra - šo - vić A - le,

73   Ko se je go - di   o - tu - de že - ni - jo,

74   O - ho, on je sta - re   maj - ke po - že - li - jo,

75 O-ho, on je sta - re maj-ke po-že-li - jo.

76 O-ho, a ti je - si je-di-ni u ma - me.

77 O-ho, pa bi i to ma-la ša-la bi - la.

78 Mo - raš li, bra - te, u-pam-ti-ti vri - me,

79 O-ho, mo-raš, bra - te, dav-no ni-je bi - lo,

80 O-ho, ka' seo'-šti - ma Đu-lić baj-rek-ta - ru,

81 O-ho, Đu-lić baj - ro sa ši-ro-ke Li - ke,

Ex. 6

A word should be said about the two accompanying instruments, the *tambura* and the *gusle*. The *tambura*, the more popular instrument among the South Slaves of Moslem faith, is a long-necked plucked lute with two strings; the *gusle*, the more popular instrument among the majority of the population, is a one-stringed and bowed lute type. The singers tune their instruments to their own voice range.

The function of instrumental accompaniment is to place the entire epic in a musical context with improvised preludes and interludes, bridge passages between melodic lines, and with support drone, or basic melodic outline in unison with the melody during singing. The *tambura*, probably a mid-eastern, Turkish import, is a rhythm instrument, whereas the *gusle*, is a melody instrument. Although both instruments fulfill the same role, they affect the music in different ways (see Ex. 2).

I have thus far discussed features characterizing South Slavic epic songs in general. Now I should like to mention briefly the creative process in which the singer is involved as he makes his selections from the elements and their variants available to him.

There are two types of performers; those who sing in the stichic manner, line by line, and form blocks of lines, and those who sing individual lines, groups of lines as well as stanzaic formations.

Mujo Velić, who was about 60 years old when Milman Parry recorded him in the Bihać region in 1935, composed entirely in the traditional stichic manner. His lines are rounded poetic and musical units which he groups into paragraphs of 25 to 75 lines. His melodies are neither litany type of recitatives nor plastic well wrought tunes. They are contour melodies moving in gentle curves, or simple tags, changing their shapes like reflections on the water. He is talented in variation, in changing his motifs, their scale notes, and modes. He is equally well experienced in the rhythmic and metric possibilities the tradition has sanctioned.

Murat Žunić whom Parry recorded in the same year and in the same Bosnian town does not show Velić's proclivity for melodic variation. He is more inclined to create stanzaic structures: couplets, tercets, and quatrains which he then recites in slow, moderate, and fast tempos. He uses the traditional introductory line beginning with a shout after which he presents his own epic line, a melody with distinct motifs in the first and second metric halves. He adheres to one main melodic formula throughout the epic. Parts of the formula are also used in tercets, whose first and second lines are nine syllables, ending incomplete by swallowing the tenth syllable, and the third line is ten-syllabic and comes to a complete ending. The two metrical halves of the first and second lines divide into 2 + 3 metrical beats and the last line into 2 + 4 metrical beats. Žunić composes a major portion of his epic in run-on lines: he sings two or three, at times even four, that is 20, 30, or even 40 syllables without break or separation. The acoustical impression gained from the perfomance is that he recites verses of 20-40 syllables in stichic manner.

Common to all of the run-on lines is that the final syllable of the last line is omitted, thus, just in this formation the opposite happens of what was described in the tercets.

Ibrahim Nuhanović's singing was recorded by Albert Lord in the 1960s. Nuhanović was old enough to have heard Žunić reciting his poems. There is indeed a close relationship between his method of composition and that of Žunić. Nuhanović's style of singing shows considerable advancement in the direction of stanzaic forms. While the ten-syllable line still remains the main unit of his compositions, it is no longer the dominant structural element. Single lines are combined or alternated with couplets, tercets and other verse groupings. He also begins his epic songs with the customary introductory line, but then he has several line types which he uses individually or in stanzaic combination with other lines. Altogether there are five such stanzaic forms whose succession shows a certain regularity throughout the epic song. He is the more versatile, the more complete composer equally at home when working with individual lines and strophic paragraphs, or forming couplets and other stanzaic forms.

It should be noted that the terms used to describe the musical events and forms in epic singing, such as scale structure, cadential endings, motivic, stichic, stanzaic forms and the like are borrowed from art music and are not known, nor do they have any meaning for the South Slavic epic singer. He is cognizant only of the poetic line and the tune applied to it. He learns the principles controlling the relationship between music and poetry orally and employs them in a semi-conscious way. Even if the formulaic patterns of verse and music have lost their meaning today, the subtle forms of melodic variation and transformation born out of the singer's natural, instinctive musical desire create their own attraction, which explains the longevity of this ancient musico-poetic art. For us the discovery of epic songs living in oral traditions offers new hope of reconstructing the performance of this ancient art, forgotten before it could fully be understood.

References

Erdely, Stephen. 1995. *Music of Southslavic Epics from the Bihać Region of Bosnia.* New York and London: Garland.

Falvy, Zoltán. 1986. *Mediterranean Culture and Troubadour Music.* Budapest: Akadémiai Kiadó.

Gennrich, Friedrich. 1932. *Grundriß einer Formenlehre des mittelalterlichen Liedes als Grundlage einer musikalischen Formenlehre des Liedes.* Halle an der Saale: Niemeyer. [Rpt. Darmstadt: Wissenschaftliche Buchgesellschaft, 1970. Mit einem Vorwort von Werner Bittinger.]

Gérold, Théodore. 1932. *La Musique au Moyen Âge.* Les Classiques Français du Moyen Âge 73. Paris: Champion.

Jakobson, Roman. 1954. "Preface." *Serbocroatian Heroic Songs.* Ed. Milman Parry, ed. and trans. Albert Bates Lord. Volume 1: *Novi Pazar: English Translations.* With musical transcriptions by Béla Bartók and prefaces by John H. Finley, Jr., and Roman Jakobson. Cambridge and Belgrade: Harvard UP and the Serbian Academy of Sciences. xi-xii.

———. 1966. "Über den Versbau der Serbocroatischen Volksepen." *Selected Writings.* Volume 4: *Slavic Epic Studies.* The Hague: Mouton.

Lord, Albert B. 1960. *The Singer of Tales.* Cambridge, MA: Harvard UP.

Stevens, John. 1990. "Medieval Song." *The Early Middle Ages to 1300.* New Oxford History of Music 2. Ed. Richard Crocker and David Hiley. Oxford: Oxford UP.

Wolf, Johannes. 1899. "Die Musiklehre des Johannes de Grocheo." *Sammelbände der Internationalen Musikgesellschaft* 1: 65-130.

4   THE SINGING OF ALBANIAN HEROIC POETRY

Wolf Dietrich

The Recording

In 1995 the economic and political situation in Albania allowed foreigners to travel around the country. Even ethnomusicological field research was to some degree possible. During a trip in September 1995 I was able to make recordings with a family in the village of Balldre, five kilometres north of Lezhë. We were told that epic singing had been practised in this family for at least three generations. The primary aim of this research was not epic singing itself, but rather the music of the gypsy groups in the country, and for this reason no other epic singers were visited or recorded during this trip.

The singers in Balldre were Lek Celaj, born about 1950, a farmer, and his father Nok Prel Celaj, aged 90, who also performed a song, accompanying himself with the same *lahuta* as his son. This instrument was not made by him or his son but had been bought earlier from a professional *lahuta* maker. The Celaj family belongs to a large Catholic minority in this area.

Although he is not a shepherd, Lek Celaj also plays the *fyell*, a side-blown, open flute of the *kaval* type, approximately 45 cm in length. That he is an experienced player of this instrument can be deduced from his technique of circular breathing, i.e. inhaling the air through the nose while playing the flute at the same time, a technique which allows continuous blowing without interruptions by breathing. Father and son Celaj sometimes sing the *kraje mahi* songs together, an old form of shepherd singing in the mountains.

The Situation of the Epic Tradition

Epic singing in Albania is found mostly in the northern parts of the country, in the regions of Malësia e Hasit and Malësia e Madhe near the borders to Kosovo and Crna Gora (Montenegro). Today even there the tradition is receding — or, put differently, if there is still any tradition alive in Albania at all, it can be found in this area. Singers like Lek Celaj occasionally perform at local festivities or during a folklore festival. Apparently a larger interest in his art does not exist among the local population.

My own experiences with epic singers in Yugoslavia show a similar decline in public interest. Some of the singers have altered the contents of their songs to attract an audience. In 1979, I made recordings (which I later published on an LP) of a singer from the village of Batusha near the Yugoslav-Albanian border. This singer had changed his verses to satiric lines about heroes and their deeds — he informed me that other singers did the same — and sung about his "anti-hero," called Bali Katravella, in the following way:

> [Bali] ... asht çue trimi, shtërngue kokërkan.
> M'i ka shtie armët prej sugjuki,
> ma ka marrë pushkën prej kakudi,
> ma ka veshë shpatë prej shevari
> ma shtërngojkë qat' gjogë veshmadhin . . .

> He [the hero] stood up to attire himself.
> In his belt he stuck his weapons made of sausage.
> He shouldered his gun made of reed mace,
> Fastened on the sword of reeds
> As his white steed he saddled the jackass . . .

The decrease of interest in epic tradition can be observed in many further details. Shortly after 1970 both RTB and Jugoton, the two state record companies of Yugoslavia, discontinued the publication of their series of *guslari* music. Even recordings of well-known singers like Boško Vujačić or Ivan Soldo disappeared from the record market.

After World War II, epic singing in Albania was recorded by the Instituti i folklorit. However, the majority of the songs published in periodicals and books date from the sixties, and recordings from recent times are rare.[1]

It is difficult to say how many recordings were published on gramophone records in Albania, because today all these publications from socialist times have disappeared. In 1995 a lot of tapes containing folk music recordings were sold in Tirana in the area around Skanderbeg Place, but these belonged almost exclusively to the following three genres:

– clarinet music (gypsy entertainment and dance music),
– songs accompanied by *çifteli* and *sharki*,
– polyphony from Toskërija and Labërija.

---

[1]See Kruta 1994; Daja 1994. On Albanian folklore and oral epics, see also Camaj 1983; Çabej 1966; Schmaus 1963; Skendi 1954. For collections of texts, see Lambertz 1958 (German translations); Sako 1967 (French translations); Sako 1968; Shala 1972.

I did not see any tape recordings of epic singers distributed at that time.

In 1986 Spiro Shituni and others published a collection of songs presented during the national folklore congresses in Gjirokastër in 1968, 1973, and 1978; the collection does not contain a single epic song, not a single *këngë kreshniqësh* (the Albanian term for heroic epic). In the eighties Beniamin Kruta, at that time director of the Instituti i folklorit in Tirana, published two records in Italy with the Cetra I Suoni Company, Rome (LPs Cetra I Suoni SU 5009 and SU 5010), containing archive material from his institute; he did not include a single epic singer. Accordingly I assume that the tradition of epic singing in Albania today is only of interest to a very small group of people, and in this light the recordings from Balldre have to be regarded as even more valuable.

In addition to the decline in public interest, the social conditions for epic singing are vanishing, too. Ninety years ago, Matthias Murko reported about the singers and their income: "Most of the vagrant singers sing for payment, most of them become vagrant singers when there is no other work. They wander about to the houses of the beys and agas. Many practise their art in coffeehouses. Even Austrian border officers sent for them before 1878 when they had Turkish guests."[2]

We know what the singers were paid: "A singer whose name was Bečir Islamović travelled for money through the Bihać area after the harvest time. He took two or three gulden in coffeehouses, five gulden for a whole night of singing in a beg's house. Often there were additional presents: waistcoats, embroidered trousers, etc."[3] Even after World War I economic opportunities, which today have ceased to exist, were found for some of the *guslari*. One example is Nikola Vujnović, Milman Parry's companion during his travels. He was an epic singer, who at that time (1935) performed in a wine shop in Dubrovnik to help increase sales.[4] Parry reports that he frequently found his singers in coffeehouses. He collected epics from Moslem, Orthodox, and Roman Catholic singers in Bihać/Bosnia, but in his own and A. B. Lord's opinion his best performers were Moslems and Roman Catholics.

The Musical Instrument *Lahuta*

According to the classification of musical instruments by Ernst Moritz von Hornbostel and Curt Sachs the *lahuta* belongs to the class of lutes. A lute is defined as a "composite chordophone, where the string attachment and the resonator are organically connected and cannot be separated

---

[2]Murko 1909, 20.
[3]Murko 1909, 20.
[4]Lord 1954, 6.

without destroying the instrument."[5] This classification does not take into account whether a lute is plucked or bowed. In common understanding, a lute is a plucked instrument, and a violin or fiddle like the *lahuta* is not regarded as a lute. This is seen in a different light in organology, where the way in which the sound is produced is of minor significance.

Within the lute family, the *lahuta* or *gusle* is a highly remarkable musical instrument — especially in Europe. Both corpus and neck are fashioned from a single piece of wood; bow and string are made from horse hair. The string is not touched or pressed with the fingertip but "struck" or "beaten" with the upper part of the fingers. Before playing, the string is rubbed not with resin but with a piece of wood to produce a certain roughness and to make the string sound with a full tone. The player's fingers always remain in the same position. Unlike the violin, the *gusle* or *lahuta* is never played with a hand position other than the first position.

The singer always plays the instrument in a sitting position, with the *lahuta* between his knees, similar to the position in which the viola da gamba is held. No other position is practised. The bow is guided with the forefinger of the right hand. It looks as if the forefinger were loosely placed on the bow, but it can actually put considerable pressure on the bow, which may cause the string to rise up to a half tone.

The technique of bowing appeared in Europe as a new invention during the tenth century, first in Byzantium. Pictorial representations from that time show (within a short period) numerous pictures of musical instruments with one, two, or three strings — all of which were bowed. Before this time not a single bow is portrayed, neither in Byzantium nor in any other place in Europe. It is not completely clear where the new invention came from, but ethnomusicology tends to support the hypothesis that the bowing technique was developed in the eastern part of Central Asia.

The soundtable (or belly) of these new bowed musical instruments from the tenth century was made of skin or wood; of these materials wood was predominantly used. The sudden rise in frequency of such representations allows us to assume that bowing was adopted relatively quickly and then, as a sort of musical fashion, tried out also on musical instruments which had been plucked before. The *lahuta* has been known in southeastern Europe since that time, and apparently has not been changed significantly since.

Today in Europe the *gusle* or *lahuta* is the only musical instrument of the lute type with a skin soundtable. Its string is still made of hair from a horse's tail (about 50-60 single hairs bundled). The fingering technique with which this string is played is unique in Europe, but can be found among players of the Ethiopian *krar* fiddle. There are other details which

---

[5]Von Hornbostel and Sachs 1914.

also point to traditions outside Europe. The bridge, for example, is usually not mounted at an angle of 90° to the string, but slanting to one side in order to bundle the horsehair of the string and thus to give the string an easier and clearer sound. In Arabian countries, Central Asia, or India movable bridges are used with many chordophones. The bridge of the Kazakh or Karakalpak *qobyz*, for example, is always placed in a strongly asymmetric position on the skin of the soundtable to avoid the so-called wolf's tones (i.e. impure tones with an unusually strong resonance in the musical instrument).

Ajkuna Bewails Omer, from the Halil and Muji Cycle

The epic songs of Albania concentrate upon the brothers Gjeto Basho Muji and Halil, whose deeds are described in numerous episodes. In Albania, songs of this type are called *kënge kreshnikësh*. The word *kreshnikësh* has been interpreted in different ways:

– Ernesto Koliqi says the word is composed of *kresh* = 'Christ', 'crusader', and the Slavic ending -*nik*;
– Stavro Skendi derives the word from the base *krajina*, a geographical region, namely the border between the Ottoman Empire and the Serbian area;
– Eqrem Çabej sees *kreshtë*, 'long hair', 'mane', as the source of the derivation, assuming that the rebels were characterized by long hair.

In this heroic song, as in many other epic songs, the *zanas* are mentioned. *Zana* is derived from the Latin word for the goddess Diana. In Albanian heroic songs a *zana* is either a tutelary goddess or sometimes an evil, sometimes a militant, spirit. A *zana* is a mortal being. Her name is taboo; usually it is referred to obliquely, because as in the case of the evil eye, direct naming could cause difficulties. Sometimes the *zanas* have a supporting function for the hero, as for example in one episode of the Muji and Halil cycle where Muji drinks milk from their breasts, which gives him supernatural powers to surpass all his rivals.[6]

The central figure in this episode is Ajkuna (or *Ajkuna te bardh*, 'the white Ajkuna', sometimes called Ajka). According to Parry she is the sister of Muji Hrnjačin ('the person with the cloven lip'); in other contexts she is Muji's wife.[7] Her seven sons all lose their lives in struggles against enemies of all kinds. Preceding this episode, Muji takes the youngest son Omer (called also *Omer i ri*, 'Young Omer') with him. Muji and Halil send young Omer to a small chapel near the border so that

---

[6] See Lambertz 1958, 9f.
[7] Lambertz 1958, 109.

he can have his first chance to prove his worth as a hero. They tell him to hide in the church and to shoot down the king on Sunday morning. Indeed Omer shoots down the priest (the Orthodox pope) as he is approaching the chapel, but then is mortally wounded by the king's guard.[8] Here Lek Celaj's song begins:

Ajkuna qan Omerin	Ajkuna bewails Omeri

Lum e lum fort për të luminë Zot,
nuk jem kan e Zoti na ka dhan.

What a mercy that there is God!
I wouldn't exist if God hadn't created us.

Ka dal drita e dritë nuk po m'ban,

The day has been breaking, but the light doesn't stay,

ka le dielli thot e nuk po m'ze.

There is sun, it is said, but it cannot be felt.

Ça ka ba aj Gjeto Bash Muji,   5
dymbdhjet shokët trimi mi ka marr,

What has that Gjeto Bash Muji done?
The hero took twelve companions with him,

n'Lugje t'Verdha njatje e ka dal.
Djalin shkjetë njaty ja kan vra

In the Green Valley they went along.
The Montenegrinians there killed the lad,

edhe në dhe, po Muje ma ka shti,
kurkush njather nuk mi ka qillu,   10
vetëm vorrin Muja tu dhërmue.

Upon the earth Muji has laid him,
Nobody else will shoot at him,
Muji alone has heaped a grave for him.

Edhe zanat pra tu ma lotu,
edhe shoktë qi po ma gjallmojn,
edhe gurtë qi po ma mulojn,
edhe ahat qi po ma rrethojn,   15
t'mir bylbylat djalin ma vajtojn.

Even the *zanas* wept for him,
His companions deplored his death,
And the stones covered him,
And the beeches stood around,
the good nightingales wailed for the lad.

Djemat edhe Muj ka shkue n'shpi,

The young heroes and Muji went home.

nana e djalit Mujne po ma vet:
Muja, djalin mua ç'ma ka gjet,
n'Lugje t'Verdha thu a m'ka met?   20

The lad's mother asked Muji:
"Muji, what has happened to my lad,
Has he stayed up in the Green Valley?"

N'Lugje t'Verdha djali nuk ka met,

"In the Green Valley the lad didn't stay,

por ka shku aty me bujt ke dajat.
Ç'ka qit gruaja prap Mujit mi ka than:
amanet ti o Muj djalin ç'ma ke ba?

He went to visit his uncles."
What did the woman answer Muji:
"Didn't you, Muj, preserve well the lad?"

Ç'ka qit Muji njather e i ka than: 25

What replied Muji to her:

---

[8]Lambertz 1958, 28f.

me vajtua kur të shkojsh për dru,
zhurm n'konakë nuk dua me mba,
se shkjetë djalin besa ta kan vra,

N'Lugje t'Verdha ti o ndaç me e pa,

njatje n'dhe po vet edhe e kam shti.30

Qyqja nana besa e pa djal,
ka nisë gruaja njather me bërtit:
sa shpejt jashtë Muja ma ka qit,
qyqe vetun rrugën ma ka marr,

ka zan vend e hana eo mi djale.   35

Nana djalin njaty ka vajton.
Kur ka shkua pra te vorri djalit,
ka nis hanën pra e ma mallkon:
tu shoft drita pra ty, more han,

si s'ma çove ti o at nat nji fjal,   40

n'Lugje t'Verdha vet o për me dal,
me hi n'vorre bashk o me gjith djal.

Noshta vorri t'dyve s'na kish zan,

noshta djali njet nukëm kish lan.

Gurit t'malit rixha i kishëm ba,   45

ahit t'malit rixha i kishëm ba,

rrahit t'zi nër kam i kishim ra,

se ka nodhun bjeshka mjaft e gjan,
ni cop vend more mu ma kishte fal
ani se.

"Weep, when you go to collect wood!
You should not clamour in the house,
Because the Montenegrinians have
    killed your son.
In the Green Valley, if you want to see
    him,
There in the earth I personally buried
    him."
The unlucky, sonless mother,
The woman now began to wail:
"How quickly Muji made me poor,
The only chance he has taken from
    me, the unlucky one,
The moon keeps watch high above my
    son."
Thus the mother wailed for her son.
Then as she went to her son's grave,
She began to curse the moon:
"May your light be extinguished, oh
    moon,
Since you didn't send me a message
    that night
To go to the Green Valley,
To step together with my son into a
    grave.
Perhaps the grave could not have
    contained us both,
Perhaps the lad would not have
    allowed me to share his grave.
To the rocks of the mountain I would
    have cried,
To the beeches of the mountain I
    would have cried,
I would have implored the black
    woodland,
Since the pasture is broad enough,
It would have given me a small place."

(Transcription and translation by Dr. Rolf Ködderitzsch, University of Bonn)[9]

---

[9]A slightly different version of this episode from Kosovo was published by D. Shala 1972,
208. The translation of this variant is found in Sako 1967, 115ff.

The Musical Presentation

The epic singer always begins with an instrumental prelude on the *lahuta*. It has a double function:
– for the singer it is a kind of last tuning, giving him security for his performance;
– during the "prelude" a certain dramatic tension is conveyed to the audience, a certain sense of expectation to hear of heroes and their deeds. As Walther Wünsch wrote, no *guslar* starts without an instrumental prelude: "A sudden and violent increase of his figurative play causes the singer himself as well as his audience to reach the 'heroic high tension' that is necessary to carry both from everyday life to the world of the song."[10]

Later, after the singer has started, the *lahuta* accompaniment is reduced to unornamented marking tones which need not be in unison with the singer's voice. As a heterophonic interval a second or a third is used.

According to Cvjetko Rihtman, the figures played on the *gusle* or *lahuta* are chosen to imitate a second partner in the local two-part singing style. Two-part singing is — with many local variants — known everywhere along the Dalmatinian coast. Ornamentation is not performed on the *lahuta* when it is used to accompany the singing, in analogy to the two-part singing technique where ornamentation is allowed for the first voice only.[11]

The majority of singers do not tune their instrument in their "natural register" but somewhat higher. The reason for this is that according to traditional aesthetics an extraordinary thing must be presented in an extraordinary way, e.g. in a masked, nasal voice. As Walther Wünsch says: "... the *guslar* stylizes and modifies his voice to attain the fascinating 'epic disposition', which is one of his strongest means of producing an effect. The visionary sound corresponds to the visionary look of the singer."[12]

---

[10]Wünsch 1934, 36.
[11]See Rihtman 1979, 95.
[12]Wünsch 1934, 31.

Illustrations:

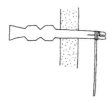

peg and upper attachment
of the string

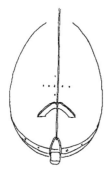

oval corpus with skin cover
pinned with pegs

sound-holes

bridge (movable)

lower attachment of the string

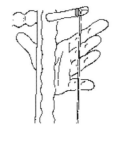

fingering technique

bowing technique

(Drawings: Bengt Fosshag)

he,   lum e lu- m e   fort per te lu-mi-ne Zot,

he, jo- e nu- ki je-me kan e   Zo- ti   na ka dhan.

he, le ka dal dri- ta   dri- te nuk po m'- ban,

he, o e ka le di-el- li thot e nuk po m'ze.

Ex.

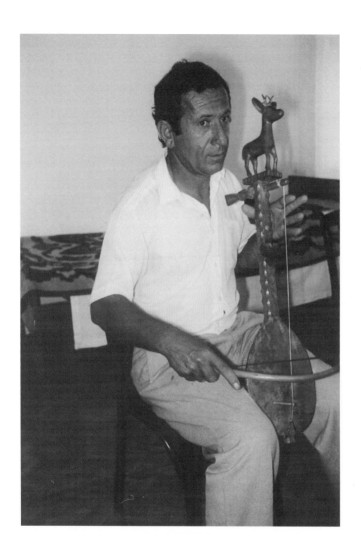

Lek Celaj (1995)

References

Camaj, Martin. 1983. "Zum gegenwärtigen Stand der Volksdichtung in Albanien." *Musikethnologisches Kolloquium zum 70. Geburtstag von Walther Wünsch (1978). Die südosteuropäische Volkskultur in der Gegenwart. Referate der 4. Internationalen Balkanologentagung (1970).* Ed. Alois Mauerhofer. Musikethnologische Sammelbände 6. Graz: Akademische Druck- u. Verlagsanstalt. 53-58.

Çabej, Eqrem. 1966. "Albanische Volkskunde." *Südost-Forschungen* 25: 333-87.

Daja, Ferial. 1994. "The Heroic-Legendary Epic Music in Albania: Its Connections with the Historic Epic of the Northern Territories." *Historische Volksmusikforschung.* Ed. Doris Stockmann and Annette Erler. Orbis musicarum 10. Göttingen: Edition Re. 133-45.

Hoerburger, Felix. 1962. "Erzählliedsingen bei den Albanern des Has-Gebietes (Metohija)." *Zbornik za narodni život i običaje* 40: 193-202.

Hornbostel, Erich Moritz von, and Curt Sachs. 1914. "Systematik der Musikinstrumente. Ein Versuch." *Zeitschrift für Ethnologie* 46: 553-90.

Kruta, Beniamin. 1994. "The Music of the Albanian Heroic Epics and Some Balkanic Parallels." *Historische Volksmusikforschung.* Ed. Doris Stockmann and Annette Erler. Orbis musicarum 10. Göttingen: Edition Re. 125-32.

Lambertz, Maximilian. 1958. *Die Volksepik der Albaner.* Halle an der Saale: Niemeyer.

Lord, Albert Bates. 1954. "General Introduction." *Serbocroatian Heroic Songs.* Ed. Milman Parry, ed. and trans. Albert Bates Lord. Volume 1: *Novi Pazar: English Translations.* With musical transcriptions by Béla Bartók and prefaces by John H. Finley, Jr., and Roman Jakobson. Cambridge, MA, and Belgrade: Harvard UP and the Serbian Academy of Sciences. 3-20.

Murko, Matthias. 1909. "Die Volksepik der bosnischen Mohammedaner." *Zeitschrift des Vereins für Völkerkunde* 19: 13-30.

Rihtman, Cvjetko. 1979. "Die Gusle in Bosnien und der Hercegowina. Beziehungen zwischen Instrument, Spieltechnik und Musik." *Studia Instrumentorum Musicae Popularis* 6: 93-97.

Sako, Zihni, ed. 1967. *Chansonnier des preux albanais.* Paris: Maisonneuve.

———, ed. 1968. *Këngë popullore historike.* Tirana: Instituti i folklorit.

Schmaus, Alois. 1963. "Die albanische Volksepik." *Shêjzat* 7: 173-90.

Shala, Demush, ed. 1972. *Këngë popullore legjendare.* Prishtina: Rilindja.

Skendi, Stavro. 1954. *Albanian and South Slavic Oral Epic Poetry.* Philadelphia. American Folklore Society. [Rpt. New York: Kraus, 1969.]

Wünsch, Walther. 1934. *Die Geigentechnik der südslawischen Guslaren.* Brünn: Rohrer.

5   CREATIVITY IN PERFORMANCE:
WORDS AND MUSIC IN BALKAN AND OLD FRENCH EPIC

Margaret H. Beissinger

Oral epic has aptly been termed "story in song."[1] Indeed, it is the *story*, not the song, which takes precedence in performance; singers of epic seek to tell good *stories*, not necessarily to sing pleasing songs. Yet music plays a fundamental role in epic. Without music, the words of epic would lack metrics and rhythm. Music elevates speech out of the quotidian and into the artistic and mythic; it heightens and empowers the messages that it conveys. At the same time, the music of oral epic has often been perceived as quite monotonous. In the Old French *chansons de geste* and in Serbo-Croatian oral epic, for example, we know that the music was repetitive and even at times tedious. Cecil M. Bowra expressed this viewpoint in the following way: "heroic poetry always seems to be chanted, usually to some simple stringed instrument . . . . The music to which poems are sung is usually not a real or regular tune but a monotonous chant in which the bard often keeps whole lines on a single note. Such indeed is said to be the regular practice in Albania, and the heroic Jugoslav chants recorded by Milman Parry are monotonous and lacking in melody . . . . Among famous Russian bards the elder Ryabinin knew only two tunes."[2] As the ethnomusicologist Fritz Bose pointed out, "the melodies of folk epic are . . . comparatively simple. The singer's intellectual energy is largely engaged in molding the text; he has little strength left for the deployment of a copious musical scheme. The tunes comprise simple, short strophes constructed of few but pithy motives."[3]

In this article, I explore the nature of music in the Romanian oral epic. Do Romanian epic singers — like those of the Old French and Serbo-Croatian genres — likewise tend toward "monotonous" (or, perhaps more appropriately, repetitious) music as they focus instead on the words that tell their stories? What is the nature of this music? What types of creativity do singers engage in as they perform? And, when and why is musical creativity employed? I maintain that, like the performers of many other oral epic traditions, Romanian singers concentrate on the words —

---

[1] Lord 1960, 99.
[2] Bowra 1952, 38-39.
[3] Bose 1958, 30.

not the music — of their songs, and for this, they produce a relatively secure and constant musical framework. I examine what "musical monotony" means in the Romanian context. But I also suggest that epic singers — especially those who are highly-skilled — periodically subvert the routine of their musical performances by generating variation in the music as they create and recreate the melodic passages of their songs. Finally, I argue that the "when and why" of the creativity that singers effect in the music is determined largely by the verbal content. Accomplished singers are directed by the words — by the poetics and narrative significance of the verses of the stories they tell. For these singers, the music responds to the patterns created through the poetics and narrative content of the words.

The Role of Music in Epic

As Albert Lord pointed out in *The Singer of Tales*, the study of epic verse begins with "a consideration of metrics and music."[4] The utilitarian function of music in epic is fundamental. It is music that provides the framework within which the narrative in verse is told; it furnishes the rhythmic backdrop for the composition of poetry in performance. But music also serves other purposes in the performance of epic; its aesthetic and emotive role is similarly central. Bose wrote that the fact that oral epic "is not recited, but sung, heightens the artistic and educational value for the listener."[5] Music places speech (unmarked) in the realm of song (marked). Gregory Nagy has noted that song is "special or marked language that is set off from speech," while speech is "everyday or unmarked language."[6] Song, in the context of oral tradition, is poetry enhanced by rhythm and melody. As Dan Ben-Amos has noted, "common to all poetic expression . . . is the deliberate deviation from everyday speech, and with it the departure from the profane . . . . The delivery of [narrative] in a metric form" — and here I would clarify *in song* —

---

[4]Lord 1960, 31. Speaking of the young South Slavic singer assimilating and mastering the art of epic singing, Lord noted that "from meter and music he absorbs in his earliest years the rhythms of epic, even as he absorbs the rhythms of speech itself," and that "basic patterns of meter, word boundary, melody have become his possession, and in him the tradition begins to reproduce itself" (32).

[5]Bose 1958, 29.

[6]Nagy 1991, 216. If we understand song as the stylized patterning of rhythm and melody, then their synchronization in effect results in what Nagy calls "a scheme where both rhythm and melody in song could be viewed as regularized outgrowths of speech that serve eventually to distinguish song from speech" (224-25). He notes further that from a functional point of view, "song would be any speech-act that is *considered* to be set apart for a special context" (216).

"indicates an intent to affect the audience emotionally."[7] Music thus enhances speech, engendering rhythmic and melodic messages of special artistic and emotive force. Finally, I would suggest that musical "monotony" and repetition also perhaps ultimately relate to ancient ritual contexts and meanings. Ben-Amos has written that "the usage of metric prosody can have a wide range of significance, varying from religious sanctions to magical power to mere play, each depending on the circumstances of delivery."[8] Epic — reaching as it does into the depths of ancient myth — is, in a sense, religious, imparting messages of profound cultural importance. Stephen Erdely observes that "the principles underlying the relation of text and music go back to times when mythic events and wonder working tales were part of ritualistic ceremonies, and reciting them in song form contributed to their effectiveness."[9] Indeed, as J. A. Westrup has pointed out, the "constant repetition" in the music of the Old French epic "has something of the character of primitive incantation, a form of magic."[10] Or, as Lord put it, it appears "likely that the story sung in verse had a magical purpose and was in some way connected with ritual. Such an origin would explain the pervasiveness of repetition of sounds . . . for such . . . characteristics are essential to the effectiveness of incantations."[11]

Even as music furnishes the requisite stable metrical framework and aesthetic conditions for the performance of narrative poetry, however, it also creates a formidable challenge for the singer.[12] Bose pointed out that music "imposes a considerable burden upon the performer. For poetry and music have each their own laws of formation, and thus every form of collaboration between word and sound, between poetry and music, is a kind of compromise."[13] The "simple" (in Bose's words; others have said "monotonous" and "repetitive") nature of epic music is, in a sense, a functional response to this dilemma; diminishing the "burden" of the singer's task facilitates performance.[14]

---

[7]Ben-Amos 1976, 229. Ben-Amos suggests that "the metrical substructure . . . serves as the definitive [poetic] feature" (228) and that this "metric speech constitutes an ontological system objectively distinct from prose" (230). He asserts that "the very existence or absence of a metric substructure in the verbal message can signify the conception the society has of a particular theme or can provide clues to the narrator's intent" (228).

[8]Ben-Amos 1976, 229.

[9]Erdely 1995, 632.

[10]Westrup 1954, 223.

[11]Lord 1974, 542. Though Lord spoke here explicitly of the *words* of oral epic, there is no doubt that the "pervasiveness of repetitions of sound" in the *music* also provided an ancient vehicle for the perpetuation of prayer, incantation, and magic.

[12]I have discussed this with regard to Romanian oral epic in *The Art of the Lăutar,* see Beissinger 1991, Chapter 6.

[13]Bose 1958, 29.

[14]As Bowra noted, "heroic poetry puts the words first and subordinates the music to them. What it uses is really no more than recitative. To use a regular tune like that of a song would

The Music of Old French and Serbo-Croatian Epic

The Old French *chansons de geste* and Serbo-Croatian epic songs (*junačke pesme*) are well-known examples of traditional narrative poetry, both firmly in the "oral epic canon." Yet, it is frequently recognized that the music of both genres was repetitious and even at times tedious.

The Old French *chansons de geste* were the great epic poems of medieval France performed by *jongleurs* in the vernacular as entertainment from roughly the eleventh to the fourteenth centuries. The heroic *Chanson de Roland*, the most celebrated example of this genre, was probably composed in the latter eleventh century. Three main cycles and numerous texts of these *chansons* remain for posterity. They typically were sung in segments of poetry — variable in terms of length — termed "laisses." The poetic line was customarily decasyllabic; final assonance often united either entire *laisses* or portions of them. As for the music to which the *chansons* were sung, only one fragment survives. It is a melody which was included in a late thirteenth-century pastoral play.[15] It is a simple tune which spans only a fourth. In addition to this fragment, Johannes de Grocheo, a scholar writing around 1300, authored a valuable account of medieval secular music which helps to piece together (to some extent) how the *chansons de geste* were performed. He wrote: "The number of lines in a *chanson de geste* is not fixed, but can be extended according to the amount of subject-matter available and the inclination of the author. The same tune should be repeated for all lines."[16] Thus, as Gustave Reese notes, the music of the *chansons de geste* "appears to have consisted of a brief snatch of a melody, which usually had one note to a syllable, and which was repeated over and over." He goes on to point out that "it was easy to fit the lines to the music since they were of equal length throughout."[17]

In other words, the same short, simple melodic formulas apparently were sung over and over throughout the performance of the *chanson de geste*. Indeed, as Reese comments, "the scarcity of the material that

---

have made the task of heroic poets much more difficult and have interfered with the clear presentation of the tales which they have to tell" (Bowra 1952, 39).

[15]The melody is found in Adam de Halle's *Le Jeu de Robin et Marion* (see Reese 1940, 204, 213). Elsewhere it has been suggested that the melody is possibly from the epic *Girart de Roussillon* (see Page 1986, 129 [includes melodic example]). It is actually a type of parody of the Old French epic but is considered a representative model of the music (see Wooldridge 1932, 262). Wooldridge also points out the existence of another extant *chanson de geste* melody for Thomas de Bailleul's *Bataille d'Annezin* (262). On the music of the *chanson de geste*, see further the chapter by John Stevens in this volume.

[16]Quoted in Wooldridge 1932, 259-60. See also Reese 1940, 204, and Westrup 1954, 223.

[17]Reese 1940, 203. An alternative interpretation is furnished by Ian R. Parker, who claims that "the reiteration of the melodic formula is true of each *laisse* but not of the poem as a whole" (see Parker 1980, 146).

remains [on the music of the *chansons de geste*] is not surprising. Probably very little was ever written down. Notated copies could seldom have been needed as reminders: the short tunes, constantly repeated, would scarcely have taxed the memories of professional performers."[18] Assessing the genre in the mid-twentieth century, Westrup has suggested that "modern taste might find it intolerable to hear a long poem recited to a constant repetition."[19]

Serbo-Croatian oral epic has been collected actively since the early nineteenth century, although it has effectively died out in today's former Yugoslavia. Numerous transcriptions of texts from the *guslari* (singers) of both the Christian and Muslim epic traditions have been published and studied. The verses are generally decasyllabic and sung in a stichic manner. While the songs of the Christian tradition of Serbo-Croatian epic are typically only several hundred lines long, those from the Muslim singers are significantly longer, often spanning even thousands of lines. Very little music of Serbo-Croatian epic has been transcribed, though in 1995, Stephen Erdely published the first thorough musical transcriptions of entire Muslim epic songs collected by Albert Lord in Bihać.[20]

It has long been recognized that the Serbo-Croatian epic — sung by *guslari* — was also rendered in chant-like, repetitive melodic lines "with few notes."[21] Béla Bartók commented in 1941 that the music of "the heroic poems makes an awfully monotonous impression at first."[22] The ethnomusicologist George Herzog noted that the "music of the Yugoslav epic poems could be called a form of chanting . . . . [T]he function of music is probably more that of providing the medium in which the text is unfolded and carried along, rather than of contributing to a formation in which the autonomy of the words is balanced with that of the music."[23] Herzog pointed out that although the number of melodic formulas in each epic song varies, four types of musical lines are generally found in the epic songs: introductory and final musical lines, "lines of continuity," and "dramatic lines."[24] The narratives are effectively rendered by way of what Herzog called "lines of continuity," those repetitive melodic formulas which dominate the musical performance and in which the least musical variety and ornamentation take place. The impulse to diversify and modify the musical contents of Serbo-Croatian epic is evident nonetheless, most notably — as Erdely tells us — as singers create "couplets,

---

[18]Reese 1940, 204.
[19]Westrup 1954, 223.
[20]See Erdely 1995; see also the contribution of Stephen Erdely to this volume.
[21]Erdely 1995, 9.
[22]Quoted in Erdely 1995, 1.
[23]Herzog 1951, 62.
[24]Herzog 1951, 62-63.

triplets, and other strophic and stanzaic forms" as well as alter the contours of the melodies.[25]

The music of Old French and Serbo-Croatian epic, then, "intolerably"
or "awfully monotonous" as it may have been, was an indispensable "in-
gredient" of performance. Functionally, it placed the words of the narratives in a repeated metrical framework; aesthetically, it situated the verses
in the realm of the marked discourse of song. It allowed for the singer's
full concentration on the story.

Romanian Oral Epic

Romanian epic — in matters of both form and content — lends itself well
to comparisons with the Serbo-Croatian and Old French genres. The epic
songs are called *cîntece bătrînești* ('old songs'). Many of the narratives
are heroic in nature. The poems are usually several hundred lines long
(much like the Serbo-Croatian Christian songs). While the genre formerly
flourished for generations, it is found at the present time only in villages
in south-central Romania. The poetic line — corresponding to the melodic
line — is normally a seven- or eight-syllable (generally trochaic) line.
Like the *junačke pesme* and *chansons de geste*, the verses of the *cîntece
bătrînești* are sung to few notes whose contours include small intervals;
the tunes are predominantly pentatonic.

Romanian and Serbo-Croatian oral epic traditions — from neighboring
Balkan cultures — reflect significant similarities in the larger historical
and cultural continuum that they share. Both are attested from at least the
late fourteenth century; their history as a genre during the past six hundred years is comparable. Like the Serbo-Croatian, the Romanian epic
mirrors the Ottoman presence in the Balkans; the core of the heroic
narrative deals with confrontations between native populations and
Turks.[26] Indeed, the Romanians share many tales and heroes especially
with the Serbo-Croatian Christian tradition.[27]

---

[25]Erdely 1995, 631. Erdely comments on how all of the singers — whose epic songs he
transcribed — generated variation in performance and thus revealed their "own personal
styles." One singer's talent "was in changing the contours of his melodies by varying its
motives, the scale notes, the mode of his tunes." Another "created couplets, triplets, and
other strophic and stanzaic forms as he changed the tempo of his singing." Finally, the third
singer was "the most versatile, the most complete composer: he was equally at home when
working with individual lines and strophic paragraphs, or forming couplets and diverse
stanzaic structures" (631-32).

[26]Needless to say, the cultural-religious orientation of the victor alters depending on the
tradition, be it Christian or Muslim.

[27]For example, narratives about Marko and Marcu; see also Fochi 1975.

Romanian epic is typically performed by traditional professional male singers — *lăutari* (sg. *lăutar*) — who are Rom (Gypsy).[28] The *lăutari* play stringed instruments (usually violin, though at times also *cobză* or its contemporary equivalent, guitar). The tradition of music and song — including epic — is transmitted within the family, from father to son, and performed for the community. Epic singers are accompanied by small ensembles of Rom musicians (two or three) who play other traditional instruments (such as violin, hammer dulcimer, and accordion).

But *lăutari* are not the only singers of epic in Romania. Non-professional singers — typically ethnic Romanian peasants — also at times sing narrative song. And while they occasionally sing the same songs as *lăutari*, *lăutari* and peasant singers are distinguished by major differences effectively rooted in the professional versus non-professional distinction. These include the singers' repertoires, the manner in which they learn their skills, the occasions at which they perform, and their styles of singing and playing.[29] Non-professional singers sing narratives that are generally shorter and more lyric than those sung by *lăutari*. They do not learn to sing and play within the family as do *lăutari*, who master their art within closely-knit male kin groups who perpetuate traditional professional music. Rarely do peasant singers excel in epic; epic is a genre for public performance, a context in which non-professional musicians less commonly play. As non-professionals, the repertoires of peasant singers generally lack the artistry of singers and musicians who market their skills of performance for their livelihood.

The repertoires of three representative Romanian singers from villages in south-central Romania form the basis for this study. They include two *lăutari* — Mihai Constantin (1912-70) and Costică Staicu (1913-83) — and one peasant singer: Niţu Voinescu (b. 1921); all were violinists.[30] The two *lăutari* (one of whom I worked with closely) performed at a variety of festive community events, particularly weddings, even through their last years. The peasant singer (also my informant) worked the land for his living; as an avocation, he sang and played the violin and performed on occasion.

The elementary unit of musical composition in epic is the melodic formula. In Romanian epic, sequences of melodic formulas make up "musical strophes." Musical strophes are structural units that are irregular in terms of length and organization; they are framed most commonly by a conspicuous final melodic formula which creates an overt cadence. Musical strophes are also frequently framed by an initial melodic for-

---

[28]For a fuller treatment of Romanian Gypsy epic singers, see Beissinger 1991, especially Chapter 1.
[29]See Beissinger 1991, 27-29, for a discussion of non-professional singers.
[30]For biographical notes on these singers, see Beissinger 1991, 8-11.

mula. Both the initial and final melodic formulas resonate with the "introductory" and "final" melodic lines of the Serbo-Croatian epic.[31] I have termed "medial" melodic formulas those melodic lines that are situated between the initial and final melodic formulas (reminiscent of the Serbo-Croatian "lines of continuity").[32]

The epic performance includes an instrumental introduction, followed by vocal sections (each of which is comprised of one or more musical strophes) and subsequent instrumental interludes.[33] The musical strophes of Romanian epic are clearly analogous to the Old French *laisses*. Furthermore, Romanian musical strophes, like the *laisses* of the *chansons de geste*, are frequently marked by patterns of final assonance — usually consecutive lines that assonate in groups of varying lengths. At the end of the song, an instrumental "finale" (often dance music unrelated to the song) is performed by all of the musicians.

"Monotony" and Creativity in Romanian Epic Music

Do Romanian singers — like the Old French jongleurs and Serbo-Croatian *guslari* — tend toward repetitive, "monotonous" music as they sing epic? The answer — in a word — is yes, but it must be qualified: some sing less predictable and routine renditions than others. In other words, some are somewhat more creative than others. Creativity in performance is here understood as the antithesis of a fixed or labored patterning of musical ideas within the musical strophe. Creativity is innovation in performance, an artistic overturning of set and routine patterns of composition. It is moments of originality on the part of the singer. This is reflected in the number of melodic formulas that are employed, how the formulas are grouped together to form musical strophes, and how the words and music connect in performance.

Constantin, Staicu, and Voinescu each clearly exhibited individual styles of epic composition, revealed in any number of different ways. Relative to the Old French and Serbo-Croatian traditions, Constantin and Staicu customarily utilized a significant number of melodic formulas per

---

[31]Initial melodic formulas in Romanian epic typically begin on an octave or seventh above the tonal center and end on a third above it. Final melodic formulas — the most stable and consistent melodic feature of the musical strophe — usually descend from a fifth or fourth above the tonal center, arriving at the tonic by the second half of the line, where it is repeated, thus effecting a clear cadence.

[32]Medial formulas customarily have an overall descending contour, frequently ending on a third above the tonic. A rough average number of medial melodic formulas per song is three or four. Taking into account the initial and final melodic formulas, singers typically employ between five and six melodic formulas in any given epic song.

[33]Vocal sections in the repertoires of the three singers viewed here are highly variable in length, from Voinescu's average of thirteen lines to Staicu's ninety; Constantin's vocal sections were roughly forty lines long.

song — an average of seven, though at times they included as many as ten. By contrast, Voinescu typically negotiated as few as three per performance, reflecting his less complex approach to the music. However, all three showed a strong tendency to organize musical strophes in recurrent groupings of melodic formulas — mainly couplets and triplets, but also quatrains. These include both groups of the same melodic formulas (such as CC or EEE) as well as recurrent combinations (AB, DDF, and so on). In other words, melodic formulas in musical strophes figure — for the most part — in relation to other melodic formulas. Here a parallel with the music of Serbo-Croatian epic again is significant. In the style of several Muslim singers whose songs Erdely transcribed, couplets and various other short stanzaic forms were part of their musical lexicon. In the case of Ibrahim Nuhanović, for example, "single lines are combined or alternated with couplets, tercets and other forms of verse groupings."[34]

Verses delivered in a spoken style of recitation (termed "parlato") function as alternatives to the melodic verses in Romanian epic. When employed in moderation, the parlato style is a hallmark of the so-called "authentic" epic style of traditional *lăutari*. It can provide an important stylistic device, furnishing an expressive break from the uniformity of sung passages or underscoring a dramatic narrative moment. But when it is excessive, it soon becomes a tedious alternative to singing. It is less taxing to speak long passages of poetry without a melodic counterpart than to sing them. For this reason, the extreme use of parlato is representative of less competent singers.[35]

In a performance of the heroic song "Miu haiducu," the *lăutar* Mihai Constantin employed eight melodic formulas plus the parlato style of recitation.[36] In terms of the cadence of the musical strophes, Constantin usually employed the final melodic formula F (in some cases repeating it), sometimes followed by a parlato verse (indicated by +) plus a melodic cadence (resembling the vocal final melodic formula F) on his violin. This provided a concrete anchor in the musical structure. He approached the beginnings of musical strophes, however, with a great

---

[34]Erdely 1995, 377.

[35]The more highly-skilled singers in this study generally employed the parlato recitation style in their epic songs in somewhat less than one-fifth of their verses. In the repertoire of a peasant singer included in another analysis (Marin Dorcea), parlato accounted for four-fifths of his verses, causing his "songs" to be rather infrequently actually sung! For a discussion of this, see Beissinger 1991, 54-55, and 132-36.

[36]"Miu haiducu" sung by Mihai Constantin and recorded by Alexandru Amzulescu on 22 February 1951 in Desa (Dolj county, Romania); text transcribed by Amzulescu (see Amzulescu 1974, 307-16) and music transcribed by me (Tape number 18a, Archives of the Constantin Brăiloiu Institute of Ethnography and Folklore, Bucharest). I am particularly grateful to the Constantin Brăiloiu Institute of Ethnography and Folklore in Bucharest (formerly the Institute of Ethnology and Dialectology) for furnishing me with this and numerous other copies of tape recordings of epic songs made by scholars in the 1950s and '60s.

deal less uniformity. Constantin sang the same couplet (AB) at the outset
of only five (out of 53) musical strophes in this song. In other words,
although AB was for Constantin a unit in his musical thought process that
introduced musical strophes, it was used discretely, simply as one way —
in addition to others — to begin musical strophes. The melodic formulas
from the first ten musical strophes of the song excerpted below reveals at
once the significant variation in Constantin's musical lexicon. (A = initial
melodic formula, B = secondary and medial melodic formula, F = final
melodic formula, C, D, E, and G = medial melodic formulas, and + =
parlato; the number on the left refers to the musical strophe. The underlining of the couplets and triplets indicates that they are recurrent in the
same recording.)

```
1     A B C C C D E F F
2     D E C C C G F F
3     A A A C C D E C G F
4     A A C D E F
5     + D E C C G F F
6     B B C C + + D E C F + + [and instrumental cadence]
7     A B B C C F F
8     D E + + + + + + [and instrumental cadence]
9     B B C C F + + + + [and instrumental cadence]
10    D E C F + + + [and instrumental cadence]
```

The musical strophes that Constantin sang were organized in an ever-
changing fashion; he was not bound by fixed sequences of melodic
groupings. It is almost as if he felt a discomfort with musical structures
that constricted him too much; he circumvented patterns that were too
fixed and routinized. And yet, he still operated within the confines of a
limited number of melodic formulas.

In the same song ("Miu haiducu") recorded from a different *lăutar*,
Costică Staicu,[37] eight melodic formulas (including the "recto-tono" style
— designated by R — in which the same tone is repeated throughout the
verse) were employed as well as the parlato style. The melodic formulas
from the first ten musical strophes are excerpted below.

```
1     R R A R R A D F
2     R A R A B D F
3     A A B A E E E D F
```

[37]"Miu haiducu" sung by Costică Staicu and recorded by Alexandru Amzulescu on 31 March
1966 in Bucharest; text transcribed by Amzulescu (unpublished) and music transcribed by me
(Tape numbers 2991b and 2992a, Archives of the Constantin Brăiloiu Institute of Ethnography and Folklore, Bucharest).

4	R A R A E A D F
5	A A R R A E D H F
6	C C D F
7	R R A R A D F
8	C A A A A E E E D F
9	R A A C D F
10	R R A A A D F

Despite the fact that short stanzaic groupings are evident, their sequence is not habitual or fixed in the musical strophes; each musical strophe is an individual and unique arrangement of melodic formulas. Furthermore, like the musical strophes from Constantin's performance presented earlier, a final melodic formula regularly provides a cadence for the musical strophe, while the beginning of each musical strophe is less uniform. The sequence of melodic formulas in each musical strophe is variable.

By contrast, singers for whom the burden of words plus music is especially taxing turn to the easiest and most dependable manner of constructing musical strophes in performance. Because they do not (or simply cannot) venture out of a relatively fixed musical mold, they pattern consecutive musical strophes which are so similar that they really resemble stanzas; in this way, they furnish a reliable framework in performance. In his rendition of "Miu haiducu,"[38] the peasant singer Niţu Voinescu employed three melodic formulas, an obviously smaller body of melodic material than in either Constantin's or Staicu's performances of the same song. Voinescu turned to strikingly similar groupings of melodic formulas in the musical strophes he constructed. Almost all of the musical strophes are framed by two consecutive final melodic formulas and an introductory couplet (usually AB or AA). The internal organization of the musical strophes is minimal, as the following chart — including the first ten musical strophes of the song — reveals. The density of repetitive groupings of melodic formulas (underlined below) is extremely high in this recording.

1	A B A F F
2	A B A F F
3	A A F F
4	A B A F F
5	A B A F
6	A F F
7	A A A F F
8	A B A B A F F

[38] "Miu haiducu" sung by Niţu Voinescu and recorded by me on 9 July 1987 in Bărboi (Dolj county, Romania); text and music transcribed by me.

9   A A F F
10   A B A F F

Voinescu repeatedly returned to an underlying musical strophe (A B A F F), varying it slightly at different times. In other words, he relied on a safe and familiar structure in the music. Furthermore, he sang short musical strophes. The average number of lines per musical strophe in Voinescu's "Miu haiducu" is between four and five, significantly below Constantin's and Staicu's (both about eight lines on the average). The longer length of musical strophes appears to mirror the singer's greater stamina for composition, as well as the tendency to compose more creatively.

Words and Music

Erdely argues that "music has, at times, its own mystical powers, its own atmosphere, but, mostly, it is adjusted in a semi-conscious, instinctive way to the poetic text and to the logic of its internal features."[39] Among skilled singers in the Romanian epic, it seems that while there is indeed creativity in the musical component in and of itself during performance, it is effectively the words which dictate the form that the music takes. What drives accomplished singers — in the moment of composition — to select the patterns of melodic formulas that they do is governed in large part by the poetics and content of the words. Distinct rhetorical and narrative patterns fashioned in the poetry frequently correspond to discrete recurrent stanzaic patterns in the music.

   The most common poetic device that simultaneously connects with stanzaic groupings in the music is final assonance; when passages in the poetry assonate, skilled singers reinforce this rhetorical unity by corresponding musical couplets, triplets, and quatrains. Lord noted that "in those languages in which morphology and syntax conspire to make a series of lines ending in rhyme, there develops a convention of maintaining this rhyme as long as the singer is able."[40] Romanian, a language characterized by morphological rhyme and assonance, clearly promotes this "convention"; Old French did as well. Indeed, it is assonance corresponding to large structural units more than any other feature in Romanian epic that finds a resonant analogue in the *chansons de geste*. In linguistic and poetic traditions in which assonance and rhyme figure largely, then, they function as key devices in the compromise between

---

[39]Erdely 1995, 632.
[40]Lord 1974, 543. Furthermore, he pointed out that "Albanian epic tradition follows this pattern" and suggested that "it is entirely possible that this practice is the cause of the *laisses* of the *chansons de geste* with their assonantal verse endings" (543).

words and music that singers generate. The acoustic effects of final assonance in the poetry correspond neatly and aesthetically to melodic structures in both the musical strophes and *laisses*.

But it is not only assonance that guides the structuring of poetic and musical lines. In the compositional style of the Serbo-Croatian Muslim singer Murat Žunić, Erdely observes that "the texts of couplets, or tercets usually reveal parallelism or some other form of contextual or syntactic relationship."[41] In like fashion in the Romanian genre, syntactic parallelism in two or more textual lines (particularly anaphora) as well as the repetition of textual lines are devices that correspond to musical groupings. Furthermore, the creative synthesis of words and music is effected through the actual mechanics of narrative verse construction: narrative ideas — reflected in discrete groups of clauses (main and dependent) and phrases — correspond frequently to distinct musical structures.

The following musical strophe (from a recording of "Tănislav" by Staicu[42]) contains eight lines which include four assonating couplets. The passage relates how the Turks, in search of the hero Tănislav, meet up with a group of girls who will unwittingly tell them of Tănislav's whereabouts. The words in italics either preceding or following the textual lines are syllables of completion, unrelated to the narrative content.

A	Iară turcii că-m' venea.	And so the Turks arrived.
A	Şî veneau dă poposeau:	They arrived and stopped for a rest:
B	Colea-n vadu Brăilii, *mă*	Over there at the ford in Brăila,
B	Colea-n dosu to' şchilii.	Over there beyond the little river port.
C	Şi iei, frate, cum şădea, *mă*	And when they stopped to rest, brother,
C	Peste trei fete dădea:	They came upon three girls:
P	*m* Trei fetiţe velingence, *mă*	Three little girls from the valley,
F	To' la pînză mi-'nălbeşte.	They all were bleaching clothes.

Each of the four assonating textual couplets is rendered in a formulaic melodic couplet (AA-BB-CC-PF). In addition to the assonance, there are other rhetorical devices in this excerpt which find melodic reinforcement. In the first couplet (AA), each line is a complete idea that propels the narrative forward. In the second (BB), both verses are parallel descriptive phrases beginning with "colea-n" (over there in), an example of anaphora. In the third couplet (CC), the story again progresses as Staicu re-

[41]Erdely 1995, 241.
[42]"Tănislav al mătuşii" sung by Costică Staicu and recorded by Alexandru Amzulescu on 10 April 1966 in Bucharest; text transcribed by Amzulescu and music transcribed by me (Tape numbers 2995b and 2996a, Archives of the Constantin Brăiloiu Institute of Ethnography and Folklore, Bucharest).

sumes an account of what the Turks are up to. The last couplet — sung to (PF) — contains a descriptive image of the girls bleaching clothes at the shore. Each textual couplet in this example — bound by assonance and parallelism as well as units of narrative integrity — is further reinforced by the unity of melodic structure. Staicu is guided in this symmetrical synthesis of words and melody by the demands of the narrative.

In a musical strophe from a different performance of "Tănislav" by Staicu,[43] the words again chart the unfolding of the melodic formulas. The following musical strophe is composed of seven lines: an assonating couplet that offers narrative progression and corresponds to the melodic formulas AB, descriptive parallel phrases sung to the triplet CCC (and marked by anaphora as "cu" — meaning 'with' — is intoned three times), and a repeated textual line that corresponds to the melodic formulas PF. The passage relates how the Turks find the hero Tănislav who, even when asleep, is so ferocious that they are petrified.

A	Pă Tănislav că-l găsea.	They found Tănislav.
B	Culcat în apă ierea:	He was asleep in the water:
C	Cu caicu priponit*î*,	With his boat attached to the shore,
C *ai*	Cu lănţuşu dă argint*î*	With his little silver dagger,
C	Cu paloşu gol pă piept*î*.	With his unsheathed sword on his chest.
P	Nu-ndrăzneau ca să-l dăştept*î*,	They didn't dare to wake him up,
F	Nu-ndrăzneau ca să-l dăştept!	They didn't dare to wake him up!
	mă	

Through this web of rhetorical and melodic verse devices, Staicu again effects a balanced compromise of words and music.

The interplay between sung and parlato verses can also be exploited expressively as the narrative veers between action and descriptive embellishment. In the following seven-line musical strophe from Constantin's performance of "Miu haiducu,"[44] two formulaic melodic couplets (DE and CF) are followed by three parlato verses. The first four melodic lines contain assonating verses that narrate what is unfolding in the story. The next three spoken lines depart from the actual narration and instead provide a parenthetic descriptive passage that assonates. This is followed by an instrumental final melodic formula. The passage below relates how the hero's sister (Calea) tucks in the prince (her brother's foe) at the

[43]"Tănislav" sung by Costică Staicu and recorded by Alexandru Amzulescu on 10 September 1965 in Blejeşti (Teleorman county, Romania); text transcribed by Amzulescu and music transcribed by me (Tape number 2878, Archives of the Constantin Brăiloiu Institute of Ethnography and Folklore, Bucharest).
[44]"Miu haiducu" sung by Constantin (see note 36).

banquet table after she has drugged him in order that she be able to depart
and warn her brother of his plans.

D	Iară Calea ce m'făcea?	And so what did Calea do?
E	Cu braţăle că-l lua. *măi*	She took him by the arm.
C	O plapomă-i aşternea. *măi*	She spread a fine woolen blanket over him,
F	Cu salteaua-l coperea:	She covered him with a thick quilt:
+	Salteaua cu floricele.	A quilt with little flowers,
+	Mi-l gîdîlă la sprîncene,	It tickled her eyebrows,
+	Făcu Calii pe plăcere.	It was a delight to Calea.
	[instrumental final melodic formula]	

Constantin was a master of exploiting parlato recitation style, frequently
contrasting melodic lines with short spoken passages in order to under-
score verses of embellishment, direct discourse, flashback, or progressive
patterns of incremental repetition. He employed the parlato style in a
discriminating and sensitive manner, creatively promoting its contrasting
effect against the melodic frame.

Voinescu's performance style — unlike Constantin's and Staicu's — reflected the greater burden that balancing words and music posed for him.
For instance, he customarily repeated large numbers of textual lines; in a
performance of "Miu haiducu," one fifth of the verses were repeated!
And, a considerable number of the repeated verbal lines coincide with
couplets in which the same melodic formula is also repeated (especially
the ubiquitous FF at the end of nearly every musical strophe). Though
repetition as a rhetorical device can be effective at times, the degree to
which Voinescu employed it reflects composition that is easier and less
taxing than more interactive verbal and musical negotiations. By contrast,
the two *lăutari* repeated textual verses sparingly and selectively
(especially Constantin), and when they did, those repeated verses were
invariably sung to two different melodic formulas. In other words, the
lăutari sought variation in the music even when the words were redundant, revealing yet another facet of creativity in performance.

The following passage from Voinescu's "Miu haiducu"[45] is five lines
long and reflects his "standard" musical strophe, beginning with his
conventional AB, moving to A again, and ending with his customary FF.
The passage relates how Prince Stephen tries to escape once he realizes
that Miu is pursuing him.

A	Ştefan-vodă că-m'fugea,	So Prince Stephen ran away,
B	Ştefan-vodă că-m'fugea.	So Prince Stephen ran away.

---

[45]"Miu haiducu" sung by Niţu Voinescu (see Note 38).

A	Dară Mihu ce-m'făcea?	But what did Miu do?
F	După iel că mi se lua,	He took off after him,
F	După iel că mi se lua,	He took off after him.

The first couplet (AB) includes a repeated textual line, followed by A, a rhetorical question. The musical strophe ends with the repetition (in both the poetry and music) of a verse that answers the question. There is a great deal of textual repetition in this short excerpt. The verses seem to be stretched to fit into the musical strophe. The repetition of groups of words, like the reliance on a fixed musical strophe, appears like a crutch for the singer; he employs these devices in order to facilitate his perform-ance. And in performance, such "crutches" do not really enhance the delivery: the repetition of verses stalls the narrative movement, and fixed sequences of melodic formulas by this point in the song sound clichéd.

Voinescu sings a high number of paratactic verses within set melodic groupings. Paratactic constructions are, of course, representative of oral epic; and yet a reliance on them can become quite routine, especially within the context of repeated musical structures. In Romanian epic this is particularly apparent due to the short length of the verse: a verse of only seven or eight syllables allows for virtually no elaboration when complete sentences are the main pattern. Such is the case with Voinescu's songs, which included very little embellishment of ideas. He did not indulge in more creative narrative construction as did Constantin and Staicu, who consistently exploited a more elaborate style — where verses expressing complete ideas were surrounded by verses containing dependent clauses and descriptive phrases that developed actions and details.

Conclusion

The juxtaposition of how professional (Rom) and non-professional (Romanian peasant) singers compose is revealing of the ways in which creativity is effected in performance. The Romanian singers who bring together the words and music in epic to form an elegant compromise are by and large *lăutari*. Even within the confines of the fundamental "monotony" of Romanian epic music, *lăutari* continually modify the structures that they sing; they are able to employ variation and innovative patterning within the traditional boundaries of epic song. By contrast, singers (typically non-professional) for whom the compromise is too great a challenge find solace in secure and predictable sequences of fewer melodic formulas. Their narratives as a whole are less creative and elabo-rate than those sung by *lăutari*. The peasant or non-professional singers do not sing epic for a living and do not perfect their skills for public consumption; they, as ethnic Romanians, are indeed *part* of the public. It is instead the *lăutari* — distinctive in society due to both ethnicity and occupation — who have exploited the art of Romanian epic singing to its fullest.

What, then, is creativity in epic music? And, taking a step back from the distinctions we can make between greater and lesser skills in individual epic singers, what affects the extent to which the music of epic is marked by "monotony" as well as creativity? Unfortunately, the evidence about music in the Old French epic is too meager to come to significant conclusions about creativity. We know simply that it was very repetitive. The Serbo-Croatian epic music also was tedious, yet there are many instances of creativity embedded within the repetitive conventions of that music; Erdely's work attests to this. And as for Romanian epic, it is "monotonous," to be sure, but relatively so, for there is also marked variety, innovation, and creativity in much of the music.

The Old French *chansons de geste* are known for their length, grandeur, and literary sophistication, presenting medieval narratives filled with personal, political, and religious strife. The Serbo-Croatian *junačke pesme* (the Muslim songs in particular) are also remarkably lengthy and include elaborate tales of return, rescue, initiation, and wedding. No one can rightly claim that either of these epic traditions is anything less than outstanding, especially when viewed from the perspective of oral composition. Although there is no doubt that the music of these two traditions perhaps was not — in an overall sense — especially complex, the narratives and their words were, and markedly so. One could argue, in fact, that the length and complexity of the *chansons de geste*, for example, find a balancing complement in the contrasting bounded and redundant music; this argument could be made to a lesser degree in the case of the Serbo-Croatian. After all, singers in both traditions wielded ten-syllable lines and sang songs of considerable duration and artistry. How could such great oral poems be accompanied in performance by anything else but music to which the singer gave little attention?

I would suggest that Romanian singers perform songs that are generally less demanding than those from the Old French and Serbo-Croatian traditions. Romanian epic is sung to shorter verses: seven and eight syllables must be filled, not ten. Furthermore, they are relatively short songs — only several hundred lines long as a rule. As a result, the narratives are not particularly complex in their development. The stamina needed to perform entire songs in the Romanian tradition, then, is somewhat less than in the Old French and Serbo-Croatian. Consequently, Romanian singers perhaps have more energy to devote to musical creativity than did jongleurs and *guslari*. It is as if the lesser demands of the poetry in the Romanian genre — with shorter verses, shorter songs, and generally simpler tales — allow fine singers to indulge in somewhat more creative

— albeit surely routinized — music-making. My hunch is that, even in the Old French genre, if we only had transcriptions, we would perceive subtle and effective modes of creativity in the music. After all, although Bartók did remark that the music of Serbo-Croatian epic was "awfully monotonous" at first impression, he also noted that once he became more familiar with it, he began to search "with great pleasure the lesser and greater . . . divergences amidst the uniformity."[46]

Oral epic is a genre in which the *stories*, not the music, are the essence. Singers of epic everywhere instinctively save their most exquisite creativity in performance for the words that comprise them. However, singers who are also adept at the finely-tuned compromises that must be made between words and music do not compose without a keen awareness of that music. Sensing the priority of the words that they sing, they sensitively adapt the music as it best serves the poetry.

---

[46]Quoted in Erdely 1995, 1.

References

Amzulescu, Alexandru I. 1974. *Cîntece bătrîneşti.* Bucharest: Editura Minerva.

Beissinger, Margaret H. 1991. *The Art of the Lăutar: The Epic Tradition of Romania.* New York and London: Garland.

Ben-Amos, Dan. 1976. "Analytical Categories and Ethnic Genres." *Folklore Genres.* Ed. Dan Ben-Amos. Austin, TX: U of Texas P. 215-42.

Bose, Fritz. 1958. "Law and Freedom in the Interpretation of European Folk Epics." *Journal of the International Folk Music Council* 10: 29-34.

Bowra, Cecil M. 1952. *Heroic Poetry.* London: Macmillan.

Erdely, Stephen. 1995. *Music of Southslavic Epics from the Bihać Region of Bosnia.* New York and London: Garland.

Fochi, Adrian. 1975. *Coordinate sud-est europene ale baladei populare româneşti.* Bucharest: Editura Academiei Republicii Socialiste România.

Herzog, George. 1951. "The Music of Yugoslav Heroic Epic Folk Poetry." *Journal of the International Folk Music Council* 3: 62-64.

Lord, Albert B. 1960. *The Singer of Tales.* Cambridge, MA: Harvard UP.

———. 1974. "Narrative Poetry." *Princeton Encyclopedia of Poetry and Poetics.* Ed. Alex Preminger. Princeton: Princeton UP. 542-50.

Nagy, Gregory. 1991. "Song and Dance: Reflections on a Comparison of Faroese Ballad with Greek Choral Lyric." *The Ballad and Oral Literature.* Ed. Joseph Harris. Cambridge, MA: Harvard UP. 214-32.

Page, Christopher. 1986. *Voices and Instruments of the Middle Ages: Instrumental Practice and Songs in France 1100-1300.* Berkeley: U of California P.

Parker, Ian R. 1980. "Chanson de geste." *New Grove Dictionary of Music and Musicians.* Vol. 4. Ed. Stanley Sadie. London: Macmillan. 145-46.

Reese, Gustave. 1940. *Music in the Middle Ages.* New York: Norton.

Westrup, J. A. 1954. "Medieval Song." *The New Oxford History of Music: Early Medieval Music up to 1300.* Vol. 2. Ed. Dom Anselm Hughes. London: Oxford UP. 220-69.

Wooldridge, H. E. 1932. *The Oxford History of Music: The Polyphonic Period of Music, Part II: Method of Musical Art 1400-c.1600.* Vol. 2. Second ed. rev. by Percy C. Buck. London: Oxford UP.

6 THE SINGING TRADITIONS OF TURKMEN EPIC POETRY

Dzhamilya Kurbanova

The roots of Turkmen folk music reach back into the depths of time. With the ancestors of the Turkmens, nomadic tribes from Central Asia, rich traditions of instrumental music as well as distinctive musical and poetic styles originated, traditions and styles which were inherited by the contemporary Turkmen people.[1]

Due to historical circumstances the Turkmens are divided into several ethnic groups,[2] a fact which had a profound influence on the formation of various musical styles in folk art, the so-called *bagshylyk yollary* (lit. 'ways of the *bagshy*'s [singer's] art').[3] The affiliation of a musician or singer to one or the other performance school can be characterized by a number of criteria: by the instruments which accompany the singing, by the instrumental prelude and interlude, by the singer's dialect, by the traditional costume, and also by the timbre of the singer's voice and by the vocal styles and ornamentations he uses.

The glottal singing mode is characteristic of the *bagshys* of all performance schools. The degree, however, with which the singer tenses the vocal chords and the way he breathes result in different sound effects, by which the singing of *bagshys* of one local school can be differentiated from that of another. In the Tashauz district, for example, the *bagshys* sing in a highly tense voice, which is called *alkym söz* ('glottal voice').

---

[1]On the ethnogenesis of the Turkmens, see Golden 1992, 205ff., 366ff., 399ff. On Turkmen music, see Uspenskiy and Belyaev 1979; Beliaev 1975, 129-74.

[2]The Turkmen language belongs to the Oghuz or southwestern group of Turkic languages and is closely related to Turkish. The major dialects of Turkmen, corresponding to the tribal composition of the Turkmen people, are: Teke, Yomud, Ersâry, Chawdur, Saryk, Salyr, and Gökleñ; see Bazin 1959. — Literary Turkmen has been written in Cyrillic letters since 1940, but recently a new Latin alphabet was introduced. In order to facilitate the reading of Turkmen words, they are transliterated in conformity with the English transliteration system of Russian adopted in this book. The following additions and deviations should, however, be noted: the vowels written as <ö>, <ü> and <ä> correspond roughly to their German equivalents; <y> denotes as in the transliteration of Russian either a semivowel as in English *yes* or an i-sound pronounced with lowered tongue and spread lips (corresponding to the sound written <ı> in Turkish). With vowels, <y> is a semivowel, as in *yol* 'way', or a palatal off-glide, as in *ay* 'moon'; in all other cases, <y> symbolizes a central i-sound, as in *yssy* 'cold'; in the combination <yy>, as in *yyl* 'year', the first <y> is the semivowel, the second the central i-sound. The velar nasal as in English *sing* is written as <ñ>; <w> is generally a bilabial fricative.

[3]On Turkmen performance styles, see also Żerańska-Kominek 1998.

Performers from Akhal, on the other hand, have a clear, ringing voice; "open" sounds are typical for them. The *bagshys* from Saryk often employ a vocalization in a high tessitura. The Turkmen *bagshys* master many specific methods of performance which are not found among other Central Asian peoples. Among them are (1) the singing style termed *dzhukguldamak*, a vocalization in one breath with an interrupted, constrained sound on the vowels "i" or "a," (2) the singing style called *khümlemek*, the singing of the syllable "khü" in a low register, and (3) singing with a closed mouth. All of these styles, which are considered an index for the mastery of singing, have their idiosyncratic differences in the various performance schools.

But apart from local peculiarities, all the schools are united by a common language, religion, way of life, and culture. In the musical heritage of any school one can distinguish two basic types: folk music proper and professional music in oral tradition. The setting and function of folk music is obvious: it is an integral part of religious and family feasts and in an everyday setting is often performed by women and children.

For the performance and re-creation of works belonging to the sphere of professional music (in oral tradition), however, special training is necessary. Only the musician who has gone through hard training to become a master and who has received the blessing of his teacher — called *pata* in Turkmen (from Arabic *fatiḥa*, 'blessing') — has the right to call himself a folk *bagshy*. Traditionally, a *bagshy* has never just simply been a singer; in him the best traits of the people are thought to be embodied. He is an expert on native culture, a master in the field of art: a poet, narrator, singer, improviser, instrumentalist, and often also a master musician.

The profession of the *bagshy*, the oldest type of bearer of the oral-poetical musical tradition, has continued into our own days. The term *bagshy* denotes both the player of an instrument and the singer. As to the *bagshy*-singer, there are two categories, the *bagshy-tirmechi* and the *bagshy-dessanchi*. A singer who performs songs from *dessans* (or epics) separately, without the prose text, or who sings songs to the words of classic poets is called a *bagshy-tirmechi*.[4] Of great interest is the way songs are selected in the performances of these singers. We have collected more than 1000 names of songs, which are far from comprising the complete repertoire of contemporary *bagshys*. However, the melodies which form the basis for these songs are less numerous. One of the most

---

[4]Turkmen epic narratives performed by professional singers are called *dessan* in Turkmen, a Persian loan-word (*dâstân*) also used in other Turkic languages. The form of these epics is generally a mixture of verse and prose; this form is widely diffused among Turkic peoples; see Reichl 1997. The term *tirmechi* is a derivation from *tirmek*, 'to gather'; lit. 'the gatherer (of songs)'.

talented musicians of the Mary tradition, Ödeniyaz Nobatov, has told us that the secret lies not in the number of melodies but in what use is made of them. Any popular melody can have ten to fourteen degrees of development, the so-called *oba* (lit. 'encampment'), on each of which several songs can be grouped together. The songs of the initial degree (*birindzhi oba*) are the lowest in tessitura, with very restrained dynamics. The higher the degree, the more dynamic the singing and the wider the vocal range.

The tessitura level of a song is defined by the base note on the fingerboard of the *dutar*, a two-stringed lute with frets. Apart from a melodic rise by chords on the instrument (*perde*, 'fret'), during the performance the *bagshy* periodically tunes the strings of the *dutar* up, each time raising the level of the base by a fourth. This is a traditional method, which is popularly called *chekim* ('a pull', also 'a puff', from *chekmek* 'to pull'). Such tunings can be carried out up to seven times, but this is already the sign of a very talented singer. In this way one melody can serve as the basis for more than 30 songs, with an increase in dynamic intensity and tessitura.

On this principle a melody can form various patterns, which can then be tabulated according to the respective *oba*. Such a classification allows us to understand how the folk *bagshy* arranges a fairly comprehensive song repertoire in his mind.[5] Apart from this, the classification also mirrors the performance of the *bagshy*, who, regardless of the melodies he selects, always starts his performance with a song in a low register and then rises by stages to songs in a high register. This model, which has evolved in the course of centuries, is followed by the beginning musician as well as by the master *bagshy*.

The *bagshys* proceed individually in the selection of melodies for their songs, where the main criterion for the selection is not the range of musical-expressive means but the right combination of the melodies with the number of syllables in the poetic stanza. There are also model songs which are realizations of a definite melody and sometimes also linked to a particular performer. This is above all true of the songs in the repertoire of Sakhy Dzhepbarov, a brilliant representative of the *Damana yol*, who left his stamp on the art of the Turkmen *bagshy*. His voice cannot be confused with anybody else's, his songs are not found in any other repertoire!

The *bagshy-tirmechi* is popular in all parts of Turkmenistan. The songs performed by him differ in their musical structure and in their metre, rhythm and melodic contour in no way from the songs performed in the

---

[5] For an example, see the table of songs based on the popular melody *Khadzhigolak* in the repertoire of Ödeniyaz Nobatov at the end of this chapter.

dessans. However, the recital of *dessans* is a special art. The latter is for the most part found only in the northern districts of Turkmenistan.[6]

The tradition of Turkmen *bagshys* performing *dessans* has ancient roots. In one of the most outstanding monuments of folk poetry, in the epic *Korkut Ata* (or *Dede Korkut*), which scholars date to the sixth or seventh century AD, the main protagonist is Korkut, a singer (*ozan*) who puts together songs and legends of the Oghuz and from whose name the epic takes its title.[7] "Grandfather Korkut" is the prototype of the contemporary *bagshy-dessanchi.* The method of alternating prose with verse passages, found in *Korkut Ata*, became subsequently widely popular in the oral traditions of many Turkic-speaking peoples.

Consequently, the art of the Turkmen *bagshy* has direct links with the art of the Oghuz *ozan*, the traditional perfomer of epics. But in addition to this tradition, the Turkmen *bagshy-dessanchi* have also transmitted scores of popular *dessans* to our days, in particular in the region of Tashauz, where the tradition is still alive. According to scholarly opinion, the memory of the Oghuz, who had dwelled here before their migration west, was also preserved in the name of the town of Tashauz, which is more correctly Tash-oghuz, i.e. 'Outer Oghuz'.

The *dessans* which are performed by the *bagshys* of the Tashauz school are the models of the recital of epic. Later, *dessans* arose in the eastern and southeastern regions of the country. The performance of epic in the central and western parts of Turkmenistan is an exceptional rarity.

In this way the recital of epic has a place in three of the five named performance schools. Among the numerous differences are also factors which connect the *dessan* performance of all three schools. These include the literary side of the epic narrative, the dramatic development of the plots, and the compositional structure of the verse passages, but also the way, examined above, of building songs on the principle of the step-wise rise in register. Let us have a closer look at these factors.

The Turkmen *dessans* were composed by poets and *bagshys.* Some of them preserved the name of the author, but the majority remained anonymous. From the point of view of the plots, the Turkmen poetico-musical tales can be classified in the following way:

1. realistic love *dessans*,
2. fantastic love *dessans*,
3. heroic *dessans*,
4. historical *dessans*,

---

[6]On the epic singers of northern Turkmenistan and their repertoire, see Seyitmyradov 1976, 9-35.

[7]For an English translation, see Lewis 1974.

5. religious *dessans,*
6. translated *dessans.*

Some of these were composed on the basis of national folklore, for instance *Shasenem and Garyp, Asly and Kerem,* and *Nedzhep-oglan,* while the plots of others were borrowed from classical Persian literature.[8] The *dessan Shabekhram* is attributed to the eighteenth-century Turkmen poet Shabende, and a poet of the same century is thought to be the author of the popular *dessan Seypelmelek and Medkhaldzhemal,* which goes back to one of the tales of *1001 Nights.*[9] The Bible story of beautiful Joseph, widely diffused in world literature, served as a basis for a *dessan* composed by Andalib, another Turkmen poet of the eighteenth century (*Yusip and Zuleykha*). Additional works that have their origin in written literature are also attributed particularly to Andalib as well as to Magrupy. They derived these well-known works, however, from oral tradition and adapted them in the Turkmen language without having recourse to the written originals.[10]

A common story-pattern of the anonymous *dessans* is the life of a popular singer or *bagshy.*[11] To this group of narratives belongs for instance the *dessan Nedzhep-oglan,* which is the biography of a Turkmen *bagshy.* In Turkmenistan one can find a great number of tombs of *bagshys,* who were venerated as holy men, as for instance the tomb of Ashyk Aydyn, the teacher of Nedzhep-oglan, the *dessan*'s hero.[12]

It goes without saying that when historical periods and events are encountered in the *dessans,* one must not conclude from this that everything that happens in the story can be authenticated. It is most likely that particular historical episodes served as an impulse for the composition of many *dessans.* Through oral transmission, however, some historical events quickly became displaced. As the formation of epic plots developed, typical scenes and formulaic patterns became established for the description and interpretation of the action and behaviour of the protagonists. In this way the *dessan* is characterized by distinctive story-patterns as well as set types of heroes.

---

[8]Extracts from *Shasenem and Garyp* and from *Nedzhep-oglan* are found in Ashyrov and Khayydov 1958. *Shasenem and Garyp* is also very popular among other Turkic peoples, in particular the Turks of Turkey, the Azerbaijanis and the Uzbeks.

[9]For an edition of *Seypelmelek and Medkhaldzhemal,* attributed to the poet Magrupy, see *Dessanlar* 1982, 7-64.

[10]For short surveys of Turkmen literature, see Benzing 1964 and Kor-Ogly 1972.

[11]For this story-pattern in Turkish folk narratives, see Başgöz 1952.

[12]*Ashyk,* an Arabic loan-word lit. meaning 'lover', is another name for the singer; it is the usual name used for the Turkish minstrel (*aşık*). See also the chapter by Emine Gürsoy-Naskali in this volume (Ch. 8).

Both the anonymous *dessans* and the *dessans* attributed to an author are performed orally by singers to the accompaniment of one or more instruments. The basic narrative line is recited in prose, while the heroes and the heroines express their feelings in verse, sung by the *bagshy* to the accompaniment of the *dutar*. The prose parts are, as a rule, simple as regards their syntactic construction and the descriptions, which are to a considerable extent enriched by the song parts with their figurative language and lexical variety.

The plot of a *dessan* unfolds according to a fixed scheme: exposition, culmination, and dénouement. The characters of the epic are as a rule static; their personality develops and results from the action, and what is told of their birth and childhood is mainly schematic. When the plot thickens, various ways of development are found in the *dessans*, while the dénouement is almost always identical. With the exception of some tragic narratives (*Shasenem and Garyp, Zökhre and Takhyr, Asly and Kerem*), the conflict is solved through the victory of the hero.

Typical of these epic works is the complication of the basic plot by introducing separate episodes into the thread of the main story, a technique which actually results in two parallel plots. Sometimes these plots are not intertwined but follow one another, as for instance in the *dessans Sayat and Khemra* and *Xüyrlükga and Khemra*.[13]

Characteristic of the composition of Turkmen *dessans* is the use of stylistic formulas and clichés which express the passing of time and the overcoming of distance. The singer enriches his tale with metaphors, comparisons, and epithets, stylistic traits which are canonical in oriental lyric poetry.

The verses of the *dessans* are for the most part composed in the form of the *murabba'*, a strophic form which consists of four lines, rhyming in aaab, cccb, dddb etc. Sometimes the *mukhammas*, a five-line stanza, also occurs. In the *dessans* the *gazel* is also found, a verse form consisting of a varying number of monorhyme *beyt* ('couplets').

In the last century, *dessans* were transmitted and popularized apart from the *bagshy* also by the *kyssachy*, a professional reader.[14] When a *kyssachy* narrated a *dessan*, he read aloud the verse parts in portions of ten to fifteen stanzas. Very often illiterate singers adopted the texts without changes from the *kyssachy*. For their songs, however, they selected no more than four or five stanzas, which also became the norm for today's *bagshys*. The verse passages of the *dessans* are basically isosyllabic and meant to be sung.

---

[13]For a scholarly edition and Russian translation of these two *dessans*, see Mirbadaleva and Kidaysh-Pokrovskaya 1971.

[14]This term, lit. 'reader of stories', is derived from Arabic *qiṣṣa*, 'narrative'.

The songs are the most stable elements of the *dessan*. Depending on the audience and the circumstances of the performance, the *bagshy* is free to shorten or lengthen the prose parts of the tale, but he never changes the songs, whose structure and number are strictly traditional. Their arrangement in the *dessan* and musical structure follows the same principle as the performance of the *bagshy-tirmechi*, that is the principle of a rise in register and an increase in dynamics.

The *dessan* usually opens with five or six songs, the so-called *tirme-aydymlar*, which have no link by subject matter with the narrative that follows. It is not by chance that the *bagshy* begins the *dessan* with such an introduction. These *tirme-aydymlar* have a number of functions. First, the singer "warms up his throat." Second, one of the introductory songs must be of a religious nature; it has the form of a traditional address to God before the beginning of a difficult and responsible mission. And, finally, the most important function is the attraction of attention. Epic tale-telling is a difficult art, which demands a high degree of competence and mastery on the part of the singer and maximal concentration on the part of the listeners. The introductory songs give the singer and his audience time to compose themselves, to gradually distance themselves from everyday concerns, to let themselves be submerged in the world of the tale and to be captivated by their favourite heroes and their miraculous deeds and wonderful songs.

In the course of his performance, the *bagshy* does not simply re-tell the *dessan*, but he also re-creates it: his art is not only a measure of his talent and commitment, but also mirrors his view of reality and the world of fantasy. Under such circumstances the contact of the singer with his audience is simply indispensible: he relies on listeners who understand and appreciate his art. This is certainly the explanation of the fact that not every *bagshy-dessanchi* agrees to sing for an audience that has no close relationship to folk music. If he does agree to sing for such an audience, he deprives himself of an important stimulus for his performance, namely the exclamations and shouts which the experts in the audience utter during his singing and which heat up the atmosphere of the performance. This helps the singer to re-create the narrative with a maximum of inspiration and devotion.

As the *bagshy* reaches the middle of the tale, he tunes the strings of the *dutar* to a higher pitch. Just as in the case of the *tirmechi*, one can hence differentiate between several tessitura levels in singing the *dessan*: songs in a low, a middle, and a high register. They represent the basic ranges of the *dessan*, between which a whole series of intermediate song positions is placed. The poems sung at culminating points in the narrative are very popular in the whole of Turkmenistan. The melodies of these songs are inseparable from the text; the listeners recognize them as soon as the introductory music is played and express their delight with approving exclamations such as "Berekelle, bagshy!" "Köp yasha!" ("Bravo, *bagshy*!" "May you live long!"), thus cheering the singer and creating an atmosphere of union between artist and audience.

The final song of any *dessan* is called "Balsayat." Such an ending is not only typical of the *dessan*; with this melody the instrumentalist and singer of any region of Turkmenistan conclude their performance. It is probably correct to say that this song is eminently suitable for a conclusion because of its optimistic character: it has a clear, rhythmical, and lively theme and a melody in a major scale, which is not on the whole typical of Turkmen music.

The *dessan* concludes with a short prayer, with good wishes for peace and well-being to everyone present.

These are the general traits, common to the epic traditions of all schools. The differences become most apparent in the manner of performing the songs and in the composition of the accompanying instruments, but also in the selection of the melodies (*kheñ*) that are used for the verse passages.

Tashauz, as has been mentioned already, is the home of the *dessan*. In that region of Turkmenistan not one wedding feast, not one ceremony is held without the singing of *dessans*. The people know and love the epics and their performers. One of the leading singers at the beginning of the twentieth century was Palwan-bagshy, from whom twelve branches of the epic *Görogly* were written down in 1937.[15] His father knew and performed forty-four branches of the epic. Their successors were Nazar-Baga Morsy-ogly, Magtymguly Karliev, Ilaman Annaev, Tuyli Otuzov and other singers from Tashauz.

The main difference between the Tashauz performance style and other Turkmen traditions is that the singer (in addition to accompanying himself on the *dutar*) is accompanied by a *gidzhakchi*, a player of the *gidzhak*, a type of fiddle. Early in his career, the singer selects for himself a suitable *gidzhakchi*, with whom the collaboration may last for a lifetime. The role of the *gidzhak* in the songs is important: the fiddle sets the tempo of the movement and gives the basic melodic line, which is played with all sorts of ornaments and melismas, sometimes even as if the *gidzhakchi* were competing in skill with the voice of the singer.

Among folk melodies which differentiate the Tashauz *bagshy* from the singers of other regions the following can be listed: "Khak uchun" (a very complicated melody; this is why it is almost never performed), "Babam Gammar," "Oyan," "Dzhelil," "Yashylbash," "Sandyk," "Tor-

---

[15]For a (partial) edition of Palwan-bagshy's version (with Russian translation), see Karryev and Potseluevskiy 1983. For this cycle of epics, see also Karryev 1968 and Reichl 1992, 151ff., 318ff.

gay gushlar," "Tay atym," "Dagy men dagy," and "Zer dokuler." These and other melodies are used by the *bagshy* for the songs of the low register (5-7 *perde*), which are then gradually raised to a higher register (12-13 *perde*). The names of these melodies come from particular poems (*Torgay gushlar*, for instance, means 'Larks', or *Tay atym* 'My foal'), but can be performed in different *dessans*. In Tashauz, the most popular branches of the epic *Görogly* are today *Kharman Däli* (Crazy Kharman), *Bezirgen* (Bezirgen), *Kempir* (The old crone), *Öwez getiren* (Öwez's adoption), *Göroglynyñ öylenishi* (Görogly's marriage), and *Kyrklar* (The forty heroes). In addition to these heroic epics, the romances *Shasenem and Garyp*, *Khüyrlukga and Khemra*, *Yusup and Akhmet*, *Nedzhep-oglan* and other *dessans* are also performed.[16] A number of *dessans* are of a religious character (*Baba-Röwshen, Zeynelarap*), but these can only be performed by a "clean" *bagshy*, i.e. one who prays the five ritual prayers (*namaz*) every day and abstains from smoking and drinking alcohol.

The duration of a *dessan* varies, depending on the wishes of the host of the feast to which the *bagshy* has been invited. Often epic works are not performed from beginning to end, but in excerpts. This concerns mainly long *dessans*. The *dessan Yusup and Akhmet*, for instance, when performed *in toto* lasts twenty-four hours; therefore the *bagshys* divide it conventionally into seven parts and perform this or that favourite episode according to the wishes of their audience.

In the school of Tashauz two styles stand out clearly: *Däli yol* ('Crazy style') and *Nagyshly yol* ('Ornamented style'). The *bagshys* of the first style pay great attention to the instrumental side of the songs. Their voice is characterized by a rough, dour timbre; in their singing leaps into contrasting registers are the norm. During the performance of the songs the *bagshy* makes quick movements with his head in different directions, an idiosyncrasy which is expressed by the epithet *däli*, 'crazy, mad'. As the the performers themselves state, this is the original style of *dessan* singing, a style which exists only in Tashauz. The famous *dessanchi* M. Karliev sang in the *Däli yol* style. Not many of his pupils (but of these, T. Otuzov, B. Mätgeldiev, Dzh. Xammyev) preserved the special characteristics of this school. The rest of the singers changed sides quite smoothly to a new trend, the *Nagyshly yol*, a style in which the influence of the Akhal school is already noticeable. It is characterized by the desire to smooth and decorate the singing and to enrich the melodies with melismas.

---

[16] Kharman Däli has recently been translated into English; see Żerańska-Kominek 1997. For an edition of *Yusup and Akhmet*, see Özkan 1989. S. Żerańska-Kominek has also edited CDs with the music of Turkmen *bagshys* performing parts of the *Görogly* cycle; see *Turkmenistan: La musique des bakhshy*, Archives internationales de musique populaire 22, VDE CD-651 (1991), and *Turkmen Epic Singing: Köroglu*, International Music Council, Anthology of Traditional Music, AUVIDIS/UNESCO D 8213 (1994).

The *Nagyshly yol* style is also found in the district of Chardzhou, on the eastern border of Turkmenistan. Here the singing of *dessans* is intimately linked to the singing of *tirme*. The traditional name of this school is *Chowdur yoly*. The manner and the method of singing of the *bagshys* belonging to this school is close to that of the singers from the Tashauz region.

The epic tradition of Mary (Merv) stands in clear contrast to the two schools described. This is a comparatively young school, which is connected to the name of the pre-eminent *bagshy* Gurt Yakubov (1929-1985).[17] Before this singer made his appearance, the performance of *dessans* was completely unknown in Merv.

In general, the singing style of the region of Merv, termed *Salyr-Saryk yoly*, is famous for its wealth of melodies and its melodious character. In this region the folk wind instrument *tüydük* is very popular, both as a solo instrument and for accompaniment. The sound of the *tüydük* also influenced the manner of singing of the Mari *bagshys*: the somewhat nasal and at the same time fluttering voice, the abundant use of vocal ornaments, and the "play" of the vocal chords. The songs and the *saz* performance of the Saryk *bagshy* are characterized by their great length, their seemingly endless melodic development and the variability of the different parts. Favourites are here, among others, the melodies "Garybym," "Nowayy," "Dilber," "Nätuwan äylär," "Khemrayym," "Ala gözli," "Serwi agadzhy."

While the particularities mentioned above are also reflected in the *dessans* of Gurt Yakubov, the singing style of this singer was nevertheless highly individual. The most salient trait of his style was the unique timbre of his voice: low, hoarse, tense, with no parallels in other schools and regions. At the beginning, his singing struck one as sharp, strange, and unusual. But once one had become accustomed to his intonation, one began to feel the singer's voice lead into unfamiliar depths of the universe and human relationships, and it became impossible to close oneself to this miracle of comprehension. As if hypnotized, the listener became absorbed in the thought and art of the singer.

Gurt Yakubov was master of an unusual memory and a special narrative talent. His contemporaries admired his ability to retain in his memory a great number of dastans, legends, folktales, and other forms of folklore. He knew more than eighty musical-poetic works, among them such complex narratives as *Baba Röwshen, Zeynelarap, Ymam Khüseyin, Leyli and Medzhnun, Zökhre and Takhyr, Yusup and Zuleykha, Asly and Kerem, Gül and Senuber, Xatam Tay.*

---

[17]On this singer, see Yagmyr 1991.

The *dessans* performed by Gurt Yakubov are in their majority of philosophical content, often with religious motifs. Until only recently, however, everything that had any connection with God was surpressed in Soviet society due to the influence of atheistic propaganda. Gurt Yakubov was also persecuted; he was forbidden to sing and to have pupils, and he was ignored in society. The singer had an unfortunate life. During his lifetime — he died at the age of 54 — he never received any official recognition, although the people always greeted his infrequent performances with enthusiasm and love. However, the main thing which depressed the singer was the impossibility of handing on his treasure of popular wisdom and his skill as a *bagshy* to a successor. With Gurt Yakubov's death a great part of his repertoire disappeared irrevocably.

The tradition of Gurt Yakubov is nevertheless alive. The continuators of his style are not very numerous, but they have succeeded in capturing his manner of singing and, what is even more important, his way of thinking as a narrator and singer. Among them, there is most notably the *bagshy*'s son, Chary Yakubov, but there are also a number of talented young singers such as Dzhumadurdy Durdyev, Gurwan Nuryev, and Allaberdi Ödeev.[18] There is already a whole school of Mary singers-*dessanchi*, named after its founder *Gurt Yakubyñ yoly* and known in all corners of Turkmenistan.

Thus the reciting and singing of *dessans* is widely popular among the Turkmen people and, according to region, has its own history, its founders and peculiarities. In the capital of Turkmenistan, in Ashgabat, various festivals and concerts often take place at which *dessanchis* from the whole country gather. Such festivals, which are evidence of a living tradition with an inexhaustible wisdom that has been passed down over the centuries, are deeply appreciated by their audiences, regardless of the regional and tribal affiliation of the singers. These performances help the Turkmens to feel their common roots and strengthen their confidence in a good future.

---

[18] Allaberdi Ödeev was present at the symposium and performed, *inter alia*, the *dessan Khatam Tay*.

Table of Songs (from the repertoire of Ödeniyaz Nobatov)

Birindzhi oba	Ikindzhi oba	Üchündzhi oba	Dördündzhi oba	Bäshindzhi oba
1 Oyan	1 Garybym	1 Nowayy (14 variants)	1 Dilber	1 Nätuwan äylär
2 Chokh yerde goyan yarym	2 Peleg ömrüm	2 Ayryldym	2 Maru-Shakhu-Dzhakhan	2 Ala begler
	3 Chykdym güller	3 Nowayynyñ düshürimi	3 Döndi	3 Kyrklar (from *Shasenem and Garyp*)
	4 Karar oldum	4 Bir zaman goygun (Yarym garasa)	4 Gözleriñ	
	5 Khalyñdan gara gözlinyñ	5 Sallanan gözel		
	6 Ay peri	5 Körpe guzy		
	7 Gardashym	7 Azady kyl		
	8 Begler	8 Khemrayym		
		9 Bir peri		

Altyndzhy oba	Yedindzhi oba	Sekizindzhi oba	Dokuzyndzhy oba	Onundzhy oba
1 Charkhybet	1 Piala	1 Yedi manzar	1 Dzhygaly	1 Söwgülim
2 Sen-Sen (from *Baba Röwshen*)	2 Saba bilen	2 Söygüli dzhenan (Bäri gel)	2 Leyli gelin	2 Kheserli
3 Meñli khanum (from *Baba Röwshen*)	3 Khany sensiñ	3 Ol yylan	3 Gözelim	3 Düshmüsh
	4 Yaranlar	4 Yadyma düshdi	4 Torgay gushlar	4 Ogulbeg
	5 Äzizim	5 Nowgül	5 Khadzhygolak	5 Bar eken
			6 Öltürer	
			7 Aslym gelmedi	
			8 Owadan gelin	
			9 Amman-Amman	
			10 Saltyk	
			11 Shelepli durno	

On birindzhi oba	On ikindzhi oba	On üchündzhi oba	On dördündzhi oba
1 Geldiñmi	1 Gazal kheñ ("Äne, men Garybyñ," "Zökhredzhan")	1 Teshnit	1 Yoluksa
2 At chapar	2 Nalayysh seniñ ("Gülle gözdzhan")	2 Khayyt yykan	2 Görünmez
3 Allaga tabshyrdym	3 Garry khan	3 Kän güldi	3 Selbiniyaz
4 Yashylbash	4 Kichi		4 Bidert yarym
5 Gyz mämeleriñ	5 Näzlinyñ		5 Khan ogul Menan
	6 Salamymny		6 Khosh gal indi
	7 Aydzhemal		7 Kim biler
	8 Shyrmayy darak		8 Öwezim
	9 Shalar bilmez		9 Balsayat
	10 Näzlinyn		10 Köne güzer
			11 Gayry shirvan

References

Ashyrov, N., and A. Khayydov, eds. 1958. *Türkmen poeziyasynyñ antologiyasy*. Ashgabat: Ylym, 1958.

Başgöz, İlhan. 1952. "Turkish Folk Stories about the Lives of Minstrels." *Journal of American Folklore* 65: 331-39.

Bazin, Louis. 1959. "Le Turkmène." *Philologiae Turcicae Fundamenta*. Ed. Jean Deny et al. Vol. 1. Wiesbaden: Steiner. 308-17.

Beliaev, Viktor M. 1975. *Central Asian Music: Essays in the History of the Music of the Peoples of the U.S.S.R*. Ed. and annotated by Mark Slobin, trans. from the Russian by Mark and Greta Slobin. Middleton, CT: Wesleyan UP.

Benzing, Johannes. 1964. "Die türkmenische Literatur." *Philologiae Turcicae Fundamenta*. Ed. Louis Bazin et al. Vol. 2, ed. Pertev Naili Boratav. Wiesbaden: Steiner. 721-41.

Dessanlar. 1982. Ashgabat: Türkmenistan.

Golden, Peter B. 1992. *An Introduction to the History of the Turkic Peoples: Ethnogenesis and State-Formation in Medieval and Early Modern Eurasia and the Middle East*. Wiesbaden: Harrassowitz.

Karryev, B. A. 1968. *Epicheskie skazaniya o Kyor-ogly u tyurko-yazychnykh narodov*. Moscow: Nauka.

Karryev, B. A., and Ye. A. Potseluevskiy, eds. and trans. 1983. *Gyor-Ogly: Turkmenskij geroicheskiy epos*. Epos narodov SSSR. Moscow: Nauka.

Kor-Ogly, Kh. 1972. *Turkmenskaya literatura*. Moscow: Vysshaya shkola.

Lewis, Geoffrey, trans. 1974. *The Book of Dede Korkut*. Harmondsworth, Middlesex: Penguin.

Mirbadaleva, A. S., and N. V. Kidaysh-Pokrovskaya, eds. and trans. 1971. *Khurlukga i Khemra, Sayat i Khemra: Turkmenskiy romanicheskiy epos*. Epos narodov SSSR. Moscow: Nauka.

Özkan, Isa, ed. 1989. *Yusuf Bey — Ahmet Bey (Bozoğlan) Destân*. Kültür Bakanlığı Yayınları 1012. Ankara: Kültür Bakanlığı.

Reichl, Karl. 1992. *Turkic Oral Epic Poetry: Traditions, Forms, Poetic Structure*. Albert Bates Lord Studies in Oral Tradition 7. New York: Garland.

———. 1997. "The Mixture of Verse and Prose in Turkic Oral Epic Poetry." *Prosimetrum: Crosscultural Perspectives on Narrative in Prose and Verse*. Ed. Joseph Harris and Karl Reichl. Cambridge: Brewer. 321-48.

Seyitmyradov, Kakabay. 1976. "Köneürgench rayonynda Türkmen fol'klorynyñ traditsion zhanrlarynyñ Sovet döwründäki yagdayy." *Türkmen fol'klory khäzirki zamanda*. Vol. 1. Ed. K. Seyitmyradov and Sh. Khalmukhamedov. Ashgabat: Ylym. 9-65.

Uspenskiy, V., and V. Belyaev. 1979. *Turkmenskaya muzyka*. 2nd ed. Ashkhabad: Turkmenistan.

Yagmyr, Oraz. 1991. *Gurt Yakup: Beyik ömürden parchalar*. Ashgabat: Altyn gushak.

Żerańska-Kominek, Sławomira, with Arnold Lebeuf. 1997. *The Tale of Crazy Harman: The Musician and the Concept of Music in the Türkmen Epic Tale, 'Harman Däli'*. Warsaw: Academic Publications Dialog.

Żerańska-Kominek, Sławomira. 1998. "The Concept of Journey (¥ol) in Turkmen Music Tradition." *Ethnomusicology* 42: 265-82.

7 THE PERFORMANCE OF THE KARAKALPAK *ZHYRAU*

Karl Reichl

The Turkic peoples of Central Asia and Siberia have long had a flourishing tradition of oral epic poetry. It was, however, only in the nineteenth century that epics were first collected and written down, most notably by Wilhelm Radloff (1837-1918), whose monumental collection of Turkic oral literature began to appear in St. Petersburg in 1866.[1] Hector Munro Chadwick and Nora Kershaw Chadwick made extensive use of Radloff's translations for the third volume of their *Growth of Literature*, devoted in part to the oral poetry of the "Tatars," in this way bringing the Turkic oral epics to the attention of a wider public.[2] The relevance of this poetry for comparative studies was not only realized by the Chadwicks but also by scholars like Sir Maurice Bowra, who repeatedly refers to Turkic oral epics in his influential book on heroic poetry, and Viktor Zhirmunskiy, who first made the acquaintance of a living tradition of oral epics when he stayed in Uzbekistan during the Second World War.[3] When the Chadwicks' discussion of "Tatar" oral literature in their *Growth of Literature* was re-issued in 1969, Zhirmunskiy wrote additional chapters on "Epic Songs and Singers of Central Asia." In this up-dating of the Chadwicks' account, Zhirmunskiy also mentions the Karakalpaks, whose oral tradition had been practically unknown in the West, no doubt mostly due to the fact that Radloff had not collected (or translated) any Karakalpak texts.[4]

The ethnonym *Karakalpak* literally means 'black hat' (*qara* 'black', *qalpaq* 'hat').[5] It is possible but by no means certain that the ancestors of

---

[1]Parts 1 to 6 of Radloff's *Proben der Volkslitteratur* [sic] *der türkischen Stämme* consist of text and translation volumes (the translations being into German); part 7, a collection of Turkic oral literature from the Crimea, consists only of texts; parts 8 and 9 were not compiled by Radloff.

[2]See Chadwick and Chadwick 1932-40, 3: 1-226. By "Tatars" the Chadwicks do not mean the Tatars of Tatarstan in Russia (with its capital Kazan) but more generally the Turkic-speaking peoples of Central Asia and Siberia.

[3]See Bowra 1952 and Zhirmunskiy's study of Uzbek oral epic poetry, written together with the Uzbek folklorist Hâdi Zarif (Zhirmunskiy and Zarifov 1947).

[4]Chadwick and Zhirmunsky 1969, 281-83.

[5]Like other Turkic languages of the former Soviet Union, Karakalpak has been written in Cyrillic letters, but recently a new Latin alphabet was introduced. For consistency's sake, Karakalpak is here transliterated in conformity with the English transliteration system of Russian adopted in this book (see above p. 4, n. 4). As to additions and deviations for the

the Karakalpaks are to be identified with the *chërnye klobuki*, the 'black hats' mentioned in Russian chronicles of the twelfth century. Historical evidence is more reliable for the sixteenth century, when the Karakalpaks (or rather the various tribes of which the Karakalpaks are composed) were part of the Noghay Horde, one of the tribal confederations succeeding the Golden Horde. At that time the Karakalpaks were found in the Volga and Don region; it was only in the eighteenth century that they reached their present home on the southern shores of the Aral Sea and the lower reaches of the Amu-Darya (the Oxus of Antiquity). Today the majority of the Karakalpaks (comprising ca. 400,000 people) live in Karakalpakistan, a part of Uzbekistan. The life-style of the Karakalpaks was originally that of the nomad of the steppes, a life-style that has left many traces in their oral literature and material culture. Typical of Central Asian nomadic society is also their social organization into tribes and clans. Linguistically and culturally the Karakalpaks are close to the Kazakhs, with whom they also share a number of epics.

There are two types of Karakalpak singers who perform epics, the *baqsy* and the *zhyrau*. The repertoire of the Karakalpak *baqsy* consists of *dastans* (as oral epics are called in native terminology) that treat of the heroic adventures of Göroghly and his forty companions and of romance-like themes such as love and separation, intrigue and fidelity. Popular love *dastans* are *Gharip-Ashyq*, *Sayatkhan and Hämre*, *Ashyq Näzheb*, and others. The *baqsy* accompanies himself on the *dutar*, a two-stringed lute and generally performs together with a second musician, who plays the *ghirzhek*, a type of spike-fiddle. Both as regards their repertoire and their manner of performance, the Karakalpak *baqsys* resemble the Turkmen *bagshys*, in particular from the Tashauz region. They also share their repertoire with the Uzbek *bakhshis* of the Khorezmian tradition. An indication of Turkmen influence on the repertoire and performance style of the Karakalpak *baqsys* is that they regularly perform the poems of the Turkmen poet Makhtumquli (ca. 1730 – ca. 1780).[6]

The Karakalpak *zhyrau* performs heroic epics rather than love *dastans*, epics often based on historical events connected to the Golden Horde and the Noghay Horde. The word *zhyrau* is a derivation of *zhyr*, 'song'; as a

---

transliteration of the various Turkic languages (except Turkish, for which the official Latin alphabet is used here), see above, p. 115, n. 2. In Karakalpak, as in other Turkic languages, /k/ followed or preceded by "dark" vowels (/a/, /o/, /u/, /y/) is velar; it is symbolized by <q>. There is also a velar fricative in Karakalpak, transliterated as <gh>.

[6]Due to dialectal differences, words shared by several Turkic languages often appear in different form; Turkmen *bagshy* corresponds to Uzbek *bakhshi* and to Karakalpak *baqsy*; Turkmen *dessan* corresponds to Uzbek *dâstân* and to Karakalpak *dästan*; Turkmen *gidzhak* corresponds to Karakalpak *ghirzhek* etc. — For the repertoire of Turkmen singers, in which also the *dastans* mentioned here are found, see the contribution by Dzhamilya Kurbanova to this volume (Ch. 6).

designation of the bard it is also occasionally found in Kazakh (where *zhyr* also means 'heroic epic'). The *zhyrau* plays the *qobyz*, a bowed instrument with two horse-hair strings. This term is found both among Turkic and non-Turkic peoples (Kazakh *qyl-qobyz*, Kirghiz *komuz*, Ukrainian *kobza* etc.); it occurs already in the Old Turkish *Book of Dede Korkut*, where Dede Korkut himself plays the *qopuz*. The instruments denoted by these various forms of the term are not always identical in structure and manner of playing; the Karakalpak and Kazakh *qobyz* is a bowed instrument, the Kirghiz *komuz* and the Ukrainian *qobza*, on the other hand, are plucked instruments. The *qobyz* is clearly an archaic instrument; it is of particular interest that the *qobyz* used to be the instrument played by the Kazakh *baqsy*. In Kazakh, the term *baqsy* does not, as in Karakalpak, Turkmen or Uzbek, denote the epic singer but rather the faith healer, the descendant of the pre-Islamic shaman. This instrument is hence a reminder of an ancient link between epic singer and shaman in the Turko-Mongolian world.[7]

Although there has been a flourishing tradition of epic poetry performed by *zhyraus*, lasting well into the second half of the twentieth century, today Zhumabay-zhyrau is the last Karakalpak *zhyrau* who acquired his art purely through oral tradition. Zhumabay-zhyrau Bazarov was born in Shomanay, Karakalpakistan, in 1927 and learned his art in the traditional way from a master singer.[8] He stayed as an apprentice singer for three years with Esemurat-zhyrau Nurabullaev (1893-1979) in Kongrat in the forties, where he acquired a repertoire of three epics and several shorter songs. Of these epics, *Edige* and *Qoblan* are heroic epics. *Edige* treats of the conflict between Edige (Idiku) and Khan Tokhtamysh of the Golden Horde. It is an epic that was probably composed some time in the fifteenth or sixteenth century.[9] *Qoblan* is like *Edige* also found in other Turkic traditions, most notably that of the Kazakhs. It belongs to the cycle of Noghay heroes and originated like *Edige* probably in the fifteenth or sixteenth century.[10] *Sharyar*, the third epic in Zhumabay-zhyrau's repertoire is in plot closely related to the folktale of the

---

[7]The relationship between the shaman and the singer of epics in the Turkic-speaking world is discussed in Reichl 1992, 57ff.

[8]The singer took part in the symposium and performed extracts from his repertoire. I have known the singer since 1981 and have recorded his complete repertoire; for reports on his repertoire and style, see Reichl 1985; 1995a and 1995b. The present chapter is based on a paper given at the First International Conference on the Music of Turkic Peoples in Alma-Ata in 1994.

[9]On the legend of Edige and the various epics on Edige, see Zhirmunskiy 1974 and Schmitz 1996. Two Karakalpak versions, one by Erpolat-zhyrau, the other by Qyyas-zhyrau, are published in Bayniyazov, Maqsetov et al. 1990.

[10]The origin of the epic as well as the poetic structure of the Kazakh versions are discussed in Nurmagambetova 1988. Esermurat's version is edited in Zhapaqov et al. 1981. A short Crimean Tatar prose tale on Qoblan is found in Bekirov 1980, 46-48.

Calumniated Wife (no. 707 in Aarne-Thompson's type index).[11] Although this *dastan* is in content quite different from the other two epics, it is performed by the singer in basically the same style.

To illustrate the singer's style, I have transcribed an extract from the epic *Qoblan*. Qoblan's first heroic exploit is the winning of a bride, the beautiful Qurtqa from the Noghay tribe. Qoblan is not the only suitor; among those who desire to wed Qurtqa is also Aqshah-khan, the padishah of Samarkand. While Aqshah-khan must return from an unsuccessful wooing expedition to the Noghay, Qoblan is victorious in the suitor contests and wins Qurtqa's hand. The following extract describes the meeting between Qoblan on his way to the Noghay and Aqshah-khan on his return journey.

Zhumabay's version of *Qoblan* is, like most Karakalpak *dastans*, composed in a mixture of verse and prose; there are, however, also pure verse epics extant, among them a version of *Qoblan*. The prose portions of the epic are spoken, while the verse portions are generally sung.[12] When singing, the singer uses a pressed, tensed, throaty voice, which is in marked contrast to his natural narrating voice. In the prose parts, Zhumabay-zhyrau tells the story in an expressive and lively voice, stressing dramatic points in the story and underlining noteworthy incidents. Sometimes Zhumabay-zhyrau declaims rather than sings verse passages (or rhythmically consistently regular passages), in particular at the beginning of an epic, in introductory passages marked by a high degree of formulaic diction. Here his voice loses its natural inflections and takes on a more stylized declaiming tone. Prose is always spoken, not sung; it is, however, often "punctuated" by short strokes of the bow on the *qobyz*. To speak prose and sing verse is the mode of performance usual for Turkic oral epics in general. There are, however, some Uzbek traditions where also the prose passages are performed to the accompaniment of a musical instrument:

> When performing the *dâstâns* the prose parts are narrated, but in a number of regions they are performed as recitative to the accompaniment of the *dombira*. We have observed such a way of performance from Razzaq-bakhshi Qazaqbaev of the village Peshqârân in the Namangan district and from Ergash-sâzanda Zakirov of the village of Charwaq in the Osh

---

[11]See Aarne and Thompson 1961, 242f. Two versions of *Sharyar* (by Öteniyaz-zhyrau and Qulamet-zhyrau) are edited in Maqsetov 1984. On the relationship of the plot of the epic to Pushkin's tale, see Nurmukhamedov 1983.

[12]For a more detailed discussion of the mixture of verse and prose in Turkic oral epics, see Reichl 1997.

district, where the prose as well as the verse of the *dâstân* is performed from beginning to end in the manner of a recitative.[13]

Depending on the "school" to which a singer belongs (i.e. who his teacher was and what his teacher's and his own relationship to other transmitters of oral epics is) and also on the *dastan* itself, the music of the verse portions might vary considerably. Zhumabay-zhyrau uses several melodies for the poems and epics he performs; of these the most common is the *tolghau namasy* ('*tolghau* melody'), which is also found in the following example (the *tolghau* is a reflective, often historical poem). According to the singer's information, the performance of this epic takes three to five nights; the first version of this epic that I recorded lasted for a total of about eleven hours, spread over several days (1990); the second version (1994) is slightly shorter.[14] As to the musical accompaniment, the *qobyz* is tuned to the voice of the singer, the higher string in the vicinity of c^1 (in the following examples b♭), the lower string a fourth down (in the examples f). The strings are played singly for the melody as well as both together for double stops.

      Sary-ala atqa er salyp,
      Ayyldy mäkkem men shalyp,
      At beline minedi-ay.
      Qabarlaspay hesh kimge
5   Zheke basy, tän özi
      Bir allagha syyynyp,
      Äyni sähär waqtynda,
      Qoblan zholgha kiredi-ay.//
      Äne, zholgha enedi.
10 Astyndaghy sary-ala at
      "Älle maydan shöllerde
      Tulparlyqty bilsin!" dep,
      "Palwannyñ keypi tynsyn!" dep,
      Här bir maydan zherlerde
15 "Zhabyrayyl!" dep añghyydy,
      Atqan da oqtan kem emes, äy.//
      Atqan oqtan kem emes,
      Hesh haywannyñ teñi emes.
      Älle maydan shöllerde
20 "Zhabyrayyl!" dep shyrqyrap,
      At üstinde Qoblanly

---

[13]Abdullaev 1989, 114 (my translation). I have heard a similar style of performance from Uighur *bakhshis*.

[14]The following passage was recorded in Nukus in 1994. — Epics are generally performed at night; compare the quotation on pp. 24f. of the Introduction.

Atlargha qamshy beredi-äy.//
Bir neshshe maydan ötkende,
Astyndaghi sary-ala at
25 Tañyrqanyp qarady-aw,
Qulaghyn tigip turady-ay.
Artyq tuwghan Qoblanly
"Ne äzhayyp boldy?" dep,
Aldy endi artyna
30 Közin salyp bayqasa,
Bir bölek zhañghyt kiyatyr,
Aldy betten qusaghan, häy.//
Ylghyy quwla qarasa,
Dawyslary elatqa
35 Uqshaydy endi bätshaghar.
"Kim eken?" dep añlasa,
Sapary oñbay kiyatqan
Aqshakhandy-aw köredi-ay.//
At aldyna keledi:
40 "Assalawma äleyküm!"
Haq sälemin beredi.
"Wa äleyküma ässalam!"
Sälemin älik alady.
"Qaydan qaytqan balasañ?
45 Neghyp zhürgen zhan barsañ?
Saparyñ qayda, shyraghym, äy?"//
Anda Qoblan söyledi,//
Anda Qoblan söyledi:
"Sapar tartyp shyqqanman,
50 Azghana üyli Qypshaqtan./
Qorghanshaday qalada
Qydyrbay shaldyñ yaratqan,
Bir alladan tilep alghan
Balasy bolaman./
55 Talaban bar Qataghan
Noghay khalqyna qyz Qurtqagha.
Talaban bolyp endi baratqan/
Men de bala/ häw bolarman-äw."///

He put the saddle on the yellow-dappled horse,
made the saddle-girth fast
and mounted on horse-back.
Without talking to anybody,
5 all by himself and alone,
Qoblan bowed to the one God
and started in the early morning
on his way.

He started on his way.
10　The yellow-dappled horse under him
said: "In every field and steppe
it shall be known that this is a winged horse!"
He said: "May the hero's heart be calm!"
In every field
15　he shouted "Zhabyrayyl!" [the Archangel Gabriel]
and was no slower than a flying arrow.
He was no slower than a flying arrow
and no animal was its equal.
In every field and steppe
20　he shouted "Zhabyrayyl!"
Qoblanly, mounted on the horse
and whipped the horse.
When they had passed several places,
the yellow-dappled horse
25　looked in surprise
and raised up his ears.
Qoblanly of extraordinary origin
said: "What strange thing has happened?"
When he looked in front and behind,
30　he saw
a heap of dust approaching,
as if coming from ahead.
As he was looking straight towards the south, he noticed
that there were voices resembling those of people,
35　the cursed fellow.
As he was wondering who they were,
he saw and recognized Aqshah-khan
returning from his unsuccessful journey.
He rode up to him
40　and greeted him respectfully:
"Assalawma äleyküm!"
"Wa äyleyküma ässalam!"
answered the other.
"Who are you, boy, where do you come from?
45　With what purpose are you riding along?
Where does your journey lead you, my dear?"
Then Qoblan said,
then Qoblan said:
"I have departed on a journey,
50　coming from the Kipchaks of the few tribes.
I am the son
whom Qydyrbay, the old man, has received from the Creator,
from the one God, through his prayers,
in the town of Qorghansha.

55   I am in love with the girl Qurtqa
          from the Qataghan tribe of the Noghay people.
          I am a young man
          who is now on his way as a suitor."

    The actual performance of this verse passage comprises six elements:
(1) The singer begins by tuning his instrument and playing various melodic snatches, the basic melody of the passage with slight variations. (2)
He then sings a meaningless line, basically on a sustained note ("hä" on
b♭), followed by a short musical "interlude" on the *qobyz*. (3) The first
seven lines of the actual text are then sung to one and the same melody:[15]

Ex. 1

    The melody of the text is stichic and not strophic. This accords with the
metrical structure of the verse passage. The verse lines (of generally
seven or eight syllables) are not grouped into regular stanzas by rhyme or
assonance. They are rather arranged into an irregular pattern of non-
rhyming and rhyming lines (e.g. *salyp* : *alyp* 1-2; *bilsin dep* : *tynsyn dep*
12-13, *kem emes* : *teñi emes* 17-18 etc.). The melody is furthermore
basically syllabic, i.e. there is one note per syllable and there are no
melismas. It falls rhythmically into two parts, corresponding to the two
parts of each verse line, which are separated by a caesura (generally after
the fourth syllable). These two parts have a clearly stressed first beat;
they can be interpreted as a sequence of a 4-beat and a 3-beat measure.
Extra syllables are incorporated into the two bars by shortening the notes.
The tonal range is comparatively small: it does not exceed a fourth (f–
b♭). The melody begins on g, which is repeated several times, descends
to f and ends on b♭; it is accompanied in unison on the *qobyz*. Line 8 has
a slightly varied melodic form:

---

[15]The following transcriptions are "emic" rather than "etic," i.e. they capture only the
distinctive features of the melodic line and not all the details of the actual performance; for
this distinction, see above, pp. 5-6. For musical transcriptions of parts of a Karakalpak
zhyrau's performance of the epic of *Alpamys*, see Karomatli et al. 1999.

8. Qo-blan   dzholgha ki-re - di-ay

Ex. 2

(4) At the end of this line there is a short instrumental "interlude" (marked in the text by //):

Ex. 3

Similar instrumental breaks occur also after lines 16, 22, 32, 38, and 46. In each case the line preceding the instrumental "interlude" is sung to a slightly altered version of the basic melody, similar to the melody given for line 8 (Ex. 2), while lines 9-15, 17-21, 23-31, 33-37, and 39-45 are sung to the melodic "formula" given for lines 1 to 7 (Ex. 1).

(5) The last part of the passage, beginning with line 47, is spoken in a high declaiming voice. In the present example the singer inserts an instrumental break after the first line of the declaimed passage (l. 47) which leads him to repeat this line when he re-starts declamation (ll. 48ff.). The spoken part of the passage is punctuated several times by a short musical phrase on the *qobyz* (marked by / in the text):

glissando

Ex. 4.

The passage ends with (6) a sequence of sustained notes on the last syllables of the text (marked by ///):

häw bo-lar man aw

Ex. 5.

This structure is typical of all non-strophic verse-passages in the epics Zhumabay-zhyrau performs. There is some variation in the melodies the singer uses, but by and large they are all of the type illustrated here. Verse passages in a different metre (of eleven or twelve syllables) and in strophic form (generally of four lines) are less frequent; they are sung to a slightly more ornate melody, which extends over more than one verse line and is hence not strictly stichic. In my recordings, this type of singing occurs, however, only rarely, and I will therefore restrict myself to the examples given here in the comparative discussion of Zhumabay's performance.

Viewed in the larger context of Turkic oral epic poetry we can see the similiarities that exist between the mode of recitation of the *zhyrau* and that of other singers, but it also becomes clear how varied the Turkic traditions are. With reference to some of the parameters for the analysis of musical styles mentioned in the Introduction (pp. 7-8), the Karakalpak *zhyrau* is in the same category as those traditions in which the singer accompanies himself on a musical instrument. Bowed instruments like the *qobyz* are rare among Turkic singers; the Altay epic singer (*qaychy*) accompanies himself on a two-stringed instrument, the *topshuur*, which is generally plucked but can also be bowed. The more usual instrument is a plucked instrument, such as the *dombira* of the Uzbek *bakhshi*, the *dutar* of the Turkmen *bagshy* and of the Karakalpak *baqsy*, the *dombra* of the Kazakh singer, the *saz* of the Azeri *ashuq* and others.[16] As we have seen, the Karakalpak *baqsy* (as well as the Turkmen *bagshy* in many traditions) is usually accompanied by a second musician; in Khorezm the Uzbek *bakhshi* is even accompanied by a small ensemble, consisting of plucked instruments, bowed instruments, drum and flute.[17]

---

[16] The nomenclature of these instruments is somewhat confusing as etymologically related terms can denote fairly different instruments. As I have mentioned above, the Karakalpak term *qobyz* corresponds to the Kirghiz term *komuz*, which is a plucked instrument. It also corresponds to the Yakut term *khomus*, which denotes a jew's-harp. Similarly, the Kazakh *dombra* has frets, as opposed to the fretless Uzbek *dombira*; both differ from the Russian *domra*, which is a type of mandolin; all these terms are forms of the word *tanbura* and are ultimately derived from Greek *pandoura*; see Sachs 1913, 375 (s.v. Ṭanbûr).

[17] For illustrations of these instruments see Vertkov, Blagodatov, and Yazovitskaya 1963; on the performance of the Khorezmian singer see Abdullaev 1989, 115f.; on the performance of the Turkmen *bagshy*, see the contribution by Dzhamilya Kurbanova (Ch. 6).

While all these singers play a musical instrument, the Kirghiz singer is unusual in performing the epic without the accompaniment of an instrument. It is generally thought that singing the epic without the help of an instrument is an archaic feature; in this the Kirghiz manner resembles that of the Yakuts.[18] There is another similarity between the Kirghiz and the Yakut singer: the way they use their hands when performing the epic. Gesticulation is an important element in the recitation of the Kirghiz singer.[19] These gestures and facial expressions have been little studied, although the theatrical style of great singers like Sayaqbay Qaralaev has been commented upon by the scholars who knew him and it has been at least partially documented by a series of photographs and a well-known Kirghiz film.[20]

The most salient traits of Zhumabay's musical performance described above concern the nature of the melody: it is stichic, syllabic, regularly "measured," with a "flat" contour, a small range (f–g–a♭–b♭) and small intervallic steps, and it consists of only a few phrases. This type of melody is widely diffused among Turkic traditions and is generally considered archaic; it is contrasted with melodies of a more song-like, often stanzaic or at least polymotif structure, with melismatic elements and a wider melodic ambitus. For Kazakh oral tradition, B. G. Erzakovich terms the singing in a stichic melody of the kind described above the "singing-recitative style" (*pesenno-rechitativnyj vid*). The musical transcriptions Erzakovich gives for the Kazakh versions of *Qoblan*, in particular of the Kazakh singer Amanzholov Erezhep-zhyrau from Karakalpakistan, show a close resemblance to Zhumabay-zhyrau's melodic style. One example may illustrate this:[21]

> Qaldyrmay ayttym düniyasyn,
> Qoydan ayttym qoshqardy,
> Tüyeden ayttym buurasyn,
> Zhylqydan ayttym ayghyrdy.

[Praying for a child, Qydyrbay promises to sacrifice various animals to a saint.] Without hesitation I promised gifts of value:/ a ram from the sheep herd,/ a male camel from the camel herd,/ a stallion from the horse herd.

---

[18]On the performance of the Yakut epic (*oloñkho*) see Kondrat'eva 1975, 155f. The Mongolian oral epic is also generally performed to the accompaniment of a musical instrument, but there are traditions where the singer sings unaccompanied. Here too, these traditions seem to represent an archaic state of affairs; see Neklyudov 1984, 124ff. Compare also the contribution by Carole Pegg to this volume (Ch. 10).

[19]See Dyushaliev 1993, 188-89.

[20]Some of the photographs are reproduced in Kydyrbaeva 1984, Plates 1-4; the film on Sayqbay Qaralaev, directed by Bolot Shamshiev, is entitled *Manaschy* ('epic singer', 'singer of the epic *Manas*').

[21]See Erzakovich 1966, 158ff.; see also Erzakovich 1975 (Ex. 6 is found on p. 429).

Ex. 6

The Kirghiz epic *Manas* is also sung to a stichic melody. This melody is characterized by its final cadence, a "triadic" descent in a succession of thirds, fourths and/or fifths. This melody or rather melodic formula is typical of the performance of *Manas* in general. It is used by all singers (generally called *manaschy* in Kirghiz), as can be seen when comparing various transcriptions taken down from different singers. Here are some variations of this melodic formula as transcribed from the singer Sayaqbay Qaralaev:[22]

Ex. 7

[22]Vinogradov 1984, 501. Compare Zataevich 1971, 189 [No. 130] (from Toqtobek Baghyshev); Beliaev 1975, 17 (from Sayaqbay Qaralaev); Dor 1982, 4 (from the Afghan Pamirs); Reichl 1995a, 172-73 (from Dzhüsüp Mamay, Xinjiang). The music of an extract from *Semetey* (the third "branch" of *Manas*), recorded in 1904 on wax cylinders from the Kirghiz singer Kendzhe Qara, is analyzed in detail in an unpublished M.A. thesis by Daniel Prior (Prior 1998). An extract from *Manas* is found on a CD compiled by Henri Lecomte, *Musique du Kirghizstan* (Paris, Musique du Monde 92631-2), band 8 (recorded from the singer Qaba Atabekov).

This melody (with its variations) is, however, only one of several. In his detailed analysis of the singing of *Manas*, V. S. Vinogradov distinguishes four melody-types. The melodic formula illustrated here is his fourth type, called *dzhorgho söz*. In Kirghiz, *dzhorgho* designates a kind of horse (an ambler); Yudakhin glosses *dzhorgho söz* as 'flowing speech' in his dictionary (*plavnaya rech'*).[23] Sixty per cent of a performed text is, according to Vinogradov, normally sung to this type of melody. Vinogradov's types 2 and 3 are far less melodic and closer to recitative. In type 2 the melody revolves round the tonic, staying within a third or a fourth; type 3 is similar in its restricted intervallic movement, but has the "triadic" cadence typical of type 4.[24] There is finally a type of recitative which is equivalent to declaiming, i.e. an essentially non-melodic utterance of verses on the same note (Vinogradov's type 1). This form of performance is found for instance at moments of climax in the story, such as battle scenes or emotional outbursts of the protagonists.[25] From my own recordings of Kirghiz oral epic poetry it emerges that the verse-portions are structured in a way similar to that described above in the case of Zhumabay-zhyrau: the singer changes in the course of his singing into a more recitative-like melody, in particular towards the end of a "laisse," and finishes the passages with a slight flourish and long drawn-out notes.[26]

A similar structuring has also been noted in the performance of Yakut epic poetry (*oloñkho*), where recitative and song alternate with one another. The singing style of Yakut singers (*oloñkhosut*) is however quite different from that found in other Turkic traditions:

> The Yakuts sing "with the throat." The diaphragm does not play the same role in their vocal art as it does with European singers. The voice of the Yakuts is always low; the singers succeed easily in singing trills and tremolos, often with fairly wide intervals (for instance, fourths) and the most unusual melismas. The timbre of the voice is for the most part low.[27]

A particularity of Yakut epic singing is that different melodic types are linked to specific situations in the narrative or specific characters (the hero of the Middle World, the figures of the Lower World etc.). In this

---

[23]Yudakhin 1965, s.v. *dzhorgho*.

[24]See his examples 7 and 8, respectively; Vinogradov 1984, 500.

[25]See Vinogradov 1984, 493f. On the music of Kirghiz epic poetry, see also Vinogradov 1958, 116ff.; Dyushaliev 1993, 159ff.

[26]Non-strophic verse passages, called "tirade" (*tirada*) in Russian, are in their metrical organization similar to the Old French *laisse* as found in the *chansons de geste*, i.e. variable in length and held together by assonance (or, in the Kirghiz case, by alliteration as well as rhyme or assonance).

[27]Peyko and Shteynman 1940, 89 (my translation).

the use of various melodic types somewhat resembles the use of leitmotifs.[28]

The patterning of a verse-passage as exemplified by Zhumabay's performance style is also found in some Uzbek traditions. The singer Châri-
shâir, for instance, changes in the course of a verse passage into a high
declamatory performance mode — termed *qaynamâq* ('boiling') in Uzbek
— before he ends with a more melismatic melodic formula and a long
note. In this tradition the *bakhshi* sings in a strained voice similar to that
used by the Karakalpak *zhyrau*, working himself up from the lower
registers of his voice to its higher registers in the course of a song. It is
interesting to note that the same voice quality is cultivated by oral singers
(*aşıks*) from eastern Anatolia when they perform the verse parts of the
Köroğlu-cycle.[29] The use of a deep, strained voice quality is also typical
of Yakut and Altaian singers; the Altaian manner of singing is called *qay*,
a word from which the Altaian term for singer (*qaychy*) is derived.[30] The
Kirghiz singer, on the other hand, generally performs in a natural voice.

Although the type of epic music which has been discussed so far is
basically stichic and hence repetitive, the performance of a good singer is
far from monotonous. Vinogradov gives the following description of
Sayaqbay Qaralaev's singing of "Qanykey's *arman*," an elegiac poem
sung by Manas's favourite wife:[31]

> Qaralaev repeats in "Qanykey's *arman*" one and the same recitative-like
> melody up to ten times, but endows it each time with new expressive nu-
> ances: now an exclamation, now a simple cry, now a loud sigh, here he
> uses strong accents, there soft, smooth transitions etc. In quick succes-
> sion major and minor thirds alternate. At times the number of syllables
> per line increases, then the musical rhythm becomes fragmented, the
> sentence longer. But the descending cadence leaves the strongest impres-
> sion: fifth, fourth, tonic. Tensing his vocal chords, Qaralaev accentuated

---

[28]For an detailed analysis of the musical aspect of the performance of Yakut oral epic poetry
see Reshetnikova 1993 and Alekseev 1996; compare also Kondrat'eva 1975, 156; on the
performance of Yakut singers see also Illarionov 1982, 96ff. Reshetnikova 1993 and Alekseev 1996 are chapters in two volumes of the series "Monuments of the Folklore of the
Peoples of Siberia and the Far East" (*Pamyatniki fol'klora narodov Sibiri i Dal'nego Vostoka*) and are illustrated by sound recordings on two small records. Examples of Yakut epic
singing are also found on a CD compiled by Henri Lecomte *Yakoutie: Épopée et
Improvisation* (Paris, Musique de Monde 92565-2), bands 1 and 2 (from the singer Semion
Grigorievich Alekseev-Ustrabys).

[29]On the performance of Uzbek *dâstâns*, see Dzhabbarov 1971; on the style of the Uzbek
bakhshi Châri-shâir from southern Uzbekistan, see Reichl 1985, 616ff. On the cycle of *Köroğlu*/*Göroghli*, see Introduction, pp. 30 and 31. For Turkish examples, see the CD published
by Ursula Reinhard *Song Creators in Eastern Turkey*, Traditional Music of the World 6
(Washington, DC, Smithsonian/Folkways SF 40432, 1993).

[30]For a musical transcription, see Shul'gin 1973, 460.

[31]Vinogradov 1984, 494; originally in Vinogradov 1958, 129 (my translation).

these notes normally by a guttural timbre, singing the last note crescendo to fortissimo and cutting it off suddenly. Sometimes he changed this recitative-like melody for another, a rhythmically and metrically more pronounced melody. The whole *arman* was structured by this alternation, adapted to the two-line stanza, the *beyt.*

Vinogradov notes that there is a more recent development in the performance of *Manas* from the chanting of the traditional melodic formulas to a more song-like singing-style influenced by lyric songs.[32] This development can be paralleled in other traditions. While in Uzbek *dâstân* poetry non-stanzaic verse-passages, in particular those in the 7-syllable metre, are sung to a stichic melodic formula, stanzaic verse-passages show a more complex melodic structure, built up of various melodic phrases. These stanzaic verse passages are often, though not necessarily, in lines of 11 or 12 syllables. There is a tendency to compose stanzas of four lines, sometimes with a refrain. The melodic elaboration of the verse-passages along the lines of lyric song is generally a more recent phenomenon; it is perfected by the Khorezmian *bakhshis*; in the Khorezmian style great stress is laid on the musical side of epic poetry, underlined also by the fact, which I have mentioned already, that the singer is accompanied by a small group of musicians. There is a close connection between the songs of the epic and folksong (also a connection to Classical *maqâm* music); often excerpts from the *dâstâns* are performed on their own, very much like songs rather than parts of a narrative. A comparable development is found in the tradition of the Karakalpak *baqsy*, whose repertoire mostly consists of love romances and *dastans* from the *Göroghly/Goroghli*-cycle. As in the love romances, the verse passages are generally monologues or dialogues, sometimes of a lyrical rather than heroic nature. Many verse-passages have their own distinct melody (*nama*). Genzhebay-baqsy, a famous Karakalpak *baqsy*, knows about eighty such melodies. These melodies have names, such as for instance (from *Gharib-ashyq*) "Aruukhan," "Khozha Baghman," "Qäwender" etc.; they are also used for folksongs.[33] Stylistically the melodies and the mode of performance of the Karakalpak *baqsy* resemble those of the Turkmen *bagshy*, as pointed out already. Melodically, the music of these epics is more ornate, more song-like. The melodies are often syllabic, but melismatic passages are also found, in particular at the end of verse-lines or stanzas. The melody generally consists of various motifs, generally four phrases, each corresponding to one verse-line. The ambitus of these melodies is wider than that of the stichic melodies. The

---

[32]Vinogradov 1984, 499.
[33]Some melodies from the love epics performed by Karakalpak *baqsys* are transcribed in Shafrannikov 1959, 132ff.

"Aruukhan" melody, for example, comprises an octave, while "Khozha Baghman" ranges even from c to f^1, i.e. over an octave plus a fourth (compound fourth). Rhythmically these melodies can be both structured in a beat-like fashion and relatively free and flowing. Love romances of this type are also found in Uzbek, Uighur, Kazakh, Azeri and Turkish oral traditions, with a similar predominance of song-like verse-passages.

It emerges from this sketch of various performance modes that they can be placed on a scale running from stichic melodies to strophic, song-like melodies; from recitative-like melodies with a fairly restricted tonal range and a melodic progression in small intervals to more ornate and varied melodies, in ambitus, tonal line, and phrasal structure; from unaccompanied singing to a performance accompanied by a small ensemble. There is a certain historical and developmental aspect to this scale. The musically elaborate style of the Khorezmian *bakhshi* is most likely a recent form of performance; there has also been a strong influence from classical Turkic (Chaghatay) poetry on the Uzbek, Uighur, Turkmen and Azeri traditions, and the frequent use of rhymed prose in the Uzbek *dastans* might very well have been suggested by Arabic and Persian models. The performance styles of the Karakalpak *zhyrau*, the Altaian *qaychy* or the Kirghiz epic singer, on the other hand, seem to hark back to a more ancient mode of reciting epic poetry, found not only among the Turkic peoples of Central Asia and Siberia, but also in the neighbouring Mongolian, Tungus and Palaeo-Asiatic traditions.

In the performance of Turkic oral epics there is a certain amount of "dramatization" to be found: through the presence of extra-verbal and extra-musical elements such as gestures and facial expressions as well as by the alternation between singing and reciting and the use of various forms of narrating and of different kinds of singing and musical accompaniment. A narrator might furthermore impersonate the characters of his story, switch into direct speech and imitate different voices. As mentioned in the Introduction (pp. 22f.), in the epic of *Alpamish*, for instance, there is a singing contest shortly before the dénouement of the story in which the hero and the heroine, but also a nasty toothless old woman take part. In these songs, which are performed in the style of wedding songs (*yâr-yâr* in Uzbek), some singers imitate the voice of the old woman and make fun of her pronunciation.[34] Despite these indications of a lively and dramatic performance, the reciting and singing of Turkic oral epics does not cross the borderline to a truly dramatic representation as found in the transformation of the *Râmâyana* and the *Mahâbhârata* into the Malay and Indonesian shadow puppet theater (*wayang kulit*) and the

---

[34]This epic is shared by a number of Turkic peoples (Uzbek, Kazakh, Karakalpak and others); see the comparative study by Zhirmunskiy 1960.

operatic dance theatre of Java (*wayang*).[35] Even dramatization to the extent it is found in the performance of the epic of *Pâbûjî* in Rajasthan is unknown in the Turkic world. As John Smith has pointed out, the performance of *Pâbûjî* consists of a mixture of singing, reciting, dancing and invoking the visual aid of a sequence of pictures on a backcloth; neither dancing nor the technique of pictorial representation are ever encountered in Turkic epic traditions.[36]

In concluding I would like to briefly comment on the role of music in the performance of the Karakalpak *zhyrau*. Although the *zhyrau*'s style resembles that of the Turkmen *bagshy*, the Karakalpak *baqsy* and the Khorezmian *bakhshi* in using a mixture of verse and prose and in alternating between singing and speaking, it differs from that style in many ways. In the latter traditions music clearly plays an important if not predominant role. There is some justification in comparing these epics (often romances rather than heroic epics) to a Baroque oratorio: the alternation between the declaiming of prose and the singing of verse recalls that of recitative and aria, with a similar emphasis on musical elaboration, and in some cases even flamboyance. Ignoring the musical side of these *dastans* leads therefore to an interpretation that ignores an important element of these epics, which are clearly composites of words and music, or perhaps more pertinently, of music and words. Studying these epics as texts only is somewhat similar to studying folksongs only as lyrics.

The matter is slightly different with epic poetry of the type represented by the Karakalpak *zhyrau*. To describe the role music plays here, it might be helpful to distinguish between a practical, an aesthetic, and a "performative" function of music. The practical aspect is obvious. Singing a text to a melody, in particular to a stichic melody, helps the singer produce metrically correct verse lines; the melody provides him with a template, a rhythmic-metric mould for his verses. The aesthetic function is of course in the foreground in those traditions, which set a high value on musicality and musical virtuosity. Some Turkic bards are highly accomplished instrumentalists and singers; this applies, for instance, to many Turkmen *bagshys*. As to the art of the Karakalpak *zhyrau*, the purely musical aspect is clearly in the background. The key to a better understanding of the role of music in his singing of the epic lies in the event character of his performance.

Oral poetry is a communicative event, framed by a context of action and interaction. There must be a particular occasion for the reciting of epic, and there is generally also a specific purpose. The feasts at which epics are performed mark notable events in human life (births, weddings) and the gathering of guests fulfils an important social function. As I have

---

[35]On the *Râmâyana* and the Malay shadow-play, see the study by Sweeney 1972.
[36]See Smith 1989.

argued elsewhere, heroic epics like *Edige* or *Qoblan* are not performed for entertainment in the superficial sense of relaxation from the worries of everyday life, but are rather reflections on tribal origins and thus have a pronounced identificational purpose.[37] The "elevation" of the spoken word into music underlines the event character of the performance: singer and hearer are bound together by the shared occasion; they participate in an event which by its special nature and its cermonial patterning assumes an almost ritual character. The comparison which comes to mind is the performance of liturgical chant. Hymns and psalms can be read as poetry, but their primary function in the religious life of a (traditional) Christian community is liturgical. They are types of prayers that are used at particular occasions (as during the Offices) and sung and chanted in a specific manner. Their performance is regulated by the ritual of which they form an integral part. Anybody who has witnessed the performance of an epic in the style of a singer like the Karakalpak *zhyrau* is struck by the almost hypnotic effect that the repetition of the same or similar melodies has on the listeners. The audience is as it were "taken into" the tale; there is no place for the detached stance of a reader who can pursue or leave off his reading whenever he or she feels the urge. Bolot Shamshiev has caught this intensive relationship between singer and listener in a scene of his film *Manaschy*, where the Kirghiz bard Sayaqbay Qaralaev continues his singing of *Manas* in the open during a thunderstorm, and everybody continues listening without seeming to notice the streaming rain. It is this performative aspect of the music of oral epic poetry which lies at the heart of the art of the Karakalpak *zhyrau*. It is an aspect which it will be difficult to reconstruct when the living voice of the singer has become silent, when the sung epic has been transformed into the printed text and our interpretation of the epic will be merely literary. The sound samples which have been collected and analysed in the course of this century will, it is hoped, at least keep the awareness of what we are missing alive.

---

[37]See Reichl (forthcoming).

Zhumabay-zhyrau Bazarov (Bonn 1997)

References

Aarne, Antti, and Stith Thompson. 1961. *The Types of the Folktale: A Classification and Bibliography*. FF Communications 184. 2nd rev. ed. Helsinki: Suomalainen Tiedeakatemia.

Abdullaev, R. S. 1989. "Bytovanie dastanov v Uzbekistane." *Muzyka eposa: Stat'i i materialy*. Ed. I. I. Zemtsovskiy. Yoshkar-Ola: Komissiya muzykovedeniya i fol'klora Soyuza kompozitorov RSFSR. 113-17.

Alekseev, E. Ye. 1996. "O muzykal'nom voploshchenii olonkho." *Yakutskiy geroicheskiy epos 'Moguchiy Er Sogotokh'*. Ed. and trans. V. V. Illarionov, P. Ye. Efremov et al. Pamyatniki fol'klora narodov Sibiri i Dal'nego Vostoka 10. Novosibirsk: Nauka. 42-72.

Bayniyazov, Q., Q. Maqsetov, M. Nizamatdinov, and Q. Mämbetnazarov, eds. 1990. *Edige: Qaraqalpaq khalyq dästany*. Nukus: Qaraqalpaqstan.

Bekirov, Dzhafer, ed. 1980. *Destanlar*. Tashkent: Ghafur Ghulam adyna edebiyat we san'at neshriyaty.

Beliaev, Viktor M. 1975. *Central Asian Music: Essays in the History of the Music of the Peoples of the U. S. S. R.* Ed. and trans. Mark and Greta Slobin. Middletown, CT: Wesleyan UP.

Bowra, C. M. 1952. *Heroic Poetry*. London: Macmillan.

Chadwick, H. Munro, and N. Kershaw Chadwick. 1932-40. *The Growth of Literature*. 3 vols. Cambridge: Cambridge UP.

Chadwick, N. K., and V. Zhirmunsky [=Zhirmunskiy]. 1969. *Oral Epics of Central Asia*. Cambridge: Cambridge UP.

Dor, Rémy. 1982. "Un fragment pamirien de *Manas*." *Central Asiatic Journal* 26: 1-55.

Dyushaliev, Kamchybek. 1993. *Pesennaya kul'tura kyrgyzskogo naroda*. Bishkek: Institut Literaturovedeniya i Iskusstvovedeniya, AN Resp. Kyrgyzstan.

Dzhabbarov, A. 1971. "Uzbekskiy dastan (epos)." *Voprosy muzykoznaniya*. Vypusk 2. Tashkent: Fan. 13-35.

Erzakovich, B. G. 1966. *Pesennaya kul'tura kazakhskogo naroda. Muzykal'no-istoricheskoe issledovanie*. Alma-Ata: Nauka.

——. 1975. "Notnye zapisi melodiy iz eposa 'Koblandy-batyr'." *Koblandy-batyr: Kazakhskiy geroicheskiy epos*. Epos narodov SSSR. Moscow: Nauka. 420-37.

Illarionov, V. V. 1982. *Iskusstvo yakutskikh olonkhosutov*. Yakutsk: Yakutskoe knizhnoe izdatel'stvo.

Kondrat'eva, S. N. 1975. "K istoricheskoy tipologii epicheskikh napevov." *Tipologiya narodnogo eposa*. Ed. V. M. Gatsak. Moscow: Nauka. 152-62.

Karomatli, F. M., T. Mirza, and S. Gabielyan, eds. 1999. *Alpamys: Doston-dan parchalar*. Tashkent: San'at zhurnali tahriyati.

Kydyrbaeva, R. Z. 1984. *Skazitel'skoe masterstvo manaschi*. Bishkek: Ilim.

Maqsetov, Q., ed. 1984. *Shar'yar: Qaraqalpaq khalyq dästany.* Qaraqalpaq fol'klory 13. Nukus: Qaraqalpaqstan.

Neklyudov, S. Yu. 1984. *Geroicheskiy epos mongol'skikh narodov.* Moscow: Nauka.

Nurmagambetova, O. 1988. *Kazakhskiy geroicheskiy epos Koblandy batyr.* Alma-Ata: Nauka.

Nurmukhamedov, M. K. 1983. *Skazki A. S. Pushkina i fol'klor narodov Sredney Azii.* Tashkent: Fan.

Peyko, N., and I. Shteynman 1940. "O musyke yakutov." *Sovetskaya Musyka* 1940.2: 84-91.

Prior, Daniel. 1998. "The Semetey of Kenje Kara: A Kirghiz Epic Performance on Phonograph with a Partial Musical Score and a Compact Disc of the Phonogram." Unpubl. M.A. Thesis. Bloomington: Indiana University.

Reichl, Karl. 1985. "Oral Tradition and Performance of the Uzbek and Karakalpak Epic Singers." *Fragen der mongolischen Heldendichtung. III.* Ed. W. Heissig. Asiatische Forschungen 91. Wiesbaden: Harrassowitz. 613-43.

——. 1992. *Turkic Oral Epic Poetry: Traditions, Forms, Poetic Structure.* The Albert Bates Lord Studies in Oral Tradition 7. New York: Garland.

——. 1995a. "Epos als Ereignis: Bemerkungen zum Vortrag der zentralasiatischen Turkepen." *Formen und Funktion mündlicher Tradition.* Ed. Walther Heissig. Nordrhein-Westfälische Akademie der Wissenschaften, Abh. 95. Opladen: Westdeutscher Verlag. 156-82.

——. 1995b. "Epensänger und Epentraditionen bei den Karakalpaken." *Kulturelle Perspektiven auf Schrift und Schreibprozesse: Elf Aufsätze zum Thema 'Mündlichkeit und Schriftlichkeit'.* ScriptOralia 72. Tübingen: Narr. 163-86.

——. 1997. "The Mixture of Verse and Prose in Turkic Oral Epic Poetry." *Prosimetrum: Crosscultural Perspectives on Narrative in Prose and Verse.* Ed. Joseph Harris and Karl Reichl. Cambridge: Brewer. 321-48.

——. (forthcoming). *Singing the Past: Turkic and Medieval Heroic Poetry.* Ithaca, NY: Cornell UP.

Reshetnikova, A. P. 1993. "Muzyka yakutskikh olonkho." *Yakutskiy geroicheskiy epos 'Kyys Debiliye'.* Ed. and trans. P. N. Dmitriev, N. V. Emel'yanov et al. Pamyatniki fol'klora narodov Sibiri i Dal'nego Vostoka. Novosibirsk: Nauka. 26-69.

Sachs, Curt. 1913. *Real-Lexikon der Musikinstrumente.* Berlin. [Rpt. Hildesheim: Olms, 1979.]

Schmitz, Andrea. 1996. *Die Erzählung von Edige: Gehalt, Genese und Wirkung einer heroischen Tradition.* Turcologica 27. Wiesbaden: Harrassowitz.

Shafrannikov, V., ed. 1959. *Karakalpakskie narodnye pesni.* Moscow: Gosudarstvennoe muzykal'noe izdatel'stvo.

Shul'gin, B. 1973. "Ob altayskom kae." *Maaday-Kara: Altayskiy geroicheskiy epos.* Ed. and trans. S. S. Surazakov, I. V. Pukhov, and N. A. Baskakov. Epos narodov SSSR. Moscow: Nauka. 454-60.

Smith, John D. 1989. "How to Sing a Tale: Epic Performance in the Pābūjī Tradition." *Traditions of Heroic and Epic Poetry. II. Characteristics and Techniques.* Ed. J. B. Hainsworth and A. T. Hatto. London: MHRA. 29-41.

Sweeney, P. L. Amin. 1972. *The Ramayana and the Malay Shadow-Play.* Kuala Lumpur: The National U of Malaysia P.

Vertkov, K., G. Blagodatov, and E. Yazovitskaya 1963. *Atlas muzykal'nykh instrumentov narodov SSSR.* Moscow: Gosudarstvennoe muzykal'noe izdatel'stvo.

Vinogradov, V. S. 1958. *Kirgizskaya narodnaya muzyka.* Frunze: Kirgizskoe gosudarstvennoe izdatel'stvo.

———. 1984. "Napevy 'Manasa'." *Manas: Kirgizskiy geroicheskiy epos. Kniga 1.* Ed. and trans. A. S. Sadykov, S. M. Musaev, A. S. Mirbadaleva et. al. Epos narodov SSSR. Moscow: Nauka. 492-509.

Yudakhin, K. K., comp. 1965. *Kirgizsko-russkiy slovar'.* Moscow: Sovetskaya Entsiklopediya.

Zataevich, A. V. 1971. *Kirgizskie instrumental'nye p'esy i napevy.* Ed. V. S. Vinogradov. Moscow: Sovetskiy kompozitor.

Zhapaqov, N., et al., eds. 1981. *Qoblan: Dästan.* Qaraqalpaq fol'klory 8. Nukus: Qaraqalpaqstan.

Zhirmunskiy, V. M., and H. T. Zarifov. 1947. *Uzbekskiy narodnyi geroicheskiy epos.* Moscow: OGIZ.

Zhirmunskiy, V. M. 1960. *Skazanie ob Alpamyshe i bogatyrskaya skazka.* Moscow: Izdatel'stvo vostochnoj literatury.

———. 1974. "Skazanie ob Idige." *Tyurkskiy geroicheskiy epos.* Leningrad: Nauka. 349-86.

8 *Dudak değmez*:
A FORM OF POETRY COMPETITION AMONG THE *Aşıks* OF ANATOLIA

Emine Gürsoy-Naskali

The oral delivery of epic poetry is no longer a living practice in Turkey. The last notice of a singer who recited the *Köroğlu* epic dates from the 1960s.[1] There might still be some epic singers in villages in Anatolia but the practice is rare.

The decline of this tradition is generally explained by and associated with the advent of modern times, the advance of technology, the complexity of societal structure and the march of progress. In 1995, when the 1000th anniversary of the Kirghiz epic *Manas* was celebrated world-wide (apart from Kirghizistan, probably most fervently in Turkey, where parks and roads were renamed after Manas, books, conferences, lectures, and broadcasts were devoted to Manas and even a special lottery was established in honour of Manas), an interesting comparison was drawn, in certain circles, between the Kirghiz and the Turkish attachment to cultural values. The Kirghiz Turks, who have maintained the recitation of *Manas* as a national feature to the present day, were considered to be more aware of their national heritage than the Turks of Anatolia, who no longer recite *Dede Korkut* or *Köroğlu*.[2] It was suggested that we, the Turks of Anatolia, revive the oral recitation of *Dede Korkut*. This implies a new interpretation of the end of our oral epic tradition, as a failure to maintain or manifest our cultural and national identity.

Whatever the interpretation may be, the recitation or singing of epic poetry, for all intents and purposes, is a tradition of the past as far as Turkey is concerned. Minor forms of oral tradition and performance — minor, in the sense of length and stature — however, survive among the

---

[1]This version of *Köroğlu* was told by Behçet Mahir and was recorded and edited by Mehmet Kaplan and his assistants; see Kaplan, Akalın, and Bali 1973. The narrative is in prose, interspersed with verse passages. For a general discussion of the *Köroğlu* epic, see Reichl 1992, 318-33; Mahir's version is briefly discussed *ibid.*, 321.

[2]For an English translation of *Dede Korkut*, see Lewis 1974; the version of *Manas* recorded by Wilhelm Radloff has been critically re-edited and translated into English by Arthur Hatto in 1990.

aşıks of Turkey. The term *aşık* means 'a person in love';[3] *aşıks* are folk poets, sometimes also referred to as *saz şairi*, in other words, 'poets who perform with a musical instrument called a *saz*'. Even though there are *aşıks* without a *saz*, these are exceptions to the rule.[4] *Aşıks* either perform individually or get together and compete with one another.

In the last few decades they have been assembling once a year for a festival, which has been held in Konya since 1966.[5] These festivals last between three days and a week. At the close of the festival, the *aşıks* run up a hill or slope and let out a shrill cry; then a sheep or ram is sacrificed in accordance with Muslim tradition.[6] The sacrifice is not, so to speak, part of the programme; the poetry part takes place indoors and the sacrifice, naturally, outdoors.

Sometimes up to eighty *aşıks* take part in the competitions held during the festival.[7] *Aşıks* compete in a number of fields.[8] Each one of these fields has its own specific rules and constitutes a distinct genre. One may classify the fields of competition into competitions based on extemporizing and into competitive performances of poetry and music which have been prepared beforehand.

Dudak değmez is a form of poetic skill which is extemporized, and one of the toughest challenges. *Dudak değmez*, or *leb değmez*, another term for this genre, means 'lips do not touch'. Competitors take turns in improvising poetry which must not contain any labial sounds; in other words, neither the bilabial sounds [b], [m], [p] nor the labio-dental sounds [f] or [v] may appear in the poetry. By way of warning or as a punitive measure a needle is placed vertically between the two lips of the singer. Should the performer pronounce one of these sounds, the needle pierces his lips: hence the name "lips do not touch." And the needle does indeed pierce the lips if the competitor is not well trained. This happened to an *aşık* from Tokat, Hasan Selmanî. He had not heard of *dudak değmez* before he took part in the singers' competion, but nevertheless got up

---

[3]Apart from this etymological interpretation which derives the word from the Arabic *âshiq*, there are other attempts at explaining the etymology of *aşık*.

[4]On the terms *aşık* and *saz şairi*, see Dizdaroğlu 1969, 18; Köprülü 1962; Alparslan 1972. On the *aşıks* and their repertoire, see also Eberhard 1955 and Moyle 1990.

[5]Halıcı 1992 is an excellent collection of biographies and select works of modern Turkish folk poets. On the competition among Turkish minstrels, see also Erdener 1995.

[6]This feature of the festival of the *aşıks* is not recorded anywhere; I was able to observe this ritual when I attended the festival in Konya in 1975.

[7]Tirmurtaş 1973.

[8]Halıcı, in reference to the festival held in 1986, quotes twelve different fields: "Atışma, Hikâyeli Türkü, Güzelleme, Doğmaca Şiir, Dudakdeğmez, Doğmaca Türkü, Kucakkama, Meydan Atışması, Muamma, Yılın Yedi Şiiri, En Güzel Memleket Türküsü, En Güzel Memleket Şiiri" (Halıcı 1986 [1992, 642]). Timurtaş 1973 lists the branches of competition as "atışma, türkü, şiir, muamma."

to compete with *aşıks* from Kars and Erzurum, who excel in this branch.[9] Selmanî had taken no notice of the warning looks of Halıcı, the patron of the festival. He was soon disqualified, as the needle had done its job, and he had to step down from the stage. Later Halıcı asked him with sympathy why he had come forth without his approval. Selmanî replied that the festival was a great experience for him; as he came from a village, he had no other way of meeting the great masters in the field. He also promised that the following year the gold medal in *dudak değmez* would be his. And so it was.[10] The following year he challenged the assembly of *aşıks* who had come from all over Turkey, making it quite clear that he wanted to be tested in *dudak değmez*.[11] He captured the audience; his words were deep in meaning and full of poetic expression. Everyone's eyes were fixed on the needle which glittered between his lips. Then came the finale when he had to "sign his poem," i.e. to name himself in the last line. The audience shouted out "tapşır!", meaning that the *aşık* should now proceed to the final quatrain (i.e. the *şah bendi*) and give his pen-name. Here, there was a certain difficulty since his pen name was Selmanî, which contains the sound [m]. He started playing his *saz*, then he smiled and continued playing with confidence: Selmanî got over the difficulty by using his real name instead of his pen-name. There was an uproar of applause in the hall. Selmanî was given the gold medal.

As to the procedure of the competition, during the *aşık* festival the competitor *aşıks* sit on the stage, facing the audience. In earlier times such meetings and challenges took place in coffeehouses, or in the homes of well-to-do patrons. The coffeehouse in Konya, named Sulu Kahve on account of the pond in it, was restored just for this purpose by Hemdem Sait Çelebi in the early nineteenth century. There might be four, five or more *aşıks* who compete at one call. There is also a jury.[12] It is either a

---

[9]It is also said that Alevi *aşıks* do not favour competitive forms of poetic performances on account of their gentle nature; hence *dudak değmez* is not popular among Alevi *aşıks*.

[10]Halıcı 1992, 641-42, 665-66.

[11]His words of challenge were:
Ey Hasan, gönülden yananlar gelsin,
Sulara katılanlar akanlar gelsin.
Dudağı iğneyle çıkanlar gelsin,
Herkes usta olan dilleri tanır.
In response, Baba Efkari gave the rhyme:
Âşıklar söylenen sözden anlarsa,
İnsanlar içinde hastan sayılır. (Halıcı 1992, 665-66.)

[12]It would be worthwhile to document the structure and itinerary of this festival. No source, for example, records the way in which the jury is formed, how many jury members there are, what points are taken into consideration during evaluation (jury members also have to assess entries which need to be handed in before the competition). The fairness of the jury's decisions is ascertained by the audience's agreement with the verdict. However, one year two jury members from Ankara had favoured participants from their home town and the other

member of the jury or one distinguished person from among the audience who gives the cue, that is the rhyme to which a poem must be extemporized. *Dudak değmez* can also be performed individually, in which case one *aşık* comes forward and is given a cue. Rhyme is termed *ayak*, and giving the cue is called *ayak vermek* or *ayak açmak*.[13] The audience is attentive to the cue line; if they think it is a particularly good line they show their liking; if, on the other hand, it is a defective cue they ask for the line to be changed to something more suitable. In competitions which require the poet to extemporize, the first competitor usually praises himself and belittles the other competitors. When the second poet takes his turn, he responds to the first singer. And in this way the relay continues. The audience is responsive: a good performance receives enthusiastic applause.

The phonology of a *dudak değmez* has a definite impact on its morphology. The wording of a *dudak değmez* has to avoid the first person, whether this be the first person personal pronoun, the possessive suffix or any conjugation ending in the first person, since these morphemes require the sound [b] for *ben* 'I' and [m] for the suffixes. Negation also becomes difficult since it requires the suffixes *ma* or *me*. Negation is possible with the verb *to be* in the present tense, where the negative particle *değil* can be used. Statements such as *there is* and possessive structures expressing ownership are also impossible as these constructions require the word *var*, which contains the sound [v].

Dudak değmez is a self-conscious and highly skilful form of composing poetry, concentrating on technical perfection at the expense of content. It exhibits the type of clever word-play one would expect from classical *divan* poetry. In fact, there have been *divan* poets who have composed *dudak değmez* poetry;[14] but *dudak değmez* is not a device of *divan* poetry

---

members of the jury had sided with them. There was discontent, and the audience reacted negatively to this decision; the unfortunate incident was not easily forgotten. See Halıcı 1992.

[13] In classical poetry, the term for rhyme would be *kafiye*. For various types of *ayak*, see Kırzıoğlu 1962 and Akalın 1966.

[14] The following *ghazel* by Ahmet Remzi Dede, once director of the Selim Ağa Library in Üsküdar and shaikh of the Üsküdar Mevlevihanesi, is an example of a *dudak değmez* in *aruz* (classical metre). The final couplet, the *makta*, does not comply with the rules:

Tarik-i aşke gir, ehl-i Hüdâ ol
Gönül, gel lâyik-i her i'tilâ ol
Dilersen dehrede âzâde-serlik
Gurûr-i câhı terk eyle, gedâ ol
Sakın izhârdan ağyâra hâlin
Yine sen derdine çâre-resâ ol.

Cidâl-i kîl ü kâle yok nihâyet
Ricâlu'llâh ile hâl-âşinâ ol
Çekil izzetle, uzlet gûşesine
Azîz ol, derd-i şöhretden cüdâ ol

and does not belong to its repertoire; it is not one of the forms a classical poet needs to cultivate and include in his collected works.

Basically *dudak değmez* is to be distinguished from other forms of extemporized poetry by the peculiar rules it imposes on its sound structure. It is typical of these rules that certain sounds are forbidden, while in other poetry certain sounds are required. Here rules regulate the insertion or the appearance of certain sound patterns, namely line initial rhyme, alliteration, and/or line final rhyme.

An extreme case of demand for the insertion of certain sounds occurs with tongue twisters, such as "she sells seashells on the seashore," or in Turkish "bir berber bir berbere gel beraber bir berber dükkanı açalım demiş." These are examples of single line tongue twisters but there are also longer texts or poems where one encounters the excess of a certain sound. This form of ditty or poetry is called *yanıltmaca* in Turkish and is to be found in all Turkic literature.[15] It obviously is a development of line initial rhyme and alliteration. *Yanıltmaca*, however, is not one of the fields in which *aşık*s compete, nor is it incorporated in the festival programme.

Both *dudak değmez* and *yanıltmaca* are manifestations of a phonetic endeavour. In both cases it is a conscious effort carried to extremes, whether it be in terms of abstention or excess. In a lengthy exercise like epic poetry, one has to take things at one's stride and in moderation. But the phonetic essence of both these forms is present in epic poetry. If epic poetry is a marathon, *dudak değmez* and *yanıltmaca* are one hundred metre hurdle races on the same track.

I will conclude by giving two examples of extemporized *dudak değmez* poetry. The first poem was composed by Murat Çobanoğlu:[16]

Dokunmaz leb lebe Remzî okurken
Dehân-i dilbere nükte-nüma ol.
(Quoted in Dilçin 1992, 499; also in Tahir-ül Mevlevî 1973.)
[15]See Gürsoy-Naskali 1994 for two Kirghiz examples of *yanıltmaca* (= *cañıltmaç* in Kirghiz) by Alıkul Osmonov. One of them is:
Bek too
Bekem too,
Bercagı
Bermet zoo.
Bermet zoo
Bermtin
Bereri
Beker go . . .
Bek zoogo,
Bermet dep,
Bekerge
Bek attı
Bergen go.
[16]Halıcı 1992, 615.

Aşkın kekliğisin dağlar içinde,	Up in the mountains, you are the pheasant of love,
Darılırsın seke seke gidersin.	If offended, skipping on one foot you go.
Gönül tarlasına uğrarsa yolun,	If your path encounters the field of the heart,
Danesini eke eke gidersin.	You cross it sowing its seeds.
Âşık tanır içten içe yananı,	The lover recognizes a man who burns inwardly,
Eğer anar isen candan cananı.	When you recall the beloved passionately.
Ne aldın, ne sattın göster nişanı,	What have you bought, what have you sold, show us the deed,
Yorgun oldun çeke çeke gidersin.	Tired you depart dragging the load.
Can içinde nice gönül eğledin,	You have entertained many a love in your soul,
Ne dediler, ciğerini dağladın.	What did they say (to you), that you branded your heart with a hot iron?
Kahreyledin gece gündüz ağladın,	Shattered, day and night you cried,
Göz yaşını döke döke gidersin.	You walk on, shedding your tears.
Âşık olan anlar kendi işini,	Those in love recognize their dilemma,
Can adar canana, seçer eşini.	They sacrifice the soul for the beloved, and pick their partner.
Aslı sihir etti döktü dişini,	Sorcery was at work and she shed her teeth,
Sen de dişin döke döke gidersin.	You walk on, shedding your teeth.

The second example is a *dudak değmez* in a fifteen-syllable line, composed by Erzincanlı Aşık Davut Sularî:[17]

Sularî'den sual etsen kainatın işini
Görür seçer er isteriz hakikat nakkasını
O diyarın sır şehrinin nasını
İnsan yüzünü gör dedi heşt dükkanı zikrederek

If you ask Sularî for the meaning of the universe,
(He will say) we want men who discern the embellisher of the truth.
Look and see the people of the secret city of that realm,
Look and see the face of man, he said, mentioning the eight shops (heavens).

---

[17]For a biography of Sularî, see Halıcı 1992, 392-95. For the musical transcription I am grateful to Metin Eke, assistant at Istanbul Technical University, State Conservatory for Turkish Music.

Su- la- rî- den su- al et- sen ka- i- na- tın iş - i- ni

Gö-rür seçer er is- te- riz hâ- ki- kat nak-ka-sı-n

O di- ya- rın sır şeh- ri-nin na-sı- nı

In- san yü- zü-nü gör de-di heşt dük-ka-nı zik-re- de- rek

References

Akalın, Lütfullah S. 1966. *Terimler Sözlüğü.* Istanbul: Varlık Yayınevi.

Alparslan, Ali. 1972. "Âşıklar Bayramı." *Çağrı Dergisi*; rpt. in Halıcı 1992, 619-21.

Dilçin, Cem. 1992. *Örnkelerle Türk Şiir Bilgisi.* Türk Dil Durumu Yayınları. Ankara: Sevinç Basımevi.

Dizdaroğlu, Hikmet. 1969. *Halk Şiirinde Türler.* Türk Dil Kurumu Yayınları 283. Ankara: Ankara Üniversitesi Basımevi.

Eberhard, Wolfram. 1955. *Minstrel Tales from Southeastern Turkey.* Folkore Studies 5. Berkeley: University of California Press.

Erdener, Yildiray. 1995. *The Song Contests of Turkish Minstrels: Improvised Poetry Sung to Traditional Music.* Milman Parry Studies in Oral Tradition. New York: Garland.

Gürsoy-Naskali, Emine. 1994. "Kırgızca Yanıltmacalar." *Bir — Türk Dünyası İncelemeleri Dergisi* 1. Istanbul: 81-84.

Halıcı, Feyzi. 1986. "Yirmibirinci Yılında Türkiye Âşıklar Bayramı." *Çağrı Dergisi*; rpt. in Halıcı 1992, 638-43.

——, ed. 1992. *Âşıklık Geleneği ve Günümüz Halk Şairleri — Güldeste.* Atatürk Kültür Merkezi Yayını 58. Ankara: Türk Tarih Kurumu Basımevi.

Hatto, Arthur T., ed. and trans. 1990. *The Manas of Wilhelm Radloff.* Asiatische Forschungen 110. Wiesbaden: Harrassowitz.

Kaplan, Mehmet, Mehmet Akalın, Muhan Bali, eds. 1973. *Köroğlu Destanı.* Anlatan: Behçet Mahir. Atatürk Üniversite Yayınları 314. Ankara: Sevinç Matbaası.

Kırzıoğlu, Fahrettin. 1962. "Halk Edebiyatı Deyimleri." I. *Türk Dili* 124, Ocak 1962.

Köprülü, Fuat. 1962. *Türk Sazşâirleri.* Ankara: Güven Basımevi.

Lewis, Geoffrey, trans. 1974. *The Book of Dede Korkut.* Harmondsworth, Middlesex: Penguin.

Moyle, Natalie Kononenko. 1990. *The Turkish Minstrel Tale Tradition.* Harvard Dissertations in Folklore and Oral Tradition. New York: Garland.

Reichl, Karl. 1992. *Turkic Oral Epic Poetry: Traditions, Forms, Poetic Structure.* The Albert Bates Lord Studies in Oral Tradition 7. New York: Garland.

Tahir-ül Mevlevî [Tahir Olgun]. 1973. *Edebiyat Lügatı.* Ed. Kemal Edib Kürçüoğlu. Istanbul: Enderun.

Timurtaş, Faruk Kadri. 1973. "'Âşıklar Bayramı' Kültüre Hizmet Ediyor." *Çağrı Dergisi*; rpt. in Halıcı 1992, 671-73.

9 THE MUSICAL CURTAIN: MUSIC AS A STRUCTURAL MARKER IN EPIC PERFORMANCE

Hiromi Lorraine Sakata

Music, with its basic elements of rhythm and melody, representing *space* and *time* in sound, has been utilized to enhance textual form and is an indispensable element in the performance of oral literature, particularly oral epics. Ruth Finnegan, in her work, *Literacy and Orality*, posits, "it is now accepted among serious students of verbal oral performance that the text alone is an insufficient guide to the art form, and that to understand it fully one must go further and also study the processes of performance/and audience reception as they actually take place in space and time."[1]

This strong relationship between oral literature and music is bound together in the concept of "performance" which includes acts of composition and transmission of the text. In our own field research experiences, we have encountered performers who find it difficult to provide song or story texts without "performing" the song or story. In the words of Albert B. Lord, "an oral poem is not composed *for* but *in* performance."[2] He strongly believed that the song is the story, "it is not merely a tale divorced from its telling."[3]

> Sulejman Makić said that he could repeat a song he had heard only once, *provided that he heard it to the gusle* [Yugoslavian horse-head fiddle traditionally used to accompany epic performances]. This is a most significant clue. The story in the poet-singer's mind is a story in song.[4]

There is evidence that this close bond between music and text, between acts of composition and transmission of text, is evident even in those genres that have been transmitted to us as written literature. A twelfth-century historical source written by Nizami, *Chahar Maqala* ('Four Discourses'), describes the composition and performance of a famous poem by Rudaki, a tenth-century Persian court poet, to Nasr ibn Ahmad

---

[1] Finnegan 1988, 125.
[2] Lord 1960, 13.
[3] Lord 1960, 99.
[4] *Ibid.*

of Bukhara. When the Amir overstayed his camp away from his capital, Bukhara, his homesick army and courtiers offered five thousand dinars to Rudaki to persuade the Amir to return to Bukhara. He therefore composed a *qasida*, and when the moment was right, "he picked up the *chang* ('harp') and in the *ushaq* mode, he commenced this *qasida* ('ode')."[5] Apparently, the performance was so effective, that the Amir

> descended from his throne, bestrode the horse which was on sentry-duty, and set off for Bukhara so precipitately that they carried his riding-boots after him for two parasangs, as far as Buruna, and only then did he put them on; nor did he draw rein anywhere til he reached Bukhara and Rudagi [sic] received from the army the double of that five thousand dinars.[6]

It is obvious from the description that Rudaki performed the verse in a musical mode (*ushaq*) which he accompanied with a harp. It is presumably this musical performance that affected the Amir so dramatically. Even in contemporary Persian, the indivisible concept of music and literature is illustrated by the Persian verb, *khandan*, meaning 'to read' or 'to sing'.

There are other examples which indicate that the very act of literary composition is dependent on musical performance. The poems of the 18th century Sindhi saint, Shah Abdul Latif, were organized by the poet himself, according to the musical modes appropriate for the performance of his poetry. His work, known as *Shah Jo Risalo* ('Compendium of Shah's poetry'), is arranged in twenty-nine chapters or sections according to musical modes known as *sur* (tone, pitch). Each *sur* represents a musical mode in which to sing the verses and/or indicates a mood or theme that is appropriate to the poem. Many of the *sur* are variants of Hindustani (classical music system of North India and Pakistan) *raga* while others are based on local, regional tunes.

Even when a work is written and not meant to be performed, the very reference to a musical performance can represent tradition, become a symbol of heroism and revolt, and define the passage of time. For example, *The Bridge over the Drina* by Ivo Andrić is a story that relies heavily on the story-telling tradition of Bosnia and Serbia in which the guslar or storyteller (who accompanies himself on the one-string horsehead fiddle, *gusle*) plays an important part in interpreting and reinterpreting history. References to music play an important part in defining the structure of the story in terms of time and place. The *guslar* marks the beginning of the construction of the bridge in sixteenth-century Bosnia when the story begins. Serbian peasants listen to the tales of a Montenegrin *guslar*;

---

[5]Nizami, *Chahar Maqala* in Javadi 1962, 124; translation mine.
[6]The poem and description as translated by E. G. Browne are included in Arberry 1958, 33.

Turkish youths dance the *kolo* across the bridge; a drum and bugle of the Austrian army can be heard playing "a new and unsual melody."[7] Songs and dances are woven throughout the narrative as though the essence of the story is told through music.

> In that great and strange struggle, which had been waged in Bosnia for centuries between two faiths, for land and power and their own conception of life and order, the adversaries had taken from each other not only women, horses and arms but also songs. Many a verse passed from one to the other as the most precious of booty.[8]

Two examples of South Asian epic performances, the *Pabuji* epic of Rajasthan, NW India, and the epic of *Kesar* (Caesar)[9] as told in Baltistan, Northern Pakistan, provide some insight into the ways sung performance adds information other than verbal narrative. Both examples include spoken and sung narrative, however, the number of tunes and the timing and placement of sung passages are determined by the performers. The *Kesar* storyteller sings a single tune at the end of each spoken narrative section. The songs themselves do not seem to add textual information, but rather, to mark the presence of the hero, Kesar.

The *Pabuji* performance differs dramatically from that of the *Kesar* performance in that it involves not only a single storyteller, but two storytellers; a painted scroll depicting scenes from the story; dance movements to certain tunes; and a sequence of sung passages to various tunes (*arthav*) which alternate with spoken narrative (*gav*). The spoken narrative recapitulates the sung events and extends the narrative further. The key words of these songs match those used in the spoken narrative section, but the structure of the sung words are determined by the structure of the tune. The song-tunes are determined by the performer for the sake of performance. According to John Smith, who is the author of an extensive study on *Pabuji*, the choice of tunes is determined by the performer's "sequential preferences" rather than by "feelings of aesthetic appropriateness."[10] He suggests that the sung passages do not add to the narrative, but rather to the performance, as a sacred ritual for the gods and as entertainment for the audience.

Although the musical performances in both of these epic traditions add nothing new to the narrative events in the tale, the time and placement of these songs are determined by the performers. They are sung at strategic points in the story, signifying characters, events, or the beginnings and endings of episodes where it may be appropriate to draw the metaphorical

---

[7] Andrić 1967, 137.
[8] Andrić 1967, 88.
[9] Also known as *Gesar* in Tibet.
[10] Smith 1991, 40.

curtain as between acts or scenes. Thus, music is used here as a marker of time and place in epic performance.

The Central Asian *Gorgholi* epic as sung in northern Afghanistan differs from the above two examples in that the whole tale is sung. How, then, is the "musical" curtain applied? The singer of the tale, known as *Gorgholikhan*,[11] accompanies himself on a two-string plucked lute known as *dambura*. His performance consists of 1) sung dramatic, narrative text, 2) lyrical sung poetry as well as 3) purely instrumental interludes. These three elements, in addition to a special vocal technique associated with *Gorgholi* singers and Central Asian bards in general,[12] are used effectively by the *Gorgholikhan* to identify important structural points in the dramatic narrative as well as the performance as a whole.

The *Gorgholi* epic is named after a sixteenth-century Turkmen hero by the name of Rushan who was a bandit-hero and an accomplished *asheq* ('bard, poet-musician'). In other parts of Central Asia, the hero is more commonly known as Köroglu ('Son of a Blind Man'), a reference to his blind father; or as Gorogli ('Son of the Grave'), a possible reference to the death of his mother in child birth.[13] The Afghan *Gorgholi* cycle concerns four generations of the hero's family, including the hero, Gorgholi Khan, his adopted son, Awaz Khan and Awaz Khan's two sons by different wives, Nur Ali Khan and Sher Ali Khan, and Awaz Khan's grandson, Jangir Khan, the son of Nur Ali Khan.

This multi-generational aspect seems to be an important attribute of most Central Asian epics. The organizational structure of the Afghan Gorgholi cycle is not clear. Many cite the number seven when referring to the number of major parts of the story known as *shakh* ('branch') while others refer to as much as thirty *shakh*. Episodes within a *shakh* are known as *dastan* ('story') or *taqsim* ('division, section').

A traditional performance of *Gorgholi* usually takes place in a guest house during long winter nights when family and friends gather around a fire to be entertained. Depending on the manipulations of the *Gorgholikhan*, the telling of a single episode may take several nights. He may stop to rest his voice and retune his instrument after every section, or, more calculatedly, he stops at some critical or climactic moment in order

---

[11]The title is contructed from the name of the epic, *Goroghli*, and reference to the singer, *khan*, from the verb *khandan*, 'to read' or 'to sing'.

[12]In Chadwick and Zhirmunsky 1969, 215, the vocal quality produced by this technique is described by Vámbéry as "certain forced guttural sounds," and Radlov as "a low guttural voice" (217). Françoise Gründ and Pierre Bois in their notes accompanying the recordings of Central Asian and overtone singing (1996) cite Roberte Hamayon 1990, 171-72, who describes the voice as "an extremely deep throat voice, resting on the production of a drone and the vocalisation of guttural sounds." See also the contribution by Karl Reichl in this volume (Ch. 7).

[13]On the Turkic *Köroğlu/Gorogly* epics, see the chapters by Dzhamilya Kurbanova (Ch. 6) and Emine Gürsoy-Naskali (Ch. 8).

to keep his audience involved, and to demand special favors of food or money. This break is known locally in Badakhshan, Afghanistan, as *bandana* and can result in much time being spent in light-hearted haggling. Many such interruptions can stretch a four to five-hour story into a two to three-day performance.

The excerpt of the *Gorgholi* tale I present in this paper is from a recording of Palawan Asil, a Tajik from Surun-e Yaftal, Badakhahan, Afghanistan. The tale was sung in Persian (Tajiki) on July 20 and 21, 1972, specifically for the purpose of recording. Therefore, the tale is sung in a rather concise manner with repetitions kept to a minimum. The season (summer), timing (evening of July 20 and morning of July 21), and atmosphere (a small audience of three or four) were far from ordinary, but Palawan Asil did not complain, nor did his performance seem to be adversely affected by the unusual situation.

As mentioned above, the telling of the tale of *Gorgholi*, like other Central Asian epic performances, involves narrative singing often described as "monotonous" or consisting of "two melodies, one executed in quick tempo, for the course of the action, the other in slow tempo and as a solemn recitative for the speeches."[14] In the case of the Afghan *Gorgholi* performance, the "two melodies" are actually two rhythmic settings based on a lyrical quatrain known as *falak*, and a narrative style that is used to tell the tale. Both melodic settings are limited to a range of a fourth or a fifth and sung in a declamatory style. Therefore, the distinguishing feature of the two settings is the rhythmic phrase structure of a single line of verse.

The typical *falak* is a quatrain of eleven-syllable lines with the rhyme scheme AABA. The *falak* represented in this epic has eleven-syllable lines sung in three phrases consisting of four syllables, four syllables, and three syllables. Each phrase is marked by a caesura represented by a syllable held relatively longer than the others in the phrase. The final syllable of a line of verse is marked by a syllable that is held longer than the final syllable of each preceding phrase. Furthermore, each final three-syllable phrase is set to a musical phrase that equals the length of the two preceding four-syllable phrases:

a- mad jof- ta ka- bu- ta- ra-(i)   (ai) az khe- le je- da   (ai)___

Ex. 1

---

[14]Chadwick and Zhirmunsky 1969, 217 and 221, respectively.

The last syllable of the last verse of the quatrain is extended beyond a sense of meter, and is exaggerated by the use of the guttural vocal technique which produces rich overtones.

(ai) em- sa- la (wa) je- da sho- da- im o por- gham de le ma (ya) wi____

Ex. 2

Thus, the musical setting of the *falak* emphasizes the poetic structure of the quatrain.

The poetic structure of the narrative lines of text which actually tell the story is different from the *falak* text in that each line is constructed of nine syllables divided into three groups of two relatively short notes and one relatively long note. The last syllable of the line is lengthened by a *dambura* melodic figure which is roughly equivalent to the short-short-long phrasing of the other groups:

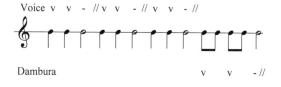

Ex. 3

Again, the musical setting of the narrative text, like that of the *falak*, defines the poetic phrase structure of each verse, emphasizing the final syllable of each phrase in a verse, and the final syllable of the line of verse itself. The ends of major sections of the tale are again highlighted by the use of very long, exaggerated endings using the guttural vocal technique which produces rich overtones.

The inclusion of *falak* quatrains, a regional song genre, seems extraneous to the tale since there is no connection between the text of the poetry and the story. What, then, is the function of these *falak*? It has been reported that the songs included in the Azeri version are all attributed to the hero, Köroğlu, an accomplished *asheq* or bard. But in the Afghan epic, there is no reference to the hero as poet-musician nor is there any connection between the *falak* and a quotation of the hero. I believe the *falak* are included not for their textual content, but rather, for their musical expression. The introduction of *falak* in the performance announces the beginning of an episode; the equivalent of the opening of the "musical curtain."

The instrumental *dambura* introduction provides an overture before the opening of the curtain. The subsequent *dambura* interludes provide brief spaces to rest the *Gorgholikhan*'s voice as well as mark intermediary section breaks. The guttural vocal quality mentioned as the hallmark of other Central Asian epic singers, is used significantly at ends of sections. When a syllable on the basic pitch is held out at the end of couplets, quatrains and sections, the guttural voice transforms into a rich timbre, which produces overtones. The *dambura* interludes, which follow these extended vocal endings, are in the style of *dambura* rhythmic vamps used in *falak* performances.[15]

I have taken a *dastan* from the performance of a *Gorgholi shakh* as performed by Palawan Asil, to show how these musical elements are used to define the structure of the story and the performance. The *dastan* describes the meeting of the hero, Awaz Khan (son of Gorgholi), with the beautiful Khal Pari, sister of his archenemy, Wazir Ahmad Khan. The *dambura* interludes represent a musical curtain that marks the two sections of the *dastan*. The first section focuses on Awaz Khan, describing his appearance, his thoughts and his speech on seeing Khal Pari sitting in a shop in the bazaar. The second section focuses on Khal Pari, her actions and her speech which lead to the climax when Awaz Khan lifts Khal Pari onto his horse, and they ride away together.

Musical Elements	Narrative, Structural Elements
Dambura introduction	Setting the stage
First *falak*	Opening the curtain halfway
Exaggerated ending on the syllable *wi---*, instrumental vamp	Ending of first *falak*, end of quatrain
Dambura interlude	Section break
Second *falak*	Opening the curtain all the way
Exaggerated ending on the syllable *wi---*, instrumental vamp	End of first couplet, end of quatrain, *falak*
Dambura interlude	Section break
Narrative singing	Start of tale; description of hero, Awaz Khan [line 1]
Rise in pitch center	Description of Khal Pari [line 12]
Return to basic pitch, exaggerated ending on the syllable *wi---*	Signals end of section describing the hero's reactions [line 35]

---

[15]An example of a performance of the *Gorgholi* epic is included in the recording by Gründ and Bois referred to (1996). It demonstrates the use of many of the same musical elements that define the various structural elements of the story and the telling of the tale.

Dambura interlude, retuning	section break
Narrative singing, return to higher pitch center	Description of Khal Pari's reactions [line 36]
Return to basic pitch, exaggerated ending on the syllable *wi---*	End of major section, *dastan* [line 59], closing of the curtain

Gorgholi[16]

Dambura introduction

Falak

Amad jofte kabutar az khel jeda	A pair of pigeons flew away from the flock
Yak sal qati budim emsal jeda	One year we were together, this year apart
Yak sal qati budim o yak ja megashtim	One year we were together and we went around
Emsal jeda shodim o porgham dele ma***	This year we parted and my heart is full of grief***
(repeat)	
***Exaggerated vocal ending*	

Falak

Bulbul ba watan takhte Sulaiman khostar ast	The nightingale at home is happier than on Solomon's throne
Kharhaye watan zilahe raihan khoshtar ast***	The thorns of one's country are sweeter than basil***
Yusuf ke ba Misr padshani mekard	Joseph who was made King of Egypt
Sad kashki gada meshod o Kenan khoshtar ast***	Had a hundred regrets, happier a beggar in Canaan***
(repeat)	

****Exaggerated vocal ending*

Dambura Interlude

---

[16]The text was transcribed into Persian by Enayatullah Shahrani. The English transcription and translation is by Nazif Shahrani.

Dastan

Yak shabam bebud o nimi shab	One night, perhaps at midnight
Khoftan bebud dade shab	Perhaps during the late evening prayers
Awaz Khan bachaye Gorgholi Sultan	Awaz Khan, son of Gorgholi Sultan
Aspe Qir zire pashna	Mounted on his horse Qir
Tofang ham dara dar shana	His gun slung over his shoulder
Naizai guldar dast toshna	A decorated lance in his hand
Az jurai tampasai gusheshna	A pair of Tanpasai jewels in his ears
Kakal hai zariham dar gardaneshna	His hair falling on his shoulders
Khanbid da rui bazarna	He dismounted in the bazaar
Shaulham amal bu no baja 10	It was nine o'clock in the night
Gozar kard rastai bazar na	He passed along the bazaar block
(change in pitch to higher center)	
Nazar kard dar labe dokan	He looked into a shop
Shista yak nozok dokhtare nazian	A slender coquette was sitting
Khodesh tanha shishta dar dokan	Sitting alone in the shop
Du rokh dara mahi asman	Two cheeks like moons in the sky
Mesuza ba misli chraghan	Glowing like a lantern
Awaz Khan did o mand hairan	Awaz Khan saw and was struck
Pas gardan jelawi qira	He turned back the rein of Qir
Begirom guft az in surat khabar	"I should learn more of this beauty," he said
Pas amad o dar labe dokan 20	He came back to the front of the shop
Pas amad o dar labe dokan	He came back to the front of the shop
Nazar kard khal pari nazian	He looked at beautiful Khal Pari
Kohare wazir ahmad khan	The sister of Wazir Ahmad Khan
Wazir dokhtare turkestan	Daughter of the Wazir of Turkestan
Tanha shishta dar labe dokan	Sitting alone in front of the shop
Har du rokhash mahtabe asman	Both cheeks like moons in the sky
Awaz Khan did kard khanda	Awaz Khan saw and laughed
Aferin guft ai kabutar	"Bravo my pigeon," he said
Sar kheli no o nim lak khana	"The head of 950,000 households
Khane dokhtare turkestan 30	Daughter of the Khan of Turkestan
Chi mekoni ala jane zinda	What are you doing, oh my dear
Tanha shishtai dokana	Sitting alone in the shop
Du rokhat kardai mahi asman	Two cheeks like moons in the sky
Dar meti kodam musulman	Which Muslim are you intending to burn
(return to basic pitch center)	
Chi jawab meti akheratna*** 35	How will you account for this on judgment day"***

***Exaggerated vocal ending

Dambura interlude, re-tunes

(change in pitch center, return to higher pitch center)

Khal pari shonid i gapa		Khal Pari heard this talk
Sharangash ai ja jonbid i dokhtar		Suddenly she moved from her place
Ganaha khamzad rui sinashna		All her jewels fell upon her breast
Salam dad in dokhtar awaza		This girl greeted Awaz
Assalam aleik guft shahzada	40	She said "Salam aleik, o prince
Manda nabashi jane zinda		I hope you're not tired, my soul
Chera tu porsidi hawale ma		Why are you asking about me
Khabar nesti ke sare dele ma		Do you not know who holds my heart
In medat haft sal bud pora		It has been exactly seven years
Dar mushqab sokhtaudam i bachi		Since I fell in love with a boy
Na didam dar haft sal guft rutna		I haven't seen your face in seven years
Shonidom hamin chand roz na		I recently heard
Tu raftai shekar zamina		You went to the hunting grounds
Pa har shabost nami dukana		I sat every night in this shop
Na ai jin tarsidom na az deo	50	I did not fear jin nor deo
Pairadan usum dami rutna		I hired men to watch on the other side
Errishab 'dialeqam dad maqsadma		Tonight God gave me what I desired"
Awaz am shonid in gapa		Awaz heard all of this
Ba zir hal abra kard khanda		He smiled lifting his eyebrows
Kham kard qamati pahlawanira	55	He bent his wrestler's frame
Ai bozui nazok war dashta		He lifted her by her delicate arm
Partaftush wai wai dar qanchogha		He threw her on his horse
Pas gardand jalawi aspi qira		He turned the rein of his horse Qir
(return to basic pitch center)		
Rast shod bazare turkmana***		And started off for the Turkmen bazaar***

***Exaggerated vocal ending

References

Andrić, Ivo. 1967. *The Bridge on the Drina*. Trans. from the Serbo-Croat by Lovett F. Edwards. New York: The New American Library.

Arberry, A. J. 1958. *Classical Persian Literature*. London: Unwin.

Chadwick, Nora K., and Victor Zhirmunsky. 1969. *Oral Epics of Central Asia*. Cambridge: Cambridge UP.

Finnegan, Ruth. 1988. *Literacy and Orality: Studies in the Technology of Communication*. Oxford: Blackwell.

Gründ, Françoise, and Pierre Bois, eds. 1996. *Chants épiques et diphoniques*. Paris: INEDIT, Maison des Cultures du Monde.

Javadi, Hasan Sadr Haji Sayid, ed. 1962 [AH 1340]. Nizami-ye Arudi-ye Samarqandi. *Chahar Maqala* [Four Discourses], in *Ganjina-ye Nasar Parsi* [A Treasury of Persian Prose]. Tehran: Tabesh Press. 117-25.

Lord, Albert B. 1960. *The Singer of Tales*. Cambridge, MA: Harvard UP.

Sakata, Hiromi Lorraine. 1983. *Music in the Mind: The Concepts of Music and Musician in Afghanistan*. Kent, OH: The Kent State UP.

Smith, John D., ed. 1991. *The Epic of Pābūjī: A Study, Transcription and Translation*. Cambridge: Cambridge UP.

10   THE POWER OF PERFORMANCE:
WEST MONGOLIAN HEROIC EPICS

Carole Pegg

This paper presents the power of West Mongolian epic performance in pre-Soviet Mongolia from two perspectives: indigenous Mongolian ideo-scapes in which epic performance, bard, instrument, text and vocal sounds were believed to have magical and ritual powers when performed within the homes of herders, and the anthropologist's interpretation, based on interviews and experiences in Mongolia, that epic performance is a central device through which identities on a variety of levels are simultaneously evoked.

West Mongolian heroic epics, *baatarlag tuul'*, are magnificent oral works, telling of brave knights who fight, and eventually defeat, the forces of evil. They are rich in poetical devices, such as vowel harmony, formal parallelism and line-initial alliteration. The latter is an ancient technical device of Mongolian literature used, for example, in the thir-teenth-century epic-chronicle *The Secret History of the Mongols* (*Mongolyn Nuuts Tovchoo*) and in later chronicles, such as *Altan Tovch* (1604) and *Erdeniin Tovch* (1662). Such literary features enabled epics to survive the seventy years of secular communism in Mongolia from 1921-1990, since they were able to be classified as "ancient literature" and mobilised as examples of creative "national" genius.

When the harsh Stalinist regime eradicated religion and attempted to create a "unified national socialist identity" from the many diverse groups within Mongolia's borders, their performance traditions were eliminated or forcibly changed. Epic performance (which had survived the spread of Buddhism into Mongolia in the sixteenth century by incorporating buddhist elements into folk-religious and shamanic texts) was abruptly halted. Under communism, the once highly-respected professional epic performer (*tuul'ch*) was reduced to living in holes in the ground and begging (Byambadorj IN), and epic texts were stripped of any references to magic or religion (Tsoloo IN).[1] Epics were collected, bowdlerised, published as composite versions (e.g. Naratuya 1986), and then per-formed and promoted as evidence of a high form of "oral literature" of a

---

[1] See Pegg 1995, 78. For the interviews (abbreviated as IN), see the references below.

unified "people," rather than of separate ethnic groups.[2] Epic studies concentrated on the secular perspectives of textual analysis and linguistics, rather than the powerful effects of ritual performance. It was perhaps ideologically convenient that a special "oral literary language" — with distinctive grammar, vocabulary and major archaisms — was identified as common to the epics of different West Mongolian ethnic groups.[3]

It is not clear whether epic performances ceased completely during the 1920s and 1930s, when there was a sustained cultural offensive which used the military to disseminate "national music" and "cultural enlightenment,"[4] or whether, as with shamanist (Baljir IN) and folk-religious practices (Tsedendamba IN), ritual performances continued in secret. The course of Altai Urianghai bard Baataryn Avirmed's career indicates that epic performances were possible by the 1950s; he began to train in 1949 and became a full-fledged bard in 1959. But religious beliefs surrounding epic performance are likely to have remained in the private rather than the public domain. As with other traditional music and song, epics had to be performed in the "new hearth for the new era," that is, in cultural centres or on theatrical stages, and re-presented as secular works of art.

My field research in West Mongolia, undertaken in 1989, 1990, 1993 and 1996, caused me to question Russian scholar Vladimirtsov's claims that the steppe aristocracy was the creator, bearer, preserver and disseminator of Oirat epics, which initially seemed a potential reason for their suppression. My suspicions were strengthened when I later read that the Russian Mongolist Burdukov noted in 1940 that Oirat-Kalmyk heroic epics were created by ordinary herders, and when I learned that this was also the view of Byambadorj, Bait Mongol Director of the Ulaangom Museum (IN). According to the bards with whom I talked, the context of performance in pre-socialist Mongolia (referred to by them as "old Mongolia") was primarily in the round felt tents (*ger*) of herders. More rarely, bards performed for princes and were sometimes retained, as was the Bait Mongol Parchin, himself a noble (*taiji*), who was not only official bard of Prince Da *Beis*[5] but also performed in the camps of Bait and Dörbet nobility.[6] Eighty-five year old blind Bait Mongol Düüdei, whose father Chuluun was a renowned bard, explained that they were obliged to perform in such contexts since they were subjects of the prince. However, within the context of the herder's home, performances, bards, instruments and texts were believed to have magical powers and to

---

[2]See Pegg (forthcoming) for a fuller discussion of the creation of identities through performance an the communist regime's use of performance as an ideological tool with which to create a "unifie socialist identity."
[3]See Vladimirtsov 1983-84, 38; Rintchen 1963.
[4]See Natsagdorj 1981,136-41.
[5]A Manchu title for a prince of the fourth rank.
[6]Vladimirtsov 1983-84, 33.

be enshrined in ritual practices. Epic performance was viewed as a powerful, ritual, supernaturally-inspired activity (Enebish IN).

I. Magical Powers of Performance, Bard, Instrument, Text and Vocal Sounds

A. Performance

It was believed that the act of performance could please the spirits of nature (*baigaliin ongod*) or exorcise them. Among Altai Urianghais — as among Buryat Mongols — epics were performed before a hunting expedition in the hope that the spirits of the forest and mountain would give them game.[7] When the performance was particularly well executed, there was no chase: the animal simply presented itself to the hunters. Epic performance was considered especially important as a means of placating spirits when settling into a winter place. The benevolence of the spirits was sought in unpredictable circumstances, for instance, Bait Mongol Parchin performed *Bum Erdeni* in 1912 before the Mongol troops besieged Hovd, as part of the war of independence from China.[8] In cases of infertility or illness in people or animals, epic performance was used to ritually exorcise demons (*chötgör*) and devils (*zetger*).

Performances were always held at night and only during certain seasons of the year. Altai Urianghais believed that epic performance during summer months would antagonize the spirits, causing storms with strong winds, rain and lightening, so they were only performed during the eighty-one days from 22 December to 15 March. By contrast, Bait Mongols believed that this applied only to certain epics. The famous Bait bard, Chuluun, performed *Bum Erdeni* and *Hüleg Baatar of Tüsheet Khan*[9] (*Tüsheet Haany Hüleg Baatar*) in summer, but he did not dare to perform in that season the third epic in his repertoire, *Khan Harangui*, which calls the son of Heaven into battle and is thought to be particularly dangerous (Düüdei IN).

When a performance had been arranged, the host provided food, as at a domestic feast (*nair*), and all in the area converged on the tent. At about ten o'clock in the evening, after receiving a ritual-scarf (*hadag*) from the host, the bard performed the invocatory praise-song. He then rested prior to delivering the main epic, which lasted until dawn. During the next day, the herders tended their animals and the bard again rested. This process continued throughout several whole days and nights.

---

[7]See Hamayon 1990; Pegg (forthcoming).
[8]Vladimirtsov 1983-84, 36.
[9]Tüsheet Khan was one of the four Khalkha Khans.

Before an epic performance, the host burned incense and juniper in a ritual of purification, and made milk-aspersions to the spirits. The audience, including children, had to remain attentive throughout the performance in order to support the struggle of good forces against evil. Among Dörbet Mongols, children were warned that falling asleep would be a sign of support for the epic's evil forces and that they might even become the souls or spirits (*süns*) of enemy soldiers. Onions were put on their eyelids to help them to stay awake. Silence had to prevail throughout the performance and it was forbidden to drink fermented mare's milk (*airag*) or milk-spirit (*arhi*). The West Mongolian epic must never be left unfinished: the evil forces must be vanquished by the good before the audience could leave.

B. Bard

The bard was believed to be magician, healer and fortune-teller — a possessor of secret or mystical knowledge — and therefore treated with great respect. A potential host had to go the bard's home, present him with a long silk ritual-scarf (*hadag*) and request a performance. The bard would then choose an auspicious day and, at the appointed time, the host would send a horse to transport him. Upon his arrival, the bard instructed the removal of anything that might detract from the efficacy of his performance. Because of his accredited powers, he was never treated as a hired performer —although afterwards he would be given gifts, sometimes of great value such as a fully equipped horse. He sat in the respected northern part (*hoimor*) of the tent and others present sat in descending hierarchical order according to age and sex. The bard's meal differentiated him from his audience: he ate lean meat on the bone and saltless black tea, rather than the fatty mutton and salty tea prized by Mongols. Prior to the performance, he would again be presented with a silk ritual-scarf by the host.

Bards were believed to be able to see into the future. Bait Mongol bard, Lhagva, for instance, recalled that a bard foretold the repression of Buddhism by communism by including in his epic performance the lines:

> The time has come when Buddha's head will be confused
> And smoke will rise from the mouth of the holy vessel.
> *Burhny tolgoi manad dunad hiij*
> *Bumbyn amnaas utaa manarah tsag bolloo.*

Lhagva also suggested that the copper insects and iron crickets referred to in epics predicted the invention of cars and aeroplanes, and warned that other predictions included the onset of a great Islamic war which would destroy the earth by wind.[10]

C. Instrument

West Mongolian epics are accompanied by the two string, fretless lute, *topshuur*, which is tuned to a non-stable interval of a fourth. When Avirmed plays, he uses the forefinger of his right hand to pluck the high-pitched string (on the right in frontal aspect) above the skin soundtable and alternates by using the thumb of the same hand to pluck the low-pitched string while simultaneously sounding the high string at the top of the neck with the forefinger of the left hand. Intervals of a fourth, fifth and sixth, g-d, a-d and b-d (descending) occur (see Ex.). The instrument is made from materials taken from an environment believed to be inhabited by spirits, and consequently surrounded by ritual. Altai Urianghai Avirmed (IN) explained how the *topshuur*'s body must be fashioned from juniper in the shape of a *tsatsal*, the wooden ladle used to asperse milk as offerings to Heaven (*Tenger*). Across this must be stretched thin, sensitive skin taken from the udders or groins of "hot-nosed" animals. The categories "hot-nosed" and "cold-nosed" are used to divide horses and sheep from cattle, camels and goats: "hot" (*haluun*) implying the closeness of kin; "cold" (*huiten*), the distance of non-kin.[11] In this way, the kinship-like relationship between certain categories of animals and humans was extended to instrument and musician. A connection was then made back to the spirits by prodding into the skin table of the instrument nine holes, symbolizing those on the *tsatsal* ladle.[12] The *topshuur* was kept in a place of honour within the bard's tent and was only allowed to be touched by him. On the day before the epic performance, the host carried this instrument, in a special box, to his home. This process was referred to as "conveying the *topshuur*" (*topshuur zalah*) and its presence within the tent was thought to be able to push away or elude danger.

---

[10]This may have been a prediction about Shambala, but it was not clarified at the time.
[11]Humphrey and Onon 1996, 58.
[12]Byambadorj 1985.

Ex.: Avirmed's "Praise Song of the Altai Mountains" accompanied by *topshuur*

D. Text

Among Altai Urianghais, Baits and Dörbets, specific epics were believed to be efficacious for particular problems. This was also the case among Buryat Mongols, where particular epics were performed before hunting or to invoke rain.[13] In addition to the fact that many magical incantations and religious formulae were enshrined within the text, the theme of an epic had specific relevance. Avirmed remembered how, among Altai Urianghais, an epic entitled *Rich, White Old Man* (*Bayan Tsagaan Övgön*) was performed to bring prosperity. The "White Old Man," lord of the local place, represents general well-being in Mongolian folk-religious belief. Another epic, *Snow White Old Man* (*Argil*[14] *Tsagaan Övgön*) — in which the main character is a horse —, was performed to increase fertility of herds. When explaining the potency of the epic *Naran Gerel Khan* (*Haan Naran Gerel*),[15] Avirmed pointed to the relevant textual affinity:

---

[13]Shoolbraid 1975, 20-21.
[14]*Argil* was used by Altai Urianghais as an intensifier (Tsoloo IN) but can also mean "rich in worldly experience or wisdom" or "big of stature" (Hangin 1986, 30).
[15]J. Tsoloo recorded *Khaan Naran Gerel* and *Bayan Tsagaan Övgön* from Choisüren in 1966.

Then the hero has to go to the mountain "Seven Plaited Black Peaks" (*Doloon Gürmel*[16] *Har Uul*), to survey his territory and check that everything is alright — whether there are any black forces there, or whether some relative has come to his domain. He sees that the sky god, Hormusta, has fallen, along with two grains of corn. From one of these is born a horse named "Pitch-Black, Chestnut Horse" (*Tas Har Heer Mor'*) and, from the other, a hero called "Black Boar of the Steppe" (*Talyn Har Bodon*). In this epic, the hero's wife must have been unable to conceive and the son must come from Heaven. The old man is delighted to find a son and suggests that they continue the celebration for another few years.

This epic was performed to cure infertile couples. The hero, born in this way, is the subject of his own epic *Black Boar of the Steppe* (*Talyn Har Bodon*), in which the hero dies and is helped back to life by his horse. Performance of this epic was therefore requested to exorcise evil spirits thought to be causing illness.

It was believed that the text must be correct and complete and that nothing must be changed, added or missed out by the performer, otherwise it would be mortally dangerous for both listeners and performer. A long training period was required — in Avirmed's case this lasted for ten years — then examination by a panel of "judges" over two whole nights, during which accuracy of textual rendition had to be demonstrated. If successful, the initiand gained public recognition of his status as a bard (*tuul'ch*), and could receive invitations to perform (Avirmed IN).

Avirmed's grandfather, Jilker, told how spirits and epic heroes assisted his memory by sending him dreams of the epic's action. To alter the epic was thought to be a great sin for which one could be punished by the spirits or by the heroes themselves. For this reason, Bait Mongol Düüdei was particularly anxious when she saw a publication of Parchin's version of *Bum Erdeni*, containing major differences in plot to her father's Chuluun's version. In Parchin's version,[17] Bum Erdeni and Huiten Höh Zev become brothers. But Düüdei described to me in detail how, in her father's version, Bum Erdeni and Hachir Har killed Huiten Höh Zev. Buryats also believed that mistakes in textual delivery would be followed by some form of punishment, and that the epic hero was present at each performance checking the "truth" of it.[18] Kalmyk performers of the *Janggar* epic (*Janggarchi*) feared sudden whirlwinds if mistakes were

---

[16]This refers to the fact that, when viewed from a distance, the mountain peaks, or vegetation on the mountains, appear to be interlocked, like the plaits of a woman's hair (Tsoloo IN).

[17]See Zagdsüren 1972 for Parchin's version, and Narantuya 1988 for a summary of that version's plot.

[18]See Shoolbraid 1975, 24.

made.[19] It is worth noting that a version of *Altai Häälah* recorded in 1986 by Tserensodnom and Gaadamba from the Dörbet bard Damia had almost no textual differences from the original, recorded from him twenty years earlier.[20]

Epic heroes, like other armed heroes on horseback, became the centre of religious cults. In the Mongolian Geser cult, thought to have originated after encountering the Tibetan epic at the end of the sixteenth or beginning of the seventeenth centuries,[21] Geser Khan was viewed as a protective deity. He was worshipped in "Temples of Geser," still in evidence in West Mongolia at the end of the nineteenth century[22] and in Ulaanbaatar today. Heissig noted that, among Eastern Mongols, parts of the *Geser Khan* epic were recited by Buddhist monks when illness threatened herds, and that the text was always kept in a horizontal "pure" place, in order not to anger the hero.[23] Geser Khan continued to be worshipped by these people until the 1930s and Geser Khan family temples survived until 1945. An active performance tradition of the *Geser Khan* epic is remembered vividly today by the older people of North-West Mongolia. For example, Jamiyan, a teacher of the Oirat script, *tod*, recalled how the performance of *Geser* both by textual and oral rendition was very popular among Dörbet Mongols. As with other epics, *Geser* was performed at night during the winter months, and "readings" were surrounded by ritual and treated with the same respect as oral performances.

E. Creating Ritual Space through Sound

Among Altai Urianghais and Bait Mongols, a low-pitched, declamatory style of voice-production, *häälah* (*hailah*) is used in epic performance (Byambadorj IN). As among the male bards of Central Asian countries, such as the *baxshi* or *zhïrau* of Uzbekistan,[24] these bards use epics as a means of contacting the spiritual world and of healing. West Mongolian bards used this unusual guttural vocal tone-colour rather than their everyday speaking and singing voices to create an imagined alternative space, linked to the real world but apart from it, in which the epic drama can unfold and the power of performance activated.

According to Mongols, the vocal sounds produced in epic performance, *häälah*, relate to two other West Mongolian musical genres: the vocal technique of overtone-singing (*höömii*) and the instrumental sounds of the

---

[19]See Bormanshinov 1982, 167.

[20]See Tserel 1964.

[21]See Heissig 1980, 93-101.

[22]Pozdneyev 1971, 204, 252.

[23]Heissig 1980, 101.

[24]Levin 1996. On the performance of the *zhyrau*, see also the chapter by Karl Reichl in this volume (Ch. 7).

three-holed, end-blown pipe, *tsuur*. Both of these genres divide the sound into a fundamental drone and a flute-like melody reinforced by a series of chosen harmonics or partials of that fundamental. In the vocal tone used for epics, overtones are also detectable, although they do not form melodies. Altai Urianghai *tsuur* player Narantsogt noted also that the air-flow used during *häälah* resembles that used when playing the *tsuur*. Listening to the sounds of overtone-singing is believed to have beneficial effects,[25] and if good sounds are produced on the *tsuur* during a domestic celebration (*nair*), Altai Urianghais believe that it brings happiness to the family. As with epic performance, the *tsuur* was used to praise the spirits of the Altai Mountains[26] and, from the first to the third day of the New Year, to ward off bad spirits for the coming year.[27] In epic performance, the pitch of the pentatonic melody performed in *häälah* lies below that of the *topshuur* [see Ex.]. Our visual notations cannot convey to the reader its essence, that is, the quality of sound.[28]

F. Imagined Ritual Landscapes of "Thirteen"

The imagined landscape created by the West Mongolian bard comprises a series of "thirteens." As a prelude to epic performance among Altai Urianghais, an invocatory "Praise-Song of the Thirteen Altai" (*Arvan Gurvan Altain Magtaal*) is performed by the bard.[29] The Altai mountain range is described as consisting of thirteen snow-capped mountain peaks,[30] with thirteen passes or "Holes of the Altai" (*Altain Nühsüv*), through which thirteen large rivers run. At the summit of each mountain is said to be located a ritual cairn or obo, at which thirteen incense-offerings (*san*)[31] are made to the thirteen Altai. Such offerings are believed to influence a person's "back and front" (*ar övör*), that is, his or her past and future lives (Seseer IN). I passed thirteen *san* when crossing the Altai between New Bulgan district of Bayan Ölgii province and Bulgan district of Hovd province in 1993. However, the ritual landscape of the thirteen Altai is imaginary. Although individuals have listed some topographical

---

[25]Pegg 1991.
[26]Nixon 1984, 663.
[27]Dulam 1987, 41.
[28]See CD, Pegg (forthcoming), for this dimension.
[29]This contrasts with the performance of epics in Buryatia, where the audiences sing in chorus an invocatory song to the performer (*üligerch*).
[30]According Tsedendamba (IN), these include Tsambagarav, Suhait (peak of Mount Sair) and Tseregt (peak of Höh Serhin Nuruu) in Ölöt territory; the Mingat's Öndör Höhii (now Altan Höhii); Tsengel Hairhan; Uvs province's Tsagaan Delgii (peak of Harhiraa); Tsagaan Shuvuut; and Gov' Gurvan Saihan.
[31]Tibetan *bsangs*.

features of thirteens, such as thirteen peaks or rivers,[32] others, such as "thirteen dense black forests" and "thirteen grazing grounds" are clearly not meant to refer to reality. Within this imaginary ritual framework, the bard creates in great detail the environment known intimately by the audience members, describing springs and rivers, valleys and ravines, trees and plants, domestic and wild animals, and evoking the relationship of humankind with nature. In so doing, he creates a performance space in which imaginery and real worlds overlap. When the bard begins this praise-song in its ritual context, he summons the "Owner of the Altai," goddess *Altan Ezen Alia Hongor*, who enters the thirteenth *san*, placed by Altai Urianghais to the south of the other twelve. The epic performance must continue until she leaves. Details of the deity and of this initial epic process are closely guarded, being only discussed annually within the family group on the morning of New Year (*Tsagaan Sar*) (Seseer IN).

The practice of offering thirteen *san* is mentioned in many epics in relation to going to the summit of mountains to pray, worshipping at obo*s* and summoning vitality. For instance:[33]

Every morning, Anaa Mergen Khan	Anaa mergen haan öglöö bür
Would ascend his Altai Sümber mountain,	Altai sümber uulandaa garch,
Make his thirteen incense-offerings,	Arvan gurvan sangaa tav'j,
Cause his splendour to shine forth,	Sür javhlangaa badruulj,
And summon his vitality.	Süld zayagaa dalaldag yum baijee.

The epic hero, Hatangardi Khan, also ascended to thirteen cairns and made thirteen incense-offerings as did the lad Gün-galuu Baatar in the tale of Hürel Khan.[34]

Offerings of thirteen *san* at thirteen obo*s* was one of the many ritual practices assimilated by Mongolian Buddhism; the central cairn was interpreted as representing Mount Sumeru and the others, the twelve *dvipas* of the world.[35] Dörbet Mongols, living close to the ruins of Tögsbuyant Monastery in Türgen district, Uvs province, told me that when there was special need, for example rain was necessary to alleviate drought, seven lamas rode on white horses to the obo on Mount Mahardag, standing close to the monastery, and offered thirteen *san*; and that at the burial of Luvsanchülten, the head lama of the monastery, thirteen *san* were offered when his body had been placed beneath the obo at the

---

[32]For instance, the rivers Bulgan, Sagsai, Hoid Chingel, Ömnö Chingel (Tsengel), Hovd and Buyant; two branches of the Tsagaan; the Öröncho (or Örömch), which flows into Xinjiang; three rivers called Erchis flowing to Russia; and the river Eev which flows from the Altai to China in the south (Baatar IN).

[33]Bawden 1982, 3.

[34]Bawden 1982,180-81, 93.

[35]Banzarov 1981, 68.

peak of nearby Mount Shan (IN). But people continued to make offerings without the presence of lamas. Dörbet Mongol Jamiyan recalled how his father made "thirteen offerings of the Altai" while reading from texts in Oirat script, in contrast to lamas who read from Tibetan script. The custom was, he said, to go to the top of the mountain, look westwards in the direction of their former homeland and then offer thirteen *san*. A special *sutra* was read which referred to many places from the Dörbets' former homeland during the Jungar State, for instance, Altai, Erchis, Hovog, Sair, Haraa, Sharaa, Boroo, Talaa, Tsultas, Tahas. These names were recited to a melody (Jamiyan IN).

Throughout the communist era, the "Cult of the Altai Mountains," with its ritual offerings of thirteen *san* continued in secret, a process described to me by a Mingat Mongol, Tsedendamba (IN), who was spending the summer of 1993 in his tent (*ger*) on Altan Höhii mountain.[36]

In the Altai Mountain region of West Mongolia, the classifications of nature and music are linked in this symbolic system of thirteens.[37] Horses are identified by thirteen colours with each colour having thirteen subdivisions and these horse colours are used to classify one of the principal vocal genres, long-songs (*urtyn duu*) into "songs of thirteen swift steeds" (*arvan gurvan hülgiin duu*). The thirteen main horse colours were listed by a group of Dörbet Mongols in the Türgen mountains: light bay (*sharga*); bay or chestnut (*heer*); piebald (*alag*); red (*zeerd*); bay with black tail and mane (*hoo, hul*); reddish-white, with a reddish tinge on the tips of the hair (*ulaan*); and so on. West Mongolian folk-song scholar Katuu listed the thirteen subdivisions of "light bay" (*sharga*), which form a category of Dörbet long-songs:[38] Fallow Bay (*Hongor Sharga*); Slender Bay (*Nariin Sharga*); Cooking-Pot Bay (*Togoo Sharga*); Agile Bay (*Gelmelzegsen*[39] *Sharga*); Elegant While Running from a Far Place Bay (*Gazryn Holoos Güideltei Gandan Sharga*); Rather Well-groomed Bay (*Tsemtsger Baahan Sharga*), etc. Despite their titles, the horse is only the subject of the first two lines, a symbol through which to link the performance with the imagined landscape; the song may be thereafter on any topic. This symbolic classificatory system of song and landscape is then mapped onto performance-practices during domestic celebrations (*nair*):

[36]See Pegg (forthcoming).
[37]Cults associated with the number thirteen are not restricted to the Altai Mountains. For instance, thirteen obos mark the entry into Darhat territory in Hövsgöl province, NW Mongolia; thirteen obos in Ushin Banner, Ordos, Inner Mongolia (*arvan gurvan hurahiin ovoo*) mark the thirteen hillocks on which Chingis Khan is said to have gathered his troops; and a recent monograph examines sacrificial ceremonies for the thirteen Ataagods made by the Hatgin clan, and points to relationships with the Borjigin clan-cult, the Jugel-cult and the cult of Chingis Khan (Qurcabagatar 1992). Buryats also have an idea of "thirteen Old Men," which are mountains with obos on top in the Baikal region (Humphrey p.c.).
[38]See Katuu 1993, 52-53.
[39]*gemelzsen*.

among Hotons, when one of the thirteen-colour horse songs is performed, subsequent songs must occur in specific order according to colour (Lhamjav IN). Similarly, there are "thirteen" kinds of *biy*-dance, the movements of which are performed mainly by the upper half of the body.

Aware of the powers of performance, Mongols used it in the above ways to make sense of and create relationships between themselves and their environment believed to comprise earthly and cosmic landscapes inhabited and controlled by spirits. They also used the powers of performance to express their social relations with other human beings, on levels including confederation, tribe (*aimag*), clan (*ovog*), lineage (*udam*), and individual (*ganz hün*).

From an anthropological perspective, an aspect of the power of epic performance is the bards' evocation and display of simultaneous connections to different levels of identity. Allegiances to Eastern and Western Mongol confederations have their seeds in the thirteenth century when Chinggis Khan established his Empire but the Oirat "tribe" was still powerful. Since that time, Eastern and Western Mongols have periodically opposed each other in war. The affiliation extended into this century when, in the 1930s, a major revolt against the revolutionary government was led by West Mongolian nobles and lamas from Tögsbuyant monastery, Uvs province (*aimag*). It is being renegotiated in post-Soviet Mongolia.

In "old Mongolia," the contents, functions and accompaniments of epics varied according to confederation. For instance, West Mongolian heroic epics (*baatarlag tuul'*) are quite different from the much shorter and story-like epics or tales (*üliger*) performed by Eastern Mongols, such as the Khalkhas. Moreover, West Mongolian heroic epic performance includes accompaniment by the *topshuur* and, occasionally, as among Zakchins, by the two-string, spike fiddle (*ikil*). Buryat Mongols also use the two-string, spike fiddle (*huur*), although, in former times, Janggar bards used the zither (*yatga*), both of which are mentioned in the text of the Janggar epic.[40] By contrast, Khalkha epics (*ülger*) are recited without musical accompaniment.

On the level of "tribe," in post-Soviet Mongolia referred to as "ethnic group" (*yas ündesten*), each performs epics of distinctive form and content,[41] although some epic cycles, such as *Janggar* and *Geser*, are also widely disseminated. Altai Urianghais, Torguts, Baits and Dörbets each have their own corpus of epics. Altai Urianghai epics include passages relating to the origins of the earth and contain many shamanic elements. Torguts have only two known epics: *Janggar* and *Üülen Tiv Havhan Har Goyoo* (possibly a chapter of *Janggar*), and these are heavily influenced

---

[40]Bormanshinov 1982, 164.
[41]Horloo 1985, 2.

by Buddhism. Dörbet and Bait epics contain many Buddhist elements and share some descriptive and conceptual motifs, but also have many distinguishing features, so may not be classed together. No Altai Urianghai or Torgut elements have been identified in the epics of Dörbets and Baits (Tsoloo IN).

The oral epic tradition is believed by bards to have been maintained unbroken over many centuries and performance skills have been transmitted primarily by males within clans and families. Altai Urianghai Avirmed's experience illustrates how the process of transmission and training was undertaken within his "tribe" and clan. At least seven generations of Avirmed's lineage are known to have been epic performers.[42] Avirmed began learning seriously at the age of thirteen, although, prior to that, he had heard epics repeatedly because of family tradition. Included in his grandfather Jilker's repertory were the epics *Rich White Old Man* (*Bayan Tsagaan Övgön*), *Snow White Old Man* (*Argil Tsagaan Övgön*) and *The Boy Naran Khan* (*Naran Han Hövgüün*), all of which are now performed by Avirmed. Because Avirmed's father, Baatar, died when the boy was two years old, his principal teacher was his paternal uncle, Shirendev. The process of transmission down the patrilineal line is symbolised by a "Ritual-Scarf of Succession" (*Ulamjlalyn Hadag*), tied to the head of the *topshuur* of the bard inheriting the role,[43] after he has passed the examination referred to above, designed to ensure accurate rendition of the inherited tradition. This was passed from Jilker to Avirmed's father's elder brother, Rinchen, and thence to Avirmed. In practice, the bard and his audience would identify on a group level with aspects of the oral performance, such as the style and contents of the lengthy narratives, as well as recognizing traditions of particular lineages and the inspired improvisations of individual bards.

In all West Mongolian epics, content and action follow a basic structure. The hero reaches manhood, and sets off on horseback to eliminate evil, put right some misdeed, and search for a devout wife. With the assistance of a good friend, or a horse (with the power of human language), he defeats monsters and bad spirits that seek to hinder his quest, and finally he wins over rivals by competing with them in the "Three Manly Games." The hero conquers evil, finds a wife, returns home and lives happily ever after. There are always two opposing sides: good versus evil, and the epics are built around the struggle between the two. Sometimes epics share the same heroes, linked by patrilineal descent, as in Avirmed's epics *Black Wrestler Dovon* (*Dovon Har Böh*), and *Black Boar of the Steppe* (*Talyn Har Bodon*); and *Zul Aldar Khan, Uyan*

---

[42]Damdinsüren 1985, 51.
[43]Davaasüren 1992.

Möngön Hadaas, recorded in 1957 from Buyan of Bulgan district, Hovd province.[44]

Conceptual and descriptive motifs are used. Conceptual motifs are complex and the subject of continuing study. They include themes such as those connected with vitality and death, the soul and various sorts of prophecy,[45] healing, petrogenesis, and mountain-cults. For many years, the Epic Symposium at Bonn has provided a forum for discussion of epic themes and motifs, and for detailed textual analysis.[46] Although conceptual motifs float within the group's epic corpus and between groups, descriptive details give a bard the opportunity to root the epic among a particular group in a particular place. Avirmed explained the intensity of detail in relation to descriptive passages of the epic *Black Wrestler Dovon*:

> The bard must first describe the five kinds of cattle, the lives of 70,000 subjects and the nature and resources of that place. After that, the hero's home and horse . . . . Then he begins the description of the feast (*nair*). This gives the bard the opportunity to describe the everyday life of herdspeople: catching and milking horses, making milk-spirit (*arhi*). Once these activities have been described, the feast begins. The bard has to dress the hero for the celebration for his clothes are distinctive. He wears a very beautiful, silk, summer gown of single thickness. The feast lasts for between sixty and eighty years, and the bard must depict all phases of it. When the hero leaves the celebration, the epic performer must change his clothes, give him arms, equip his horse. This is all done in minute detail.

Everything, including details of clothes and everyday life, must be described both for the hero and opposing monster or evil spirit. Through detailed depiction of the daily existence of nomadic herdsmen, made meaningful by creative expression, the audience had access to a vast corpus of knowledge of the history and customs of their own group. At the same time, though, the bard was free to improvise with certain passages according to his ability and, for a variety of reasons relevant to a particular situation, may decide to stress one aspect of his identity rather than another: "Mongol" rather than "Turk," "Western" rather than "Eastern" Mongol, "Altai Urianghai" rather than other kinds of Urianghai, his family rather than his neighbours, or his individuality expressed in textual improvisations. Through the power of performance, embracing performance traditions, descriptive poetic embellishment of the main action and

---

[44]Horloo 1985, 3.

[45]Bawden 1982, 9-24.

[46]See, for instance, the various volumes on Mongolian heroic epics edited by Walther Heissig (Heissig 1979, 1981, 1982, 1985, 1987, 1992).

an inspired, creative delivery, the bard was able to express these simultaneous or partial identities.

Since the peaceful democratic revolution of 1990, Mongols have been re-awakening and reinventing the pre-socialist traditions of "old Mongolia" as part of the renaissance of diverse identities denied to them by the former socialist regime. No longer appropriated by a centrally-controlled system as the bearers of archaic, literary texts which represented a "national" genius and a single unified socialist identity, bards are able to perform epics in ritual contexts, to discuss openly the traditional ideoscapes into which epic performances are being re-embedded, to transmit the tradition within families (Avirmed is now teaching his son Dorjlalan, his nephew Oldoh, and his younger brother Seseer) and to use it as a means of expressing diverse identities.

Düüdei, Uvs aimag, 1993 (photo C. Pegg)

Avirmed, Hovd province, 1989 (photo C. Pegg)

Seseer, Duuv district, Hovd province, 1990 (photo C. Pegg)

Interviews

Avirmed, B. 53 yrs (a) 09.07.89 in his shop in Hovd town; (b) 14.07.89 in his *ger* in Hovd town, W. Mongolia.

Baatar. Altai Urianghai. 11.07.93 at the "Festival of Three Manly Sports" (*naadam*), Bulgan district, Bayan Ölgii province, W. Mongolia.

Baljir Udgan. Darhat shamaness, 80 yrs. 14.1093 in her *ger* by the river Harmai, Hövsgöl province, NW Mongolia.

Byambadorj. Bait Mongol. Director of Ulaangom Museum, Uvs province, W. Mongolia (a) 24.08.90 in the Museum; (b) 05.09.90 in Buddha's tent (*Burhan ger*) behind the Museum; (c) 29.09.93 in his flat in Ulaangom.

Düüdei. Bait Mongol. 25.08.90 in her *ger* in Uliasny Hev, the winter camp about 5 km east of Ulaangom, Uvs province.

Enebish, J. Torgut Mongol academic. 30.06.89 in the Mongolian Academy of Sciences, Ulaanbaatar.

Jamiyan. Dörbet Mongol (a) 20.08.90 in Harhiraa Hotel, Ulaangom, Uvs province; (b) 08.08.93 in his home in Hovd town, Hovd province, W. Mongolia.

Lhagva. Bait bard. 02.09.90 in his *ger* on top of a mountain in Manhan district, Uvs province.

Seseer, H. Altai Urianghai bard. 08.07.93 in his *ger* in Duut district centre, Hovd province.

Tsedendamba. Mingat. 24.07.93 in his *ger* on Altan Höhii mountain, Hovd province, W. Mongolia.

Tsoloo, J. Zakchin Mongol. 31.07.90 in the Institute of Language and Literature, Mongolian Academy of Sciences, Ulaanbaatar.

References

Banzarov, D. 1981 [1846]. "The Black Faith, or Shamanism among the Mongols." *Mongolian Studies* 7: 53-90.

Bawden, Charles R., trans. 1982. *Mongolische Epen. X. Eight North Mongolian Epic Poems.* Asiatische Forschungen 75. Wiesbaden: Harrassowitz.

Bormanshinov, Arash. 1982. "The Bardic Art of Eeljan Ovla." In Heissig 1982, 155-67.

Byambadorj. 1985. "Uvs nutgiin topshuur ihliin tuhai zarim medee" [Some information about the *topshuur* and *ihil* of Uvs]. Unpublished manuscript presented at the 7th Symposium on Asian Music, Ulaanbaatar and given to me in Uvs province, by the author.

Damdinsüren, Ts. 1985. "On the New Edition of the Mongolian Version *Geseriada.*" In Heissig 1985, 593-99.

Davaasüren, Y. 1992, "Töriin Soyorholt Tuul'ch" [State Prizewinner Epic Bard]. *Ardyn Erh*, 30 Jan: 2.

Dulam, S. 1987. "Conte, chant et instruments de musique. Quelques légendes d'origine mongoles." *Études Mongoles et sibériennes* 18: 33-47.

Hamayon, Roberte. 1990. *La chasse à l'âme. Esquisse d'une théorie du chamanisme sibérien.* Nanterre: Société d'ethnologie.

Hangin, G. 1986. *A Modern Mongolian-English Dictionary.* Indiana University Publ., Uralic and Altaic Series 150. Bloomington: Indiana University.

Heissig, Walther, ed. 1979. *Die mongolischen Epen. Bezüge, Sinndeutung und Überlieferung. Ein Symposium.* Asiatische Forschungen 68. Wiesbaden: Harrassowitz.

———. 1980 [1970]. *The Religions of Mongolia.* Trans. from German by G. Samuel. London: Routledge.

———, ed. 1981. *Fragen der mongolischen Heldendichtung. I.* Asiatische Forschungen 72. Wiesbaden: Harrassowitz.

———, ed. 1982. *Fragen der mongolischen Heldendichtung. II.* Asiatische Forschungen 73. Wiesbaden: Harrassowitz.

———, ed. 1985. *Fragen der mongolischen Heldendichtung. III.* Asiatische Forschungen 91. Wiesbaden: Harrassowitz.

———, ed. 1987. *Fragen der mongolischen Heldendichtung. IV.* Asiatische Forschungen 101. Wiesbaden: Harrassowitz.

———, ed. 1992. *Fragen der mongolischen Heldendichtung. V.* Asiatische Forschungen 120. Wiesbaden: Harrassowitz.

Horloo, P. 1985. "Traditions and peculiarities of Mongolian heroic epics." In Heissig 1985, 1-8.

Humphrey, C., with Urgunge Onon. 1996 [1995]. *Shamans and Elders.* Oxford: Clarendon.

Katuu, B. 1993. *Mongol Tuuliin Belgedel* [The Symbolism of Mongolian Epics]. Diss. Institute of Language and Literature, Mongolian Academy of Sciences, Ulaanbaatar.

Levin, Theodore. 1996. *The Hundred Thousand Fools of God: Musical Travels in Central Asia (and Queens, New York).* Bloomington: Indiana UP.

Narantuya, R. 1986. *Eriin Sain Han Harangui.* Ulaanbaatar: Ministry of People's Education.

———. 1988. "Mongol Tuuliin Bürtgel." *Aman Zohiol Sudlal* [Folklore Studies] 17.1-6: 79-1154.

Natsagdorj, Sh., ed. 1981. *BNMAY-yn Soyolyn Tüüh 1921-40* [Cultural History of Mongolia]. Ulaanbaatar: State Publishing House.

Nixon, A. 1984. "Tsuur." *The New Grove Dictionary of Musical Instruments.* Vol. 2. London: Macmillan. 663.

Pegg, Carole A. 1991. "The Revival of Ethnic and Cultural Identity in West Mongolia: The Altai Uriangkhai *tsuur*, the Tuvan *shuur* and the Kazak *sybyzgy.*" *Journal of the Anglo-Mongolian Society* 12: 71-84

———. 1992a. "The Epic is Dead, Long Live the üliger?" In Heissig 1992, 194-206.

———. 1992b. "Mongolian Conceptualizations of Overtone-Singing (*xöömii*)." *British Journal of Ethnomusicology* 1: 31-55.

——. 1995. "Ritual, Religion and Magic in West Mongolian (Oirad) Heroic Epic Performance." *British Journal of Ethnomusicology* 4: 77-99.

——. (forthcoming). *Mongolian Music, Dance and Oral Narrative: Performing Diverse Identities.* Seattle: U of Washington P [with compact disc].

Pozdneyev, A. M. 1971 [1892-96]. *Mongolia and the Mongols.* Vol. 1. Ed. John R. Krueger. Trans. from Russian by J. R. Shaw and D. Plank. Indiana University Publ., Uralic and Altaic Series 61. Bloomington: Indiana University.

Qurcabagatar, L. 1992. *Qatagin arban gurban Ataga tngri-yin tayilga* [The Hatgin Clan Sacrificial Ceremonies for the Thirteen Ataagods]. Huhhot: Inner Mongolia Culture Publishing House.

Rintchen, B., ed. 1963. *Folklore Mongol 2.* Asiatische Forschungen 11. Wiesbaden: Harrassowitz.

Shoolbraid, G. M. H. 1975. "Form and General Content: The Burjat-Mongol Epic." *The Oral Epic of Siberia and Central Asia.* Indiana University Publ., Uralic and Altaic Series 111. Bloomington: Indiana University. 18-39.

Tserel, B. 1964. "Altai Hailah." *Terüünii Malchin.* Ulaangom.

Vladimirtsov, B. Ya. 1983-84. "The Oirad-Mongolian Heroic Epic." *Mongolian Studies: Journal of the Mongolian Society* 8: 5-58.

Zagdsüren, U. 1972. "Preface to Mongol Script Version of *Bum Erdeni* and *Dani-Hürel.*" *Aman Zohiol Sudlal* 7 (10). Ulaanbaatar: State Publishing House.

Recordings:

Desjacques, Alain. 1986. *Mongolie. Musique et chants de l'Altai.* Orstom-Sela CETO811. LP.

——. Mongolie. *Mongolie. Chants Kazakhs et tradition épique de l'Ouest.* Ocor 558660. LP.

Pegg, Carole A. (forthcoming). CD to accompany *Mongolian Music, Dance and Or Narrative: Performing Diverse Identities.*

11 SINGING EPICS AMONG THE PALAWAN HIGHLANDERS (PHILIPPINES): MUSICAL AND VOCAL STYLES

Nicole Revel

The Singing of the Epic *Mämiminbin*

During our 1970-72 stay in the Palawan Highlands, *Mämiminbin* was the first epic that the singer Mäsinu sang for us.[1] On that November evening, I immediately perceived that we were in the presence of a vocal and narrative tradition different from the one we were familiar with from having recorded the singer Usuy. Mäsinu continues the tradition of his grandparents in Mandalawän, Sunggud, the father of his mother, and of Lapung, Ranggi, the brother-in-law of this maternal grandfather, as well as the beautiful chanting of Kundipal of Ilug, whom I also met and recorded at that time (see Table 1).

The singing of the tale is characterized by a much faster delivery and a voice less serene and also less shadowy than Usuy's; a natural voice, whose timbre is "high-pitched mixed with low-pitched" (*gintangan ät mäsning bäkäq mälämbäg*), as well as firm and constant. The tension and equilibrium of his vocal gesture do not vary according to the characters or moments of the epic in the course of one and the same night.

> My breath is of average length, not as long as Usuy's. If I forced it, if I pushed it, I would be out of breath before ending my utterance. Usuy had a "high-pitched" (*mäsning*) voice and "his breath was long" (*mäbwat ginawa yä*); his singing was "melodious to hear" (*mäligu kingän myu*); it was "beautiful" (*mägayun*)! His narrative had many inversions (*tuturan yä, mäkansang bäliwät-bäliwät*), "because he was trying to balance the voice's effects and the narrative" (*sabab nägtitimbäng lyäg yä bäkäq tuturan*).

Usuy used a large number of "fillers" (*dalahitän*), enabling him to sing to the end of his breath while maintaining a perfect mastery of his melodious voice and the utterance of a semantically very sophisticated story, "embellished" by the numerous fillers.

---

[1] On the transcription of Palawan, see below pp. 204f.

Mäsinu's father, Intaräy, was also a singer of tales, but he died prematurely in a cholera epidemic. Although he inherited his father's voice, Mäsinu did not really learn from him. It was with his three grandparents and Märadya Kälang in Kangrian, the grandfather of his wife Lamut, thus his "grandfather" by marriage, that he acquired his repertoire.

However, an apprenticeship calls for a particular attitude, characterized by the "ardent desire" to learn (*iräg*) and by perseverance. Without this attraction, this inclination based on auditory pleasure, and intense repetitive practice, on which memory is based, the internalization of these long chanted narratives cannot be reached. This embodiment of orality is a major experience (for Mäsinu's repertoire, see Table 2):

> In the past, I whistled to myself in the house, in the fields or in the forest. I whistled tunes, imitated the voices of the characters and "repeated them ceaselessly to set their memory in my body" (*ulit-ulit ampang mägsunsunran na baran*). "Reiteration" (*pägsansawlingan*) allows "memorization" (*pägrändäm*).
>
> I learned *Mämiminbin* and *Tyäw* by ear in this way, from my maternal grandfather Sunggud in Mandalawän. His voice was "very high-pitched" (*mäsning banar*) and his "narrative was very clear" (*mätlang tuturan yä*).
>
> In Kangrian, at the beginning of my marriage, I listened to Märadya Kälang for two years, my wife's grandfather, Lambung and Lunggayaq's father. He sang *Ugang-ugang* and *Datuq ät Tägpalawan*, which I memorized.
>
> From my grandfather Payas, my father's first cousin in Kämantiyan, I learned *Käsawakan* (Broken branches). His voice had a "low timbre" (*mälämbäg*) and his narrative was "straight to the point" (*mätignaq tuturan yä*).
>
> From Ranggi, my mother's uncle in Amrang, I learned *Ladpan*. His breath was short.
>
> From Payas' younger brother in Kämantiyan, with Kabut who was also a first cousin of my father's, I learned *Ulu ät Danum* (Source of the River); his voice was "high-pitched" (*mäsning*) and "his narrative clear and direct" (*mätlang bäkäq mätignaq tuturan yä*).
>
> In Kämantiyan I had the chance to hear Mäqisläm, his voice was half-high and half-low, like my voice, and his narrative had neither "inversions" (*bäliwät*) nor "melodic ornaments" (*kaya lilibu*), and I memorized *Lumalayag* (The Sailing Outrigger Boat Datuq), as well as *Käkulasyan* and the long story of "Binyag and the Muslims."
>
> In this same village, I heard and memorized *Mängingirang* (The Hunter with Dogs) and a long excerpt of *Limbuhanän* with Bägsäk, who had "a long breath" (*mäbwat lyäg yä*) and "a low timbre" (*mälämbäg*).
>
> When Kundipal visited us, I learned with him a repertoire that came from the Ilug valley, from the other side of *Käbätangan* (Mount Mantalingayan). Thanks to him, I learned *Käpangdangan* (The Pandanus For-

est) and *Käbätangan*. His voice was very high-pitched but his narrative was beautiful, sparse, clear, and transparent. I very much admired his way of singing.

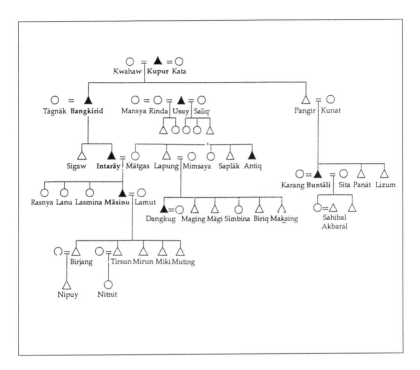

Table 1: Genealogy of the bards (▲)

Epic	Duration	Recording/ editing status
Mämiminbin	½ night	transcribed and translated
Tyäw	½ night	transcribed and translated
Käswakan	½ night (excerpt)	transcribed and translated
Binyaq bäkäq		
Käqislam-islaman	2 nights	synopsis
Lumalayag	1 night	synopsis
Ulu ät Danum	1 night	synopsis
Käkulasyan	½ night	synopsis
Käpangdanan	½ night	synopsis
Mängingiräng	½ night	synopsis
Käbätangan	1 night	synopsis

Ugang-Ugang	½ night	no synopsis
Datuq ät Tägpalawan	½ night	no synopsis
Lädpan	1 night	no synopsis
Limbuhanän	1 night	no synopsis

Table 2: Mäsinu's repertoire

The quality of voice, timbre and ornamentation, as well as the quality of the narratives and their unity of meaning and composition, are all equally appreciated. The syllabic delivery allows the ear to capture and comprehend the narrative, because music and text are in tight correlation, united by a reciprocal constraint.

The epic *Mämiminbin*, as sung by Mäsinu, is structured in blocks formed by correlated words and notes, generally emitted in a quick syllabic delivery, and characterized by an opening formula, followed by repetition of the same note, and a closing formula on a long note.

At the beginning of the chant, one perceives a first block formed by two units (correlated words and notes), separated by a short breath. These two successive units are of variable length, as the following blocks show. A longer pause allows the latter to be brought out.

One can observe that a four-hour chant, lasting for half the night (and corresponding to a text of 111 typed pages), is textually as long as a performance by Usuy which lasted for about seven hours (110 typed pages). The minimal unit, however, is still the "breathing group" as I defined it in 1983.[2] This "breathing group" had caught my attention from the very first days of transcribing the epic *Kudaman* in 1971.

Different "motifs" can be noticed, motifs that depend on the characters embodied by the bard. In Mäsinu's chant, there is no melismatic ornamentation or varying pitch on one syllable, in contrast to certain melodic phrases sung by Usuy in *Kudaman* and *Ayäk*, or the melody of *Pulyäg*. In any case, the Highlanders say that Mäsinu's voice could "make circumvolutions" (*mälikäg-likäg*), and his narrative, whether in its dialogues or narration, is appreciated for its high quality. It has "content" or rather "flesh"(*mäqunäd*); it is "direct" (*mätignaq*), "clear" (*mätlang*) and consistent. Hence, it is also appreciated for its seamless elegance during performance and rigorous link between sequences in the unfolding of the plot.

There is a genuine "plot outline" (*upama ät batangan*), an "Ariadne's thread," if I may make this analogy (*iqibutän ät tuturan*), to move the plot along to the "heart of the epic" (*mata ät tultul*, literally 'the eye of the epic'). Several "itineraries" (*dalan ät tultul*) or "pathways of the epic

---

[2]Revel-Macdonald 1983, 38-44 ("Le texte et la musique").

narrative" (*panäw ät tultul*) come to his mind, from which he makes his choices.

Mäsinu's song, in contrast to Usuy's, has a verbal texture that is dense in meaning and quite devoid of fillers, which would allow a more ornamented vocal expression, but also require a longer breath.

As an illustration I will give two examples. Ex. 1 is the chant of the hero of the epic, Ex. 2 the chant of Mämiminbin's pets, the Pagoda Doves (*Balud* or *Putyän*) (for texts and translations, see below). The musical transcription was made by Dr Jose Maceda. In the melody, an interval structure f-g-a-c can be observed.

Ex. 1:

Hin a- tin kwan yä Ba-a- lud ma-a- ya la-mang bärä- san ku dim- yu bä.

faster

Hin sabab kwan yä näkwit nä dag pä-säsa-nang ku at-wä ät lungsud

Sä- ä- lu- us ka-yang ga pägbä-sän ku dim-yu bä.

Hin sägwaq kwanyä ba-qa-tin- si da- a- kä- n bä-paq di-ki

Hin nä längku mäsän-da-lan ät sä- läd a- täy ku bä.

Mänunga kwan yä i- pu-hun ku dimyu mängäbyaqku nä ät

mändu- u- ru- ruk ät dä- pu-gan ku bä.

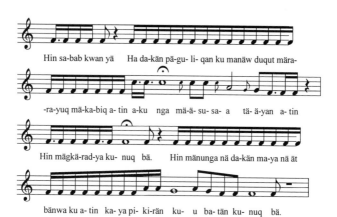

Hin sa-bab kwan yä   Ha da-kän pä-gu- li- qan ku manäw duqut mära-

-ra-yuq mä-ka-biq a- tin a-ku   nga   mä-ä- su- sa- a   tä- ä-yan a- tin

Hin mägkä-rad-ya ku- nuq bä.   Hin mänunga nä da-kän ma-ya nä ät

bänwa ku a- tin   ka- ya pi- ki-rän   ku- u ba- tän ku- nuq bä.

Ex. 2:

Hin nä kwan yä ampuq banar na-ri   it bä-räs känyä ä bä ät Balud in   bä

Hin damänkwanyä kaya nä pä- lan iba kay   ba-tän tu-mi-räng

kä nä damän in   bä.

Hin a- tin mägkädya- ri nä kwan yä näsambungankäy ikäw sägwaq

kas kä di- mu   ät pä- ä- ä-nga-gäw ga- si   Hi sa-bab mä-ya-qat

mä-su- gid ät mä- ra-yuq mä- ka- biq bä.

Hin damän di-ki ga- si   ba-tä- än   a- ti- in ku-nuq kä iba käy di- mu   bä.

Hin a- tin bäq bängsa kay la- mang   taqäw   batän mäsäwran kay nä sän- tin   bä.

The Musical Accompaniment

The musical accompaniment of the ring flute, *päbayaqan ät bäbäräk*, is played by Kälulut, who, knees pulled to his chest, lies beside the epic singer and plays the notes slightly after the bard. When listening to them, it becomes clear that the flute player and the singer have not tried to tune up before starting. The flute accompaniment traces the chanted narrative and has no autonomy. This acolyte flute "voice," which I have mentioned in the past in the context of the authentic tradition of the Highlanders' epic singing,[3] began to disappear in the 1970s. Twenty-nine years later, it has now completely disappeared in the Mäkägwaq and Tämlang valleys to where I return regularly.

The hypothesis put forward by B. Lortat-Jacob with reference to the Balkans that "to the epic genre of oral traditions corresponds an epic form" seems to be partly verified by the Palawan tradition.[4] His twelve general points which relate function and structure to one another are of relevance here, notably points 2, 3, 4 and 10. They concern the theatricalization of the solo voice, the shortness of breathing pauses, to be discussed later, the links and constraints uniting the narrative and the music, and the syllabic delivery and its relative slowness connected to the comprehension of the text. In the case of the Palawan, a metric form is absent but the vocal motif of each character is constitutive for the genre. Syllabism, or the use of a repeated note within a narrow range, and the reduced resort to melisma also characterize Mäsinu's singing.

The dynamics are also regular, but the various motifs identifying the characters and their dialogues in direct style alternate with an impersonal tone. This tone, which the bard gives to his voice and the narrative as the plot and the action of the characters progress, is slightly distanced; it is the "neutral" tone necessary to the epic genre.

Finally, one can also observe a "simultaneous sequencing of music and text," but this seems to be constant, like a sound icon, a melodic formula

---

[3]See Revel-Macdonald 1983; Revel 1992.
[4]Lortat-Jacob 1992, 10-13.

specific to the character but variable in the setting of sequences depending on the "paths" (*dalan*) chosen by the bard to bring the intended action in his narrative to a close.

In spoken languages, sound, life and movement give us iconic representations. Hence, I was able to show the importance of ideophones in Palawan culture.[5] Iconic representations certainly come into play here, as ideophones are an attempt to reproduce the sounds of the world, of birds, of natural elements, and to denote a specific quality of the object or thing represented. I am referring here to C. S. Peirce and his subdivision of the sign into icon, index and symbol. This trichotomy designates different aspects of symbolism and not different kinds of symbols. This subdivision should be understood as a functional distinction; in Peirce's words: "I call a sign which stands for something merely because it re-sembles it, an *icon* . . . . So in contemplating a painting, there is a moment when we lose the consciousness that it is not the thing, the distinction of the real and the copy disappears . . . ."[6] The icon has an expressive sym-bolism which contrasts with the referential symbolism where the arbi-trariness of the sign is absolute and manifest. Nonetheless, there is no universal icon.

As Aristotle wrote, "poetry seems to owe its origin to two particular causes, both natural. From childhood men have an instinct for represen-tation, and in this respect man differs from the other animals that he is far more imitative and learns his first lessons by representing things."[7] The basic notion is that of *mimesis* applied to an artistic activity, mainly music, dance, and the performing arts: "We have, then, a natural instinct for representation, and for tune and rhythm . . . and starting with these instincts men very gradually developed them until they produced poetry out of their improvisations."[8] Through the imitation of an object, or a model, one obtains the re-presentation of this model, in this case, the emblematic profile of each character in the sung narrative.

Here, the imitation is realized by the solo voice and the sound of the flute, thus by rhythm, melody and language. If the icon is an image of its object, in the proper sense of the Greek word *eikon* 'to be similar, to resemble', then melodic formulae identifying characters are indeed icons, sound images, substitutes for puppets, endowed with a figurative symbol-ism, given that sound motifs identify the heroes.

Mäsinu's performance demands "attentive listening," at once auditive and abstract, throughout the night. One has to follow the "journey," the itinerary of the characters. There is a genuine mental strategy at the base

---

[5]See Revel 1993, 15-20, and Revel (forthcoming).
[6]Peirce 1933, 211 (3.362).
[7]Aristotle, *Poetics* 1448b; quoted from Fyfe 1932, 13.
[8]Fyfe 1932, 15.

of all memorization, which the singer uncovers and which the analyst has to decipher.

The little ring flute, *bäbäräk*, is distinct from the longer ring flute, *suling*. It is reserved in this area for the "bird touch," or "bird scale" (*läpläp bägit*). Made from a section of bamboo (*bungbung, bingsag* or *sumbiling*) with a narrow cavity and a ring from another section of bamboo, the flute shows in its construction — that is, in the placement of its holes and the distance between them — an implicit theory of the scale. Hence, one is confronted with a certain savoir-faire which reveals the possession of a musical theory. There are three holes on the frontal side of the tube and one hole on its dorsal side. When a *bäbäräk* is made, after the middle hole is bored on the dorsal side with a red-hot iron rod, the second, third, and fourth holes are pierced on the frontal side at equal distances.[9] The equidistance between the holes equals the unit of measurement called "one finger-joint" (*luwäd*) or one "thumb-joint" (*änanaklaq ät käramut*), starting from the middle hole. According to Mäsinu, only Bäblag in Käkabwatan and Kälulut in Banglas knew how to accompany the voices of "the epic heroes" (*tutultulän*) on the flute.

When the men go to collect the almaciga resin in the *käbäktikan*[10] forest, they spend entire nights out beneath the stars or the moonlight. The beauty of the almaciga tree forests, the humming of the wind across the tops of the trees, the friction of the branches, the *ringär*, those voices emanating from the aerial canopy are intense poetic moments captured by the bards. They draw their musical inspiration from this soundscape. This attentive listening to the beauty of natural sounds generated a musical scale for the lute and the little ring flute, *bäbaräk*, reserved for their imitation, the "bird scale."[11] This leads to the creation of new vocal melodies through the experience of the *paläpläp*, the favour of a *Taw Mänunga*, the gift (*bingäy*) of a "Good Spirit of the Forest," an Invisible Being from the Mountains, who gives knowledge and know-how to true human beings. This revelation through "dream" (*taginäp*) — or rather by a state of illuminated consciousness between waking and sleeping — has the forest as its privileged place, where one receives gifts from the Good Spirits. It is a place where one gets something by hunting, food gathering, or fishing. It is the place of exchange *par excellence* between the two human kinds who, according to myth, were to follow a prohibition to marry from Ämpuq, but transgressed it.[12] Consequently, the "true human beings" that we are have lost the ability to see the "other beings" around

---

[9]Revel 1992, 30-34.
[10]*Käbäktikan* 'the forest of Almaciga trees' < *bäktik*, Agathis damara (Lamb.) (L.C. Rich).
[11]See the bilingual French/English booklet of the CD ed. by Nicole Revel-Macdonald and Jose Maceda in 1988 [1991].
[12]Revel 1992, 15-52; Macdonald 1974.

us, with whom the rules of equal and courteous sharing must always be respected.

Melodies, as well as narratives, vary according to the singer of tales. Part of the sung performance is left to the "imagination" (*kira-kira*) or creativity of the bard. In this way, Usuy developed new melodies in *Kudaman*. When Buntäli sung this epic and transmitted it to Usuy, there were only three "melodies" (*lyäg*). Usuy enriched it by creating as many melodic motifs as characters, which were quite numerous. After Usuy's death, Buntäli no longer attempted to sing *Kudaman*. Instead, he devoted himself passionately to the performance of *Datuq ät Pänärangsangan* (Sunset Datuq), an epic of six to seven nights, which I have also recorded and completely transcribed and which will soon be translated. However, in 1997 Buntäli passed away. Concerning the epic *Limbuhanän*, Jose Rilla has listened to several versions of it, with various sung motifs identifying the heroes, and they were different for each singer. Hence, I believe that I can confirm that "the melodic-rhythmic formulae are modular, in the interplay of variants."[13]

Buntäli's version of *Kudaman* treated in song the ritual of making honey wine (*simbug*). Each year in the Highlands, the blooming of the huge trees calls for a feast of thanksgiving for *Ämpuq ät Burak*, the "Master of Flowers," and the celebration of the *Simbug* ritual in his memory. Usuy transposed the action into the framework of the ritual of the "Commemoration of the Master of Rice" (*Tamwäy ät Ämpuq ät Paräy*) and the making of "rice beer" (*tinapäy*) for seven years in a row.

One can observe that the statement by B. Lortat-Jacob holds true that "[t]he text and the music, insofar as neither the one nor the other is fixed in time, are in a relationship of structural homology. Here, the setting into a sequence of music and text can theoretically be reformulated in a different way in each performance."[14] Each vocal icon has to correspond exactly both to the character embodied by the singer and to his utterance. If this matching is not perfect, the narrative becomes incomprehensible and the audience confused or scornful. In his interpretation of *Mämiminbin* in 1972, Mäsinu made two hundred and eleven shifts in melodic motifs in three and a half hours.

---

[13]Lortat-Jacob 1992, 12.
[14]*Ibid.*

Listening to the Epic

For all present listening to the epic is a source of deep emotional, intellectual and aesthetic pleasure. "One can be moved to tears," say the Highlanders, and the audience's expectations are high, both for the beauty of the voice and the abstract rigour of the action revealed by the sung narrative.

> In the past, the Highlanders always wanted to listen to a *tultul* and all of them asked me to come, my father-in-law, my brothers-in-law, in Amrang, Banglas, in Kangrian. I used to sing often . . . . When you came to live in Bungsud, I sang often. Starting in 1986, I was headman of the village (*pänglimaq*) and I was involved with the Piadpo agricultural project in Samarinana in the foothills. Then, I only sang very rarely. When you came back to see me, I sang again.
>
> Nowadays I feel that the youngsters no longer listen. I sing and they sleep. It is impossible to sing for very long if one does not hear the *tubag*.

This "presence in return," this response, this accompaniment by the others, this sharing shows the interest and wonder of a warm, involved audience. Should the bard be greeted with silence, he feels worried and anguished. It is like "the response of a dead tree stump" (*pägsimbat ät tuwäd*), "but behind it hides a *Länggam*, an 'Evil-doer', who does respond!" The latter becomes a menace and the bard stops and interrupts his song. Better to abstain, to remain silent . . .

Similarly, it would be impossible to sing an epic on one's own. The *tubag*, the brief comments and exclamations of a captivated audience, the shared humour, joy and sadness, are indispensable to the bard as he sings. They provide psychological, intellectual and emotional support. It is an act of sharing. The host usually comes to sit near the bard, who is lying down, and he joins him and accompanies him. When there are many visitors — many guests on the eve of a wedding ceremony before the jural discussion —, the bard sings. Then community sharing reinforces the cohesion of the social group and of alliances that are being woven whilst listening to just such a story.

This sense of belonging and cultural identity are reaffirmed during the major rituals of *Tambiläw ät lungsud*, a ceremony for curing "the world" represented by several hamlets, and during the *Tambiläw ät tabang*, a ceremony with a shamanistic voyage "to cure" a sick person, who is surrounded by his relatives and friends. For such occasions, the men prepare *lutlut*, a unique ceremonial dish made of sticky rice, cooked with coconut milk in bamboo internodes. All night, they look after the cooking of dozens of bamboo pieces. Gongs are played, and then the bard chants a *tultul* in the presence of a large audience, which he has to entertain until daybreak. While they watch over the cooking of *lutlut*, the ritual meal *par excellence*, men and women listen to good music, which makes them joyful, and to magnificent stories, which make them think.

A visitor is welcomed with the same playful and thought-provoking attitude. To please him, to make his arrival special, and to be as hospitable as possible, the bard chants a *tultul* and sometimes invites the visitor to sing in return. In this way, one reaffirms a moral identity and a highly esteemed code of values, which are considered worthy of perpetuation and praise, the *Adat ät Kägunggurangan* (The Tradition of the Ancestors).

During each performance, the bards listen to one another, in this way enriching their repertoires. When they return to the hamlet — after a sojourn marked by hard labour in daytime and poetry in the night — the men check the wild boar traps (*bawäg*) which were laid in the forest, and if they have been successful, they will spend the following night in the large meeting house listening to an epic or tale (*susugirän*), for everybody's amusement and entertainment. The lovesongs from the coast, the *kulilal* songs, are always excluded from these hunting wakes. The *Adat ät pinäri* (The Custom of Prey) in the "wilderness" (*talun*) demands an immediate offer of thanksgiving from the Highlanders to Läli, the Master of Boars (*Ämpuq ät Byäk*). Because it is necessary to maintain an equilibrium in the biotope, one has to soothe the Master of Game, seduce him, avoid his fury, and gain his favour. After all, one has "preyed" on a pet of his and one has to give him a generous and courteous gift in return, an "offering of thanksgiving" (*päsalamat*). While, in the presence of Mädyatu, the eldest, the food was shared out equally to all members of the hamlet, the head and "hindquarters" (*tuwis*) rested on a trellis above the hearth and had to roast all night on a low fire. On the evening of October 21, 1972, Mäsinu lay down, as is the custom, on the lateral floor of the tiny hut of Dankug, his left arm folded across his forehead and his body completely relaxed, diaphragm open, his leg bent, with just a piece of cloth for a blanket, and sang *Tyäw* (The Mayna Bird), a story of hunting and adultery.

A thanksgiving offering in an epic is coupled with "sympathetic magic" (*päsiring*). In the *tultul* of the Highlands, the heroes only eat boar and never young tree shoots; among islanders, they enjoy meaty and succulent slices of fish. The men capture boars, while the women (*Linamin*) do "fishing" (*mänyud*), in keeping with the Bihang ways based on the myth of the formation of landscapes, the myth of *Tambug*.[15] One sings to appease the Master of Game, to respect a relationship of joint exchange with the supernatural world, and to bring luck. Hence, it is a symbolic

---

[15]See Revel 1992, 110-19; Macdonald 1988, 17-93.

efficacy that is aimed at, an attempt to unite the human beings and the Master of Prey on several different levels of both the lived experience and the symbolic, in a fair, balanced, and hopeful relationship, one that is close to Siberian shamanism, as described and analysed by R. N. Hamayon.[16]

Following the example of the heroes, only one thing will do to satisfy "the appetite" (*säbläk*): to catch a wild, meaty boar, the most succulent and rarest accompaniment to rice in daily life! The chant is a gift in return, endowed with symbolic efficacy for the days to come.

The Recording and Preservation of Song, Performance, and Text

The beauty of oral poetry is experienced during its performance — it is ephemeral and changing, rigorous and spontaneous. In a recent study of *Kudaman*, I proposed the notion of "multiple drafts," a notion which I find important and to which I would like to return here.[17]

In a situation of oral communication, the notion of "multiple drafts" is inherent to our condition as speaking beings. In daily life, one's utterances are made in a precise context in space and time, with a specific intention and according to a particular emotional climate. As utterances follow one after the other, decisions are made and modulated by the context and the relationship. The receiver is taken into consideration and the discursive situation is genuinely a situation of interlocution. When the bard sings a narrative, he, too, finds himself in a lengthy discursive process and in a situation of interlocution. We have just seen how without an audience physically present, and intervening by speech, the bard would be unable to get to the end of the story that he wishes to transmit and make heard. As he performs, the bard must engage and captivate his audience from the very beginning. Through the ease of his diction, the eloquence of his words, and the constant perfection of his vocal gesture, he must establish and maintain a privileged state of communication all night long.

In order to convert a long aural story into a visible text, how does one present it graphically? What are the prosodic units of this "open text," which is free from the constraints of the written code? How is one to project them onto the space of a page? One has to capture the spoken text by listening and then realizing it in visible form. One has to find a way of symbolizing the singer's playing with words, his breathing, his manner of

---

[16]Hamayon 1990.

[17]See Revel 1996, in particular 123-27 (a paper originally given at the Turku Workshop, June 1993, under the title "On Mental Text, Oral Performance, Written Transcript and the Notion of Multiple Drafts").

chanting the semantic cohesion of a story, broken up into multiple utterances and phrases, as well as his art of speaking, i.e. diction, and his art of singing, i.e. music and voice.[18]

When listening, one must simultaneously feel the pleasure from the chanted text and have an understanding of it. The Palawan singer of tales is fully aware of this. To be listened to and understood, he must reach a constant and perfect vocal gesture, one of sustained intensity and quality.[19] The vision of the text has to reflect a measure, one or several melodic units, a stream of utterances linked to the "actants" and to the slowly unfolding action and the thickening plot. A special bond unites them in a continuum of sounds, silences and meaning.

The Palawan language is part of the Austronesian family of languages, extending from Formosa to Madagascar and to Easter Island through Oceania. The Philippine languages are part of the Western branch of this vast family and are divided into three groups: the languages of the North, the Centre, or Meso-Philippines, and the languages of the South. Typologically, these languages belong to the agglutinative type, which, in an interplay of affixes (prefixes, infixes, suffixes) and inflexions, generates compound words from root words or (real or virtual) derivational bases. This is to say that these languages have a complex morphology as well as a pronounced case system.

As the phonological system of the Palawan language had been established during my first months of field work among the Palawan Highlanders (1970-71), I could immediately proceed to a phonological transcription of the epic into alphabetical characters. The system of transcription is the following:[20]

The Palawan phonological system comprises sixteen consonants in four correlated series, voiceless: /p/ /t/ /k/ /q/, voiced: /b/ /d/ /g/, continuous oral consonants (and semivowels): /s/ /r/ /l/ /h/ /w/ /y/, and nasal consonants: /m/ /n/ /ng/. From the point of view of place of articulation, these consonants can be classified into five groups: bilabial, apico-alveolar, prepalatal, velar, and glottal consonants. The transcription of the glottal stop is /q/; the transcription of the velar nasal stop is /ng/.

The vocal system includes four vowels which form oppositions by two distinctive features — anterior vs. posterior — and by two levels of aperture — open vs. closed:

---

[18]For the notion of "open text", see Tedlock 1983, 7: "Not a text whose notion closes in upon features that can be assigned certified membership in self-sufficient codes such as those of syntax and scansion, but a text that forces even the reading eye to consider whether the peculiarites of audible sentences and audible lines might be good speaking rather than bad writing."

[19]See Revel 1993.

[20]Revel-Macdonald 1979, 46 and 60; Revel 1985.

$$/i/ \qquad\qquad /u/$$
$$/a/ \quad /\ddot{a}/$$

The sign /ä/ corresponds to a back [a]. Stress is not distinctive.

In addition to phonological features, prosodic features must also be identified and properly analysed. Typical of the performance of Palawan singers is their full mastery of a vocal technique based on breathing groups of utterances of variable lengths. These consist of sentences inserted between an opening syllable [*hin*] and either the closing syllable [*bä*], as in Mäsinu's style, or else [*in*], as in the styles of Usuy and Buntäli. The closing syllabe is an "auditive" punctuation signalling the end of a vocal utterance endowed with meaning. Simultaneously, it has the value of a rhyme, for it creates a homophony at the end of each breathing group of words, no matter what their length. It is followed by a respiratory pause, a silence of variable length and weight. Through a lexicometric analysis, we compiled the following descending frequencies: 941 [*hin*], 71 [*hu-*], 49 [*ha-*], 31 [*hi-*], 15 [*hud-*], 13 [*han-*], or 1120 opening syllables through an "exhaled attack." This represents the same number of intakes of breath, followed by the air passing through the vocal cords before they are fully closed. In fact, it is an exhaled [h] which is sung and not an aspirated one. There are 1192 occurrences of [*bä*] as closing syllable.

The transcription I propose of semantic and vocal units which are not governed by regular metrics is attentive to and follows the presence of each silence, no matter how short, and of each intake of breath by the bard. Each block or breathing group of words ends with a [*bä*] and a slightly longer breath. A new line not preceded by a period in a breath unit indicates that the silence is brief and resumption of the text instantaneous. It means that the entire stanza which makes up the breathing group of words is not yet finished. The unit of metre is hence not the verse line, governed by measurable metre — there is no regular metre in the strict sense in these epics — but an utterance in prose of variable length, either in the direct style of the dialogues or in the narrative style of descriptions and addresses to the audience.

Singing the epic, which consists essentially in shaping a dialogue, incorporates bisyllabic words which we may call "fillers" or "tags."[21] These are more or less necessary, depending on the bard. The variation in frequency of these words is closely tied to his breath capacity and the length of the "breathing group of words" which he emits. Usuy, who had a very long breath capacity, used many fillers and as many melodic

---

[21]Basically meaningless words that fill up the line (*chevilles* in French).

ornamentations; they disrupt the translated text considerably. As a comparative accompaniment to the sung text, I also chose to re-establish the syntactic text, stripped of fillers, when *Kudaman* was published (1983). Nonetheless, the translation of dialogues and narrative parts was almost completely barren of these often problematic "short words." Thanks to my increased experience, I was less hampered by the fillers in Mäsinu's translation, also because he has a smaller breath capacity and a quicker delivery of speech. Still, I chose to remove them in French and in English because from listeners of a song one becomes a reader of dialogues, finally reading out loud. I kept *kunuq*, 'they say' or 'the story tells', and *kwan yä*, 'he says'. The fillers common to the two bards, as well as to Buntäli, whose repertoire I know well, are presented here. With the aid of lexicometrical analysis, I have set out the following hierarchy of frequencies: *atin*: 633 instances; *gasi*: 359 instances; *kunuq*: 353 instances; *batän*: 183 instances; *täyän*: 191 instances; *sälus*: 152 instances; *banar*: 67 instances. There is also *kwan* + a personal modality or proper name preceded by the particle of the personal name, *si* or *ni*, which has 699 occurrences and which I often left for clarity in the dialogues. These words, which are monolexemes and not compound words, do actually have a meaning and belong to definite grammatical categories:

> *atin*: 'this', demonstrative pronoun;
> *gasi*: 'also', aspectual particle of manner;
> *kunuq*: 'he says', direct utterance modality;
> *batän:* 'sorry', 'excuse me', modality of politness;
> *täyän*: 'may it please God!', 'so may it be!', wish and verbal modality of past conditional;
> *sälus:* 'mercy!', 'pity!', exclamatory particle;
> *banar*: 'truly', 'honestly', intensifying adverb.

In the epic, these words become charged with an emphatic value proper to the sung narrative. Furthermore, they support both the "melodic lines" sung by the bard and become ornamentations supporting his thinking process by according him a few fractions of a second to correctly utter his message while singing the story. Aspectual particles, exclamative particles, and interlocutive particles can all be treated as enunciative particles[22] of the sung narrative, giving it density and beauty. I will thus treat them more as prosodic particles which, in the absence of metre in Palawan epics, have a phatic and stylistic function.

In order to verify the transcription I am proposing here, I am presenting a sound document in its visual form as it appears on a computer

---

[22]Defined by M. J. Fernandez-Vest as "markers of discourse distinctive for their prosody, distribution, and specific meaning" (1994, 4-5).

screen. The photographic documents of the sound waves analysis in Ex. 2 were made by using Sonic Solution software programs thanks to the collaboration of the Audiovisual Department of the Bibliothèque Nationale de France. A copy has been deposited in the International Archives for Oral Traditions of the Nordrhein-Westfälische Akademie der Wissenschaften in Düsseldorf. The sound image develops on two axes, which are visualized and heard simultaneously: the vertical axis shows the amplitude, which is always maximal on full screen, and the horizontal axis shows the time, which varies with the musical segments. One can zoom in on segments of variable length, going from a general view of the whole song down to the most infinitesimal detail. This visualization allows a perfect montage and could be a great help to the transcriptor. It helped me to verify the adequateness — or inadequateness — of the transcript I had made; it reveals all the breath marks, pauses and "breathing groups of words" which I had perceived as the distinctive unit in the *tultul* of the Highlands.[23] Here, the opening formula is indeed [*hin*] and the closing formula becomes [*bä*]. Thus, eighteen photographs were made for illustration purposes. Starting from the melodic segments of each of six characters, one perceives the shape of the sound wave. We have proceeded by breathing groups and photographed three or two blocks covering the screen, depending on the characters.

In conclusion I would like to give as Ex. 3 and 4 the sound waves of the musical transcriptions presented above (see Ex. 1 and 2). The texts and translations follow the respective graphs.[24] For the transcription of the text, it is to be noted that a period indicates a brief pause at the end of a sung utterance and that [*hin*], beginning a new line, indicates a a brief intake of breath.

---

[23]Revel-Macdonald 1983, 43; this notion was formulated as early as 1948 by Michel Leiris and taken up again by Gilbert Rouget in 1966.

[24]In Ex. 1 the musical transcription of *käradya ät* in the last but one line of the text is missing; in Ex. 2 only the first two "stanzas" of the text are transcribed.

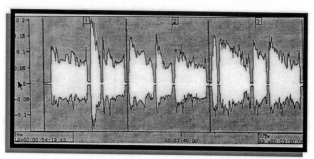

Ex. 3

Text:

[1]   Hin atin kwan yä Balud maya lamang bäräsän ku dimyu bä.
      Hin sabab kwan yä näkwit nä dag päsäsanang ku atwä ät lungsud
      Sälus kayang ga pägbäräsän ku dimyu bä.

[2]   Hin sägwaq kwan yä baqatinsi dakän bäpaq diki
      Hin nä längku mäsändalan ät säläd atäy ku bä.
      Mänunga kwan yä ipuhun ku dimyu mängäbyaq ku nä
      ät mändururuk ät däpugan ku bä.

[3]   Hin sabab kwan yä
      Ha dakän päguliqan ku manäw duqut märayuq mäkabiq atin aku nga
      mäsusa täyän atin
      Hin mägkäradya kunuq bä.
      Hin mänunga nä dakän maya nä ät käradya ät bänwa ku atin
      kaya nä pikirän ku batän kunuq bä.

Translation:

[1]   So, my little Pigeons, he says, I have something to tell you.
      I have lived for a long time in this world and found no happiness in it,
      yet I never whispered a word of it to you.

[2]   However, he says,
      My heart can no longer bear this loneliness.
      It is right that I tell you, and you first of all, that I am leaving in search
      of someone who will know how to make a home for me.

[3]   For, he adds,
      I will return from travelling, whether far away or nearby;
      all this work is such a problem, said he.
      It is good that someone takes care of my house for me.
      For then I will no longer need to worry about it.

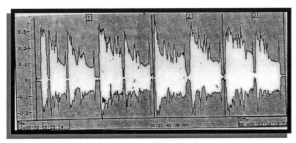

Ex. 4

Text:

[1] Hin nä kwan yä Ämpuq banar nä ari it bäräs känyä bä ät Balud in bä.
Hin damän kwan yä kaya nä pälan iba kay batän tumiräng kä nä damän in bä.
Hin atin mägkädyari nä kwan yä nä sämbungan kay ikäw, sägwaq kas kä dimu ät pängagäw gasi.
Hi sabab mäyaqat mäsugid ät märayuq mäkabiq bä.

[2] Hin damän diki gasi batän atin kunuq kä iba kay dimu bä.
Hin atin bäq bängsa kay lamang taqäw batän mäsäwran kay nä säntin bä.

[3] Hin tämäd diki bängsa kay damän taw atin bä.
Kunuq pägnununga bä dimu bä.
Anday ga kwan yä mänglägäs kunuq gasi bä.

Translation:

[1] Of course, Master, replied the Pigeons.
As for us, we will be without our companion since you are leaving us.
We may give you our consent but do not take the wife of another.
For that would be badly spoken of, both here and far away.

[2] As for us, we cannot be your travel companions.
If only we had the appearance of humans we would know how to behave abroad.

[3] But we do not look like humans.
Be careful, they say;
And above all, do not take anyone by force.

References

Fernandez-Vest, M. J. 1994. *Les particules énonciatives dans la construction du discours.* Paris: Presses Universitaires de France.

Fyfe, W. Hamilton, ed. and trans. 1932. Aristotle. *The Poetics.* "Longinus." *On the Sublime.* Loeb Classical Library 199. Rev. ed. London: Heinemann.

Hamayon, Roberte. 1990. *La Chasse à l'âme. Esquisse d'une théorie du chamanisme sibérien.* Nanterre: Société d'Ethnologie.

Lortat-Jacob, Bernard. 1992. "De la berceuse à l'épopée: questions de genre." *Revue de Musicologie* 78: 5-25.

Macdonald, Ch. 1974. "Mythes de création Palawan. Analyse structurale d'un mythe et de ses rapports avec le chamanisme." *Archipel* 8: 91-118.

———. 1988. *L' éloignement du ciel. Invention et mémoire des mythes chez les Palawan du sud des Philippines.* Paris: Maison des Sciences de l'Homme.

Peirce, Charles Sanders. 1933. *Exact Logic (Published Papers).* Vol. 3 of *Collected Papers of Charles Sanders Peirce.* Ed. Charles Hartshorne and Paul Weiss. Cambridge, MA: Harvard UP.

Revel-Macdonald, Nicole. 1979. *Le Palawan. Phonologie. Catégories. Morphologie (Philippines).* Paris, SELAF 1979: 46 et 60. Thèse de III cycle soutenue en juin 1974. Paris V, Université Réné Descartes, Sorbonne.

Revel-Macdonald, Nicole, and Jose Maceda, eds. 1988. *Musique des Hautes-Terres palawan, Philippines.* CD avec livret bilingue français/anglais. Paris: Musée de l'Homme. [1ère éd. 1988, 2ème ed. 1991.]

Revel [Revel-Macdonald], Nicole, ed. and trans. 1983. *Kudaman. Une épopée palawan chantée par Usuy,* Les Cahiers de l'Homme Paris: EHESS.

———. 1985. *"Burak ät bäräs." Fleurs de paroles. Histoire Naturelle Palawan.* Thèse d'état en Lettres et Sciences humaines, soutenue en 1985, Paris V, Université Réné Descartes, Sorbonne.

———. 1992. *Fleurs de Paroles. Histoire Naturelle Palawan. Chants d'amour/ Chants d'oiseaux.* Paris: Peeters/Selaf.

———. 1993. "Esthétique des voix épiques palawan." *Pour une Anthropologie des Voix.* Ed. N. Revel et D. Rey-Hulman. Paris: INALCO/ l'Harmattan. 109-34.

———. 1996. *"Kudaman:* An Oral Epic in the Palawan Highlands." *Oral Tradition* 11: 108-32.

———. (forthcoming). "Morphogenèse des langues: les idéophones." *Cognition incarnée, cognition située? Le témoignage des langues orales.* Table Ronde organisée par M. M. J. Fernandez-Vest au Congrès international des linguistes. Paris: Société de Linguistique de Paris/Céderom.

Tedlock, Denis. 1983. *The Spoken Word and the Work of Interpretation.* Philadelphia: U of Pennsylvania P.

WORD AND MUSIC:
THE EPIC GENRE OF THE *FULƁE* OF MASSINA (MALI)

Christiane Seydou

The abundant and varied literary production of the *Fulbe* of Massina (Mali)[1] offers a wide range of genres, some of which — including a musical component — precisely illustrate through the relationship between word and music the statuses and functions peculiar to this type of artistic expression.

The epic genre, which necessarily associates words with instrumental music, is the best example of this combination. However, before examining this genre specifically, it will be useful to define the place of the epic in relation to the other genres with which it forms a system that makes up the "lines of forces" of the Fulani culture in that region, in order to illustrate its most obvious traits.

The Literary Genres

I. "Spoken" Genres

A. Without Musical Accompaniment

a) Prose

It appears that the genres which rely solely on verbal expression are those which transmit knowledge and rules of social or private behaviour, and as such influence the thinking and the mental setup of the society: these are proverb, riddle, motto, aphorism, and prose narrative genres such as historical chronicle and especially the folktale (in all its dimensions, from the animal fable to the philosophical tale), the cultural importance of which for African societies is well known.

---

[1] The name of the West-African people whose epic poetry is the subject of this study is *Fulbe* in the plural, and *Pullo* in the singular; in French they are often called *Peul*, in English *Fulani*. Their language is called *Fulfulde*, in English also *Fula*. The letter <ɓ> denotes an implosive [b], a sound which can be described roughly as a [b] preceded by glottal closure.

b) Poetry

Poetic creation is highly elaborate amongst the *Fulɓe* of Mali; three main genres are distinguishable, of which two are completely "spoken":
– the *mergol* (pl. *mergi*), poetry which is declaimed in a monotone, is very rhythmical and deals with all subjects; it represents a genuine repository of the language and the culture;
– the *jammooje na'i* or "eulogies of bovines" (composed by young herdsmen), is characterized by a rapid and continuous mode of recitation that is based on the rhythm of breathing. It is further distinguished by a highly elaborate search for sound effects that take the very music of the words as their fundamental artistic criterion.[2]
– A third poetic genre, religiously inspired poetry, is not a purely spoken genre, for it calls upon vocal music (see II. A).

B. With Musical Accompaniment

The epic — which will be the subject of our discussion — belongs clearly to the narrative genres, although it also contains mottoes and, sometimes, elements belonging to the historical chronicle, as well as folktale-motifs; yet its foremost feature is, as will be seen, its necessary association with a precise expression of instrumental music.

II. Sung Genres

A. A cappella

A cappella singing is practised especially in the feminine sphere, be it in the playful context of children's singing — a repertoire of common heritage — , in the context of family life, or in indirect communication, such as lullabies or pounding songs, which are products of personal and individual improvisation.

Moreover there is an eminently scholarly genre which also resorts to a cappella singing: singing, that is, religious poetry, which assumes a highly codified form as far as metrics and rhyme are concerned. Borrowed from Arabic models, religious poetry prohibits all instrumental music, which is considered utterly profane and in some respects even "diabolic."

---

[2]See Seydou 1991.

B. With Instrumental Accompaniment

The *Fulɓe* delegate to "caste people" most of the instrumental music production; thus dance music is performed by an orchestra made up of "caste" musicians. Nevertheless "individual" music may be played by young *Fulɓe* who were born free, who play the flute or a small one-string lute, often all by themselves or in an evening get-together amongst friends, but never in a public exhibition.

Singing takes place in the same circumstances: combining word and music, it is practised either by the "griots" on festive occasions of public character or by young people, at more private gatherings amongst class-mates of their own age. Such gatherings take place exclusively prior to their coming into the world of adults, which is marked by marriage. The songs of the former are varied: praise songs or circumstantial songs accompanied by three- or four-stringed lutes (*hoddu*), festive songs sup-ported by a whole orchestra etc. As to the latter, these songs are accom-panied by a small one-string lute (*molaandu*), and the percussion part is performed simply by striking silver rings against half gourds placed upside down on the ground. The latter songs are characteristic of playful activities and the "text," essentially allusive, serves a restricted group-function referring to shared situations and experiences, carrying an in-tense emotional impact.

Through the range of the different types enumerated here, it can be noted that the contrast of certain situations will enlighten us about the status of music in relation to literary expression. The genres which do not involve any musical element, neither instrumental nor vocal, are those (e.g., folktale, chronicle, proverb . . .) which aim at the intellectual and mental faculties or imagination rather than at the emotional conscious-ness. They have a basically informative or "pedagogical" function, even if only implicitly. Where language is taken as sonorous material in itself, the music of the words suffices and the poetry is only declaimed (e.g., pastoral poetry). Where the content is essential (e.g., religious poetry), instrumental music is rejected as profane, even impious, and the affective effect, destined to better touch the audience, is taken over by vocal mu-sic: the voice is considered an instrument which can be mastered, con-trolled and submitted to the human will — in contrast to the lute which, according to legend, is connected with the world of spirits, that is the jinns. Finally, where the text has a semantic and pragmatic purpose, as is the case with the epic, the words are not kept separate from an expression of instrumental music, which "carries meaning" and "functions" just as well.

The Epic

1. The Griot

Amongst the *Fulɓe* of Mali, as well as the other neighbouring peoples (Malinke and Bambara), the epic is the apanage of a group known as "griots," a socio-professional class of musicians and verbal artists which is part of the wider class of people regarded as belonging to a "caste."[3] In Mali, it is the category of *maabuuɓe* griots (weavers and/or griots versed in genealogies and traditions) which keeps the monopoly of this knowledge and art. It should be noted that the use of the lute (*hoddu*, three-stringed lute), common to the *maabuuɓe* and *wammbaaɓe* griots (musicians and singers), is not exclusive to the recitation of the epic. On the other hand, a narrative, however heroic its protagonists may be, will not be a proper epic if it is not accompanied by a lute. But not every *maabo* griot is equally talented at words and music, so the performance of an epic may require the partnership of two artists, the one declaiming, the other playing the lute. Ideally, the text and musical part are performed by one and the same griot, which is the optimal way of harmonizing the effects of the words and the instrument.

2. The Motto

In traditional Fulani society, one of the main functions of the *maabo* griot is to play on his lute the musical motto of his "master." This is the head of a family to which, from father to son, he is bound in a very particular relationship of alliance and clientship that is founded on mutual dependence: economic dependence for the griot, social and psychological dependence for the "master."[4] The effect of this musical motto on the latter is made obvious by the verb designating the griot's performance: *yarnude*, 'to water', literally 'to make (someone) drink' (his music). For it is not a matter of hearing or listening to one's own musical motto, but of being "watered," "irrigated" with it, the verb *yarnude* evoking well that impression of physical impregnation and the feeling of the soul being flooded. It is also said that, through the motto, the *maabo* "takes," "seizes" (*nanngi*) his "master"; in fact the listener feels himself totally overwhelmed by the hearing of *his* motto. This musical motto, which is a kind of emblematic and highly glorifying designation, has a correspond-

---

[3]See Camara 1976.
[4]See on this subject the introduction of *Silâmaka et Poullôri*, ed. Christiane Seydou 1972, 9-38.

ing verbal motto, a concise, pithy and metaphorical formula, which is a sublimated definition of the person and identifies him in an ideal manner.[5]

To the musician's talent, the griot adds the mastery of words. Through the power of his words and specific status, the *maabo* wields with the motto a means of influencing not only the personality of the person whom he addresses, but even his destiny. Indeed, by declaiming the motto or by playing it on the lute for him, the griot compels the person to conform to the ideal image thus given of him. And through the exaltation produced by the motto, he forces him into fulfilling his most authentic self. Many anecdotes and episodes of epic narrative illustrate this.

3. The Epic: A Collective Motto

In this society, the epic seems to function as a collective motto, the epic narrative being an extended metaphor of what constitutes the distinctive identity of the Fulani people: the *pulaaku*. In fact not only are the heroes and their actions fully representative of the identifying ideology in which each Fulani recognizes himself, but everything tends to compel the audience, carried away by shared exaltation, to identify with the ideal image of those — always paroxysmal — characters and exploits.[6]

This parallel between the individual's motto on the one hand and the epic on the other, which is its equivalent for the community, is further supported by the fact that the epic narrative is sustained from beginning to end in its declamation by a musical theme, which is nothing but the hero's motto. Every melodic theme — which has proper name (*Ndonndoore, Saygalaare, Njaru*, etc.) — introduces and precedes the narrative itself, indicating immediately to the audience the person it will concern. Motifs common to the whole range of epic texts (e.g., muster drums, military cavalcades, vultures feeding on the dead on the battlefield, the implacable rhythm of destiny at work) are sometimes grafted onto this canvas, which is woven at will from an infinity of variations on the basic theme. At other times more personal and less conventional interpretations appear, kinds of original descriptive tableaux where language sometimes gives way to music. This is illustrated by the struggle of the hero Silâmaka with a monstrous snake, which the griot describes only with two verbs: "(the snake) throws him to the ground and coils itself around him." After this, ceasing to recite, the griot lets the strings speak under his fingers, stringing the notes out into long coils and striking the body or the hide of the lute in furious slapping. The Fulani public, experiencing these narratives throughout their lives, can recall the development of the story simply from hearing these musical themes and per-

---

[5] See Seydou 1977.

[6] How is the epic genre defined? For an example, see Seydou 1982.

ceive its significance. And the words of the griot come to fill out, as a superimposition, such and such an episode of the *geste* concerned in its verbal aspect.

The very concept of the epic genre in fact comprises this fundamental, constitutive element: the musical expression, more precisely, the instrumental music of the lute (*hoddu*). For, even if the text has a well determined structure and the hero a specific type of behaviour, this is not sufficient to define completely the narrative genre as epic. The epic requires the musical accompaniment supplied by the lute to be regarded as such. Both the griot and his audience consider moreover that the lute "speaks" (they say: "the lute speaks"). And just as for the individual the verbal motto is frequently considered to be a basically superfluous exposition of his musical motto (which is sufficiently evocative and significant in itself), so the text of these narratives, declaimed on a sober tone, is sometimes perceived as a sort of gloss on the musical score, a paraphrase of the discourse of the lute, or, in any case, a doublet of it. This explains the interpretation of a certain griot who accompanied himself on the lute. He announced each passage of the narrative and anticipated them with the appropriate musical theme and particular melodies, explaining after a few bars that "what you are hearing here is the drums," "here, it is the vultures that are feeding" etc. These were the only moments when the narrator, setting up a sort of doubling of his function, made himself the interpreter of what his fingers caused the lute to say.

But the lute can do more that just "speak"; just like the words of the griot, which "take hold of" the person whom they address, so does the lute exercise a power, an influence, over the listener. In fact the emblematic character of the melodies played on the lute confer to these tunes a double import: semantic, because they designate the heroes and their history (well known to the public), but also pragmatic because, in evoking in the listeners a shared emotion, an internalised exaltation, they plunge them in a kind of fervent communion, into a celebration of their cultural identity and the desire to perpetuate it. When one observes the attitude of every listener to the melodies of the *hoddu*, it becomes clear that the aesthetic conception of the process of musical creation mingles here with the semantic and pragmatic intention of the interpreted melodic phrase. Certainly, the art of every musician is recognizable in his ability to multiply the variations on the basic theme, to match words and music or to fill out the words with the notes of the strings etc. However, the admiration that a griot can arouse is measured essentially by the silent exaltation which he generates in the depths of the soul of everyone who, at that privileged instant, feels intensely that he is partaking in a community. He shares with this community the ideal of the *pulaaku*, the reference for his identity, for which the epic, as much as its melodies played on the lute, is one of the most effective cultural vectors.

4. The Lute

The importance accorded by the Fulani to the lute and to the *maabo* in their socio-cultural system is also evidenced by the place which these two subjects occupy in their literature. While the epic texts themselves provide evidence for this, a particularly significant characteristic, inherent in the epic genre and in the status of its performer, may be emphasized: every performance of an epic narrative by a griot constitutes in itself a genuine act of self-reference. Just by playing on his lute the musical motto of the hero and in declaiming his verbal motto, the narrator inserts himself directly into the narrative. As if playing the role of the hero's griot, he introduces from the outset a confusion of identities, times and deeds, which confers to the epic its ever immediate value and effectiveness.

Furthermore, in the *Geste of Ham-Bodêdio*[7] (one of the best-known heroes in the Fulani world) for example, some scenes are included in the narrative that recount the invention of the hero's musical motto and verbal mottoes. Here again, we see that the music precedes the words for the definition of the character, and that the *maabo* griot plays a major role in his destiny. In fact, it is usual in all epics that the narrator endows the griots taking part in the plot with a significant task in their roles as messengers, confidants, counsellors, negotiators etc. But it is, above all, their determining influence on the hero's fate that is in evidence when they impel him to action by playing his motto to him, or, on the contrary, in leaving their lute silent, they prevent him from launching into an adventure judged doomed fo failure. In the cycle of Ham-Bodêdio, this function of the griot is particularly well illustrated in the initial episode where the epic action starts effectively only after the hero is endowed with his musical motto.

This episode, presented at length by the narrator, conveys the supernatural character attributed to musical creation (for the translation of an extract, see the appendix below). In fact, because he has heard one night an unknown and unusual melody and not succeeded in discovering its author, Ham-Bodêdio orders all the griots of his fief, under the threat of death, to retrieve the melody — a melody which however none of them has heard. There follows a vain quest until the last of them, almost returning empty-handed, is hailed in the deep of the bush by the jinn which had created the melody and who reveals it to him in the course of a secret

---

[7]Ed. Seydou 1976 (with 2 disks). For the invention of the musical motto, see pp. 65-81; for that of the verbal motto, see pp. 299-309.

experience in the form of an initiation, following the most classic process, that is:

> – trial by ordeal: resistance to fear of strangeness, obeying the summons of the unknown, complete submission during the apprenticeship;
> – relinquishing the "old self": blind obedience to the injunction to break his lute and to forget all his prior knowledge;
> – reward and rebirth of the "new self": restoration by the jinn of a new lute extracted from a termite hill and, after the griot's lustration with magic spells, the gift of the sought-after melody.

The griot, a submissive pupil of the jinn initiator, then sees his fingers miraculously imparted with brand-new knowledge which will belong only to him ever after. And, having returned to the service of the hero, his master, he becomes that hero's official griot by virtue of having the musical motto.

In the same *geste*, another episode presents the invention of the hero's verbal motto. On the eve of a battle, having demanded a suitable motto, Ham-Bodêdio begins to slaughter the griots because every metaphor they proposed carried a possible negative interpretation. Finally, one of them discovers an image describing Ham-Bodêdio without any ambiguity and elicits his agreement at last. Not without winking to the audience, the narrator identifies himself with the triumphant and sole surviving griot, thus deliberately and explicitly entering the game of self-reference which we mentioned above. Nevertheless, this episode, with some tuned-down avatars in other versions of this epic, only appears to stigmatise the haughty, independent, violent, excessive and out-of-norm character of the figure in question, whereas the discovery of his musical motto appears to determine the whole epic narrative itself. In so far as there is no epic glorifying a figure for whom there is no musical motto, in fact, only those who have deserved one can be celebrated. And if one wants to narrate the glorious feats of a character whose "melody" one does not know, it is necessary to choose amongst the epic heroes available the one to whom this figure can be assimilated and whose musical motto can be used as a "signature tune."

Regarding the musical instrument itself, we cannot but mention a famous text, the *Fantang*,[8] which is illustrative of the importance of the lute, and which we mention here although it does not stem from the *Fulɓe* of Mali but rather from those of Senegal.

---

[8] See Ndongo Siré Mamadou 1986.

The term *Fantang* designates a particular melody constituting the official musical motto of the pastoral *Fulɓe* and of the *pulaaku* (or *pulaagu* in *pulaar* of Senegal). This melody, played by the griots, accompanies the narrative description of the first appearance of the musician-eulogist as a profession and of the institution of the relational system binding together *Fulɓe*, griots and craftsmen.

This legendary narrative, declaimed in the epic manner, begins with a long evocation — in motto form — of cattle, and then introduces three brothers, who own in common the herd inherited from their father. The eldest, Hammadi, then the youngest, Demba, find the profession of cowherding too tough; only the middle brother, Samba, decides to dedicate himself to it entirely. From then on, each of the brothers pursues his favourite occupation. The eldest, Hammadi, who spends the day wandering in the bush, provides his brother with wooden utensils for milking or watering his animals; he becomes the wood-workers' ancestor and stands here for the prototype of "caste-craftsmen." More complex is the narrative concerning the discovery and the appropriation of the lute, which will lead to the establishment of the status of the griot and of a new type of relationship between the middle brother, Samba, and the youngest, Demba. Of particular interest to us here is the supernatural character of the first appearance of the musical instrument:

> One day, Samba, lying under a baobab in the middle of his herd, is woken up by a vulture perched on the tree and playing the lute. Hurling a clod of earth at him, on which he has spat incantations, Samba makes the bird drop the instrument and he seizes it. Imitating the vulture, Samba takes pleasure in playing it until the day when, surprised by Demba and unable to resist his younger brother's entreaties, he hands it over to him. The latter, who has a fine voice, henceforth travels through the country, celebrating on his lute the cows and his brother the cowherd, in exchange for which he receives gifts and subsistence and becomes the prototype of the griot.

Other versions have Demba himself discovering the vulture, which, having drunk the milk from the gourds entrusted to his care, perches on a tree, draws a lute from under his wing and plays the musical motto of cattle. But it is always the brother Samba who deprives the bird of his instrument to give it to his younger brother, thus announcing symbolically the dependent relationship between the griot and the *Fulɓe*. In fact, Samba provides the griot Demba with not only the musical instrument but also, in his own person, the subject about which the griot performs his verbal art, that is, praise of the cow-herd and his cattle. Samba also provides Demba with the privileged addressee who, in exchange for his words, takes economic responsibility of him. Thus, when Demba wants to take a wife, he goes to solicit his brother's help to get the carrying ox required by custom. Samba then demands that, in exchange for his gift, Demba sings his repertoire to him.

It is, however, remarkable that the master of the lute in this narrative is a vulture, which, perched on a tree, plays it with skill to celebrate the cattle. While certain texts report that the lute is in itself a symbol of the original brotherly trio by way of the very elements which constitute it — the case made by the wood-worker, hide and strings from the animals of the herd, sounds from the fingers of the musician who makes it speak —, here one can find no mention whatsoever of manufacturing. It rather appears as a sort of magic object about which Samba (or Demba) has had a fortuitous revelation and which he has then forcibly taken from its owner, making it fall from the sky, as it were. Regarding the practice of the musical art, this follows the traditional technique of apprenticeship, with the musician striving to reproduce by himself the melody which he has heard played by the vulture. In one of the versions it is specified that this melody is in fact that of the *Fantang* and that the bird "sings in homage to the cow-herds." This music and song, which seem to be a sort of act of kindness on his part for the milk which he has just drunk to quench his thirst, produces total fascination over Demba, the future griot. No doubt this is a fascination of an aesthetic nature, but it is also much deeper, as this scene seems to foretell the destiny of the griot, praiser of the very people that he will strip of their goods.

Thus this legendary narrative presents the discovery and use of the lute as a preliminary step to the establishment of a social organisation depending on the distribution of functions that induce a distinction of status and the fixing of specific relations between the categories so defined. This quasi-mythical justification of the structures of Fulani society confers to the *hoddu* a determining role: it is from the lute's appropriation by the middle brother (who has chosen the tending of herds), then his handing it over to the youngest brother (who has a fine voice), that the whole system of relations between the *Fulɓe* and the "people of caste" originates, as well as the particular alliance of the *Fulɓe* and the griots.

It is clear then how intricately the status, attributes and role of the griot in the functioning of the social system, and above all the type of relation which ties him to the *Fulɓe*, are bound up with the form and function of the epic genre and most particularly with that which the musical interpretation of the lute represents in this society. Compared to other musical instruments, the lute constitutes the distinctive sign of the griot to which the *Fulɓe* obviously attach a specific importance in their "ideological" universe. Indeed, if the motto and the epic are the privilege of the griot, it is because, by means of their textual contents and their musical performance, they are so effective, the first on the person, the second on the community, due to the special power attributed to the words of the griot and the notes of the lute.

Conclusion

In the epic genre, characterised by the necessary association of a "prosaic," declaimed discourse and instrumental music entrusted to the lute, it has been seen that the latter is not just a simple musical accompaniment or aesthetic ornament of the narrative, but that it constitutes *per se* an entirely self-contained artistic and socio-cultural activity. This activity, having its own existence, doubles the expression of the words, and can even replace it at the functional level.

Furthermore, in the light of the texts mentioned above, the music of the lute takes on a particular dimension since here musical creation is given a non-human origin. And one cannot refrain from thinking on the one hand, *mutatis mutandis*, of the Platonic myth of inspiration, and on the other of the usual process of all initiation. As to the instrument itself, it has been seen that it was not considered the work of an artist or a craftsman, but the product of a revelation and hence of supernatural origin. Lute and music are clearly situated in the demonic universe, the use of such an instrument implying an incursion into the world of the unknown and an ambiguous relationship with occult powers. This gives a good insight into the images attached to musical art and to the power of those strings, whose effect is so strong on men's souls and which the griots alone — by virtue of their specific status, their training and their knowledge — can tame and use at will.

Appendix

From *La Geste de Ham-Bodêdio ou Hama le Rouge* (Seydou 1976, 71-76).

One night a jinn comes and sits in the hero's lobby; he starts playing a melody on his lute. Awakened by the music, Ham-Bodedio takes hold of a weapon and rushes down from the upper floor, where he was lying; the jinn stops playing. Ham-Bodedio goes back upstairs; he hears the melody again, goes down again and the same scene recurs three times; unsuccessfully. In the morning he summons all the griots of his fief and declares that he grants them one week to find the melody he heard that night: "If I have not heard it by next Thursday, in the evening no musician will be alive any more." All the griots set out in search of that melody, unsuccessfully. One of them Ko Birayma Ko, comes back, empty-handed too, when:

> He soon came where Black-River and White-River meet.
> A wooded earth-bank was there;
> A termitary stood on it.
> Soon he reached it and he was about to go beyond the place
> when the jinn came out and hailed him.
> As soon as he hailed him Ko turned his head.
> The jinn hid.
> Ko said: "Hallo, you!
> You who called me, whoever you are, if at least you had stayed here, I would see you!
> Nothing more can trouble a man doomed to die today!
> What is in store for me when I am back scares me much more than you, who called me and then hid!"
> And he proceeded on his way. The jinn hailed him again.
> He turned his head and saw him.
> His head reached the sky and his feet stood here on the earth.
> He did not hesitate for a second,
> he did not step back,
> without balancing or shuffling he moved forward
> till finally he bumped into him.
> The jinn rose and they were face to face;
> they greeted each other.
> The jinn said: "Ko Birayma Ko!" The latter said; "Yes!"
> He said: "I am the one who called you,
> this is only because, what you are looking for, is here in my own hand."
> Ko said: "And what is it I must look for?"
> He said: "A melody which was played in Ham-Bodêdio's lobby, in the night, last Wednesday, that is what you are looking for."
> Ko said: "That is right. That is what I must look for."
> The jinn said: "Sit down." He sat down.
> He pressed on the termitary, a lute came out of it; they tuned their instruments.
> They started to play the melody of Saygalare again and again.
> He said: "This is the melody you have been looking for. Now stand up and go!
> We, jinns, name it Saygalare.
> Everyone of God's creatures living here below, every son of Adam (i.e. every human) will hear it from you. Stand up and go!"
> Ko stood up;
> he left and went farther;

he sat down and started strumming the strings of his lute
and he realized that everything he had hitherto known by heart had de-
serted his fingers, all the more Saygalare! He realized that nothing was
left to him.
He turned round
and went back
where he had left him; he arrived and said to him: "Peace on you!"
The old jinn said to him: "Peace on you!" He said: "If you are not a
joker, what you gave me
let me know it
and give back to me what I used to have, and let me play the lute too!!"
The jinn said: "Ko!" and Ko said: "Yes!"
He said: "Raise your lute above your head, throw it and smash it!"
Ko hit his lute on the ground, the lute split.
The jinn pressed on the termitary;
a lute came out of it;
he pressed on the termitary and one more lute came out;
he pressed on the termitary and there was a spring, which came out of it.
He pressed on the termitary,
a bag of magic charms came out; he pressed on the termitary, a calabash
came out.
He took the calabash, he drew water from the spring,
he took the charms,
he untied them in the calabash, he told Ko to drink; he drank.
He told him to wash; he washed.
He told Ko to take one of the lutes; he took one of the lutes.
They played the first chords of Saygalare
and they started playing
more and more.
He said: "Ko!"
Ko said: "Yes!"
He said: "Stand up and go back!
Stand up and go! Now you have it!
No one will ever be able to take Saygalare from you; even I will not; nor
will anyone else.
You are the one
from whom every creature of God will hear it."

(Translated by Isabelle Trotte)

References

Camara, Sory. 1976. *Gens de la parole. Essai sur la condition et le rôle des griots dans la société malinké.* Paris, The Hague: Mouton.

Ndongo Siré Mamadou. 1986. *Le Fantang: Poèmes mythiques des bergers peuls.* Paris: Karthala-IFAN-UNESCO.

Seydou, Christiane, ed. and trans. 1972. *Silâmaka et Poullôri: Récit épique peul raconté par Tinguidji.* Classiques africains 13. Paris: Armand Colin.

————, ed. and trans. 1976. *La Geste de Ham-Bodêdio ou Hama Le Rouge.* Classiques africains 18. Paris: Armand Colin.

————. 1977. "La devise dans la culture peule: évocation et invocation de la personne." *Langage et cultures africaines. Essais d'ethnolinguistique.* Ed. G. Calame-Griaule. Bibliothèque d'anthropologie. Paris: Maspero. 187-264.

————. 1982. "Comment définir le genre épique? Un exemple: l'épopée africaine." *Journal of the Anthropological Society of Oxford* 13: 84-98. [Also in V. Görög-Karady, ed. *Genres, Formes, Significations. Essais sur la littérature orale africaine.* Oxford: Anthropological Society of Oxford.]

————, ed. and trans. 1991. *Bergers des mots: poésie peule du Mâssina.* Classiques africains 24. Paris: Armand Colin.

13 THE PERFORMANCE OF OLD NORSE EDDIC POETRY: A RETROSPECTIVE

Joseph Harris

The phrase "eddic poetry" refers to a collectivity conceived as a genre, but like the "ballad," at least the anglophone ballad, the genre's unity is a construction of recent times and reflects our sense of stylistic similarity among verbal objects of very varied origin, age, and *sitz-im-leben*. The term "edda" is used in one manuscript of the *Prose Edda* (also known as *Snorra Edda* or *Younger Edda*), where the initial rubric reads: "This book is called Edda. Snorri Sturluson has compiled it in the manner in which it is arranged here."[1] The chronology of Snorri's life (1178/79-1241) is usually interpreted as placing the composition of his Edda about 1223 or 1220-30. The application of this name (its meaning is uncertain and disputed) to the *Poetic Edda*, an anthology of poetry in two manuscripts of the late thirteenth and early fourteenth centuries, dates only from the seventeenth century and reflects the belief of antiquarians of that time that Snorri's "book called Edda" was derived from the poetic anthology (or its source), which was held to be older. Later scholarship reversed and/or complicated the relationships between the "younger" and the "elder" *Edda*.[2]

At the core of what is called "eddic poetry," then, is a metaphor, and the extension of the genre term to similar verse outside the *Poetic Edda* is a simile. By the broadest definition the term would apply to all verse in the four ancient meters of the North, *fornyrðislag*, *málaháttr*, *ljóðaháttr*, and *galdralag*. In practice, however, the reference is usually to the major anthology, the Codex Regius of the *Poetic Edda* or, by its official name, Gml. kgl. sml. 2365[4to], a manuscript returned to Iceland in recent decades from Copenhagen, its home since the mid-seventeenth century. Probably one of the most important anthologies in world literature, its approximately thirty poems pose great problems for the literary historian, among them just how many poems there are and what features they really have in common that justify, if they do, the common genre label. Perhaps the most important problem, that of the date or dates of the poems, is inextri-

---

[1]Faulkes 1982, xiii. For up-to-date references, see also Faulkes 1993.
[2]These literary historical relationships are clarified in general works such as Harris 1985 and 1984.

cable from the matter that concerns us here, their performance. For we must assume that eddic poems, though found in manuscript, laboriously transcribed, and edited for presentation to the modern reader in familiar-looking book form, were essentially a type of oral poetry. The logic for this claim does not depend only on their formulas and general resemblances to the kinds of poetry, especially epic, collected in oral situations in the field, though the eddic poems do resemble foreign oral poetries to a certain extent. Instead the conclusion of orality derives from certain elementary facts of the cultural history of the region. A brief rehearsal will help to set the scene.

Iceland was settled from Norway between about 874 and 930 and converted to Christianity in the year 1000 — according to the traditional chronology. Only then could writing in the usual sense have been introduced, for it is only a small exaggeration to say that the acquisition of literacy was a function of the introduction of the religion of the Book.[3] Literacy was slow in coming, however, and we learn nothing about any writing in Iceland before the winter of 1117-18 when the oral laws were copied down. Iceland's written literature, which is surely one of the greatest medieval literatures, begins to flourish late in the twelfth century, and the main manuscript of the *Poetic Edda* is part of this vibrant literary culture. Dating from about 1270, only a portion of its written sources can with certainty be traced back beyond Snorri, and then only to about 1200. But the poems anthologized here include archpagan masterpieces such as *Hávamál* and *Vǫluspá*, and even in the younger heroic poems there is no certain allusion to Christianity. So even without the evidence of language and the realia alluded to, most of which reflect the Viking Age and not the High Middle Ages, there would be a gap to be explained. The flourishing period of the pagan poems, not to mention their "origin", must have been before 1000. If they are oral poems, how did they resist the rule of renewal in oral literature, what Walter Ong calls "homeostasis"?[4]

An impressive recent study of a certain group of eddic mythological poems (Gunnell 1995) argues that they were dramatically enacted during the period of what I just called the gap and that our texts are actually transcriptions of recent performances. Though Gunnell's argument is inventive, I find this scenario difficult to reconcile with the new Christian culture which, in skaldic poetry, had suppressed allusion to the gods during the first century and a half. Albert Lord touched on this dilemma when he wrote: "The date of any *text* of an oral traditional poem is, consequently, the date of its performance, that being the date of its composition. The date of the *specific song* would be the date on which some

---

[3]On the native form of literacy in runes and its possible relevance to poetry, see below and Harris 1996 with references there.
[4]Ong 1982, 46-49.

traditional singer for the first time adapted existing themes and configurations to other specific people and events, that is to say it would be the date of the first performance. This is ordinarily beyond our ken."[5] Most scholars of eddic poetry could, I believe, agree with the latter part of this statement concerning the birth of a new "specific song," especially with the hopelessness of dating with any precision something "beyond our ken." In the first part of the statement dealing with transmission, "date of its performance" refers to a poem's most recent performance, and I believe that most scholars of eddic poetry would have difficulty in accepting this doctrine, with its fluidity and union of composition and performance.

Instead the eddic tradition has been regarded as a predominantly memorial one, where composition and performance can be distinguished from each other and where intertextuality can even include something like literary borrowings.[6] It must be admitted that before Parry and Lord eddic scholars unanalytically and unreflectingly applied assumptions derived from writing cultures, but since the 1960's an eddic scholarship informed by the Oral Theory has *nevertheless* concluded that the South Slavic slipper does not quite fit our princess. Earlier there were even efforts to explain some aspects of eddic tradition by means of the one type of writing that *did* exist in the North before Christianity, runic writing.[7] This native alphabetic system was used mainly for relatively brief inscriptions in stone, metal, and wood, but some scholars speculated that preservation of poetry in runes could explain what I called the cultural gap, and some slight support was offered by a few saga passages where poems are said to have been inscribed on rune staves, the most famous being Egill Skalla-Grímsson's *Sonatorrek*. The theory of runic transmission continues to lead a shadowy life in eddic scholarship, but it seems a little more plausible since the discovery in the 1960's of many hundreds of such rune staves in the Norwegian port of Bergen, a few of which do preserve poetry. The theory is perhaps due for a reexamination, but as of now it is still almost universally rejected.

So far I have touched on a number of eddic problems: 1) the codicology of the existing manuscripts and deductions about the written history of the poems; 2) the relation of that written history to the oral phase, and the role of writing, including especially runic writing, in the actual composition, as well as in the preservation of poems; 3) putative dramatic performance at the pre-literary stage; 4) formulas and oral composition in

---

[5] Lord 1993, 865; emphasis mine.
[6] Harris 1985 contains a summary of the history of research in this area; some of the landmarks are: Heusler 1941; Einarsson 1963; Lönnroth 1971; and Harris 1983. Very recently Acker 1998 gives a still fuller survey and builds new conclusions about the formula in eddic poetry.
[7] Reviewed in Harris 1985 and 1996.

the Lordian sense at that stage vs. deliberative composition and memorization. But I repeat that the eddic corpus is so heterogeneous that it may be that no generalizations beyond the circular ones concerning meter and diction may apply to all members.

Our understanding of the relationship of eddic verse to the other major form of poetry in Old Norse, skaldic, is of importance for further thoughts on performance. "Skald" is the normal Old Norse word for poet; like the West Germanic *scop/skopf,* this designation comes from the poet in his most dangerous role, that of scold and scoffer. Skalds were composers of satire and, especially, of its inverse, eulogy; and most surviving early skaldic verse is praise poetry fostered in the Norwegian courts or stylistically similar occasional stanzas. Though the skaldic corpus is much larger and even more varied than the eddic, it is the royal praise poems that best characterize the "genre" as a whole. Skaldic and eddic poetry are usually contrasted along the following lines: eddic poetry is anonymous, timeless, traditional, treating of legendary subjects, remote from life, often "epic" in that sense, while skaldic poetry is usually attributed to named poets who compete for attention and may influence each other, fixed in time and place, treating occasions such as praise of a king and therefore close to life, and rarely narrative. Yet recent scholars find many reasons to see the two "genres" as closely linked, mutually influential, often mastered by the same poets, and existing in a sort of poetic continuum. The much more copious information about the oral life of skaldic poetry supports deliberative composition and memorial transmission for eddic poetry and perhaps a level of individual creativity and application to life that the appellation "traditional" tends to underplay.

And what, finally, can we say about music in relation to eddic poetry? In the old literature skalds are never connected with harps, harping, or singing, and scholars like Heusler (1941) assumed that skaldic verse was by nature unsingable: the skald took his stand before his prince and demanded a hearing for the long eulogy he had composed in advance, and he declaimed it in a loud voice; or else he improvised, not always rapidly, a single stanza attached to some scene or action. Either way there was no room for music. The main references to the oral performance of eddic verse are a little more ambiguous on this subject. The poems recited at an Icelandic wedding in 1119 are not said to be accompanied, and the most remarkable feature of this performance is the embedding of the verses in prose sagas, their prosimetrical nature.[8] Another instructive passage, however, gives an extensive picture of a wandering minstrel who entertains with prose and prosimetrical narration, with eddic verse, and finally with harp music; but the music does not seem to accompany

---

[8] Harris 1997, 134-35.

the poetry.[9] Elsewhere the sparse references to harps and harping unassociated with song are rather unlike the picture offered by Old English verse and by the earliest continental references, where poetry and the harp go hand in hand.[10] A recent study of the performance of skaldic verse confirms the unmusical model,[11] but for eddic verse the orthodox view has probably been that while Old Germanic verse — in other words the lineal predecessor of both Old Norse and West Germanic poetry — was to some extent performed to the harp, the two arts detached themselves in the Scandinavian Viking Age. This would leave eddic and skaldic spoken poetry an unmusical island in a sea of oral performance where, most theorists would argue, "unsung" poetry must be derived by special (melody-deleting) development from normal song.[12]

Evidence for a contrary view might begin with the five known melodies to which examples of eddic and skaldic verse were apparently sung. But when? And how old is the music itself? Published in Paris in 1780 in Jean Benjamin de Laborde's *Essai sur la musique ancienne et moderne*, these tunes were collected in Copenhagen about 1778 from an Icelandic scholar, Jón Ólafsson frá Svefneyjum, who later published a book on Old Norse poetry wherein he makes it clear that he considers the old poetic language to be "the language of song," Danish *Syngesproget* (1786). A brilliant debunking study of this whole complicated affair was published by the contemporary Icelandic scholar Jón Helgason (1972), who concluded on a note of extreme doubt, even about the possibility that the melodies preserved something ancient. Jón Helgason whimsically compared the situation to a man who calls expectantly toward the cliffs: ancient Nordic? old Germanic? and gets back an echo, late Icelandic.[13] But Jón Helgason's skepticism is balanced by the equally brilliant affirmative studies to which he was replying, studies by the Germanic philologist Dietrich Hofmann and the medieval musicologist Ewald Jammers.[14] From their many-nuanced specialist examinations of the text-tune fit, the historical situation, and the tunes themselves, a layman may conclude that the late Icelandic custom of singing these old verses may have had medieval precedents and even that the preserved melodies may well, at least in part, represent evolved forms of medieval tunes. The fact that the circumstances around the choice of verses for Jón Ólafsson's performance raise suspicions can be divorced from presumptions about the age of the tunes and of the custom of singing similar texts. The Icelandic musicologist Hallgrímur Helgason is also emphatically positive

---

[9]Harris 1997, 133-34 and references there.
[10]Finnur Jónsson 1907-8; Andersson 1934.
[11]Gade 1994.
[12]See Nagy 1990, 30, 46-47; Hanson and Kiparsky 1997; Reichl and Harris 1997.
[13]Jón Helgason 1972, 47.
[14]Hofmann 1963; Jammers 1964; Hofmann and Jammers 1965.

about the age of the music.[15] Skepticism still seems the wiser course, but I do not believe that the last word has been said.

If eddic verse, or some of it, was musically performed in the medieval period, what did it sound like? Fashions will have evolved from the fifth and sixth century when Latin references to Germanic performances suggest (as *Beowulf* later does) that even a king might take up the harp (or properly the lyre) to sing an elegiac poem or that praise poetry was perfomed to the harp.[16] In fact one could argue that harp accompaniment does not at any time guarantee real singing in our sense of the word, and Jammers speaks chiefly of *cantillatio* (approximately *parlando*). Tuneful "singing" is mentioned in Norse sources, by the way, but the context is almost always one of magic. Instead the typical verb associated with the performance of eddic vese is *kveða*. This word is linked to *kvæði* and probably to *kviða*, both words for types of poems, but the verb *kveða* is also uniquely used in the modern language for the production — in a kind of half-singing or unaccompanied melodic recitative — of the long rimed romances called *rímur*. It seems, especially given Jammers's ideas about early Germanic *cantillatio*, that *rímur* melodies and manner of perform-ance may furnish better clues than the tunes of 1780. The oldest pre-served *rímur* texts are from the late fourteenth century, but the melodies are noted much later.[17] The *rímur* constitute a difficult subject for non-Icelanders, and it would probably be true to say that relatively little historical work on the field is also competent on the musical side of this musical-epic tradition,[18] but two books from the 1980's give a good musicological survey.[19]

I close by repeating that *if* Viking Age eddic poetry was, in its per-formance aspect, a purely spoken genre (whether simply recited or in some way dramatically declaimed), it stood rather isolated — isolated from its own Old Germanic ancestors and its West Germanic cousins and from its most immediate successor, the *rímur*, not however from its closest relative, skaldic verse. It seems possible that a narrow-ranged recitative-like performance style in Viking Age eddic verse would provide the logical and musicological links required to account for most, not all, the data. Modern recreations must of course be met by gratitude as well as skepticism.[20]

---

[15]Hallgrímur Helgason 1975; 1980, esp. 22-23.
[16]See, for example, Andersson 1934.
[17]Beginning in the late nineteenth century, according to Nielsen 1982, 29.
[18]For introductions, see Stefán Einarsson 1955; Hughes 1980. A brief older musicological study is Bjarni Thorsteinsson [Þorsteinsson] 1934.
[19]Nielsen 1982; Hallgrímur Helgason 1980.
[20]Recreations such as the musical one and the dramatic one offered at the conference: the five medieval Icelandic melodies interpreted by Anna Þorhallsdóttir, *Folk Songs of Iceland*

References

Acker, Paul. 1998. *Revising Oral Theory: Formulaic Composition in Old English and Old Icelandic Verse.* New York: Garland.

Andersson, Otto. 1934. "Nordisk musikkultur i äldsta tider." *Musik og musik-instrumenter.* Ed. Otto Andersson. Nordisk kultur 25. Stockholm: Bonniers. 3-23.

Bagby, Benjamin. 1995. "The Reconstruction of Eddic Performance." *Edda Eins: Geschichten und Gesänge aus dem Norden.* [A program.] Echternach: Editions phi.

Einarsson, Stefán. 1955. "Report on Rímur." *Journal of English and Germanic Philology* 54: 255-61.

——. 1963. "Harp Song, Heroic Poetry (Chadwicks), Greek and Germanic Alternate Singing: Mantic Song in Lapp Legend, Eddas, Sagas and Sturlunga." *Budkavlen* 42: 13-28.

Faulkes, Anthony, ed. 1982. Snorri Sturluson. *Edda: Prologue and 'Gylfaginning'.* Oxford: Clarendon.

——. 1993. "Snorra Edda." *Medieval Scandinavia: An Encyclopedia.* Ed. Phillip Pulsiano et al. New York: Garland. 600-2.

Gade, Kari Ellen. 1994. "On the Recitation of Old Norse Skaldic Poetry." *Studien zum Altgermanischen: Festschrift für Heinrich Beck.* Ed. Heiko Uecker. Berlin: de Gruyter. 126-51.

Gunnell, Terry. 1995. *The Origins of Drama in Scandinavia.* Cambridge: Brewer.

Hanson, Kristin, and Paul Kiparsky. 1997. "The Nature of Verse and its Consequences for the Mixed Form." In Harris and Reichl 1997, 17-44.

Harris, Joseph. 1983. "Eddic Poetry as Oral Poetry: The Evidence of Parallel Passages in the Helgi Poems for Questions of Composition and Perform-ance." *Edda: A Collection of Essays.* Ed. R. J. Glendinning and Haraldur Bessason. Winnipeg: U Manitoba P. 210-35.

——. 1984. "Eddic Poetry." *Dictionary of the Middle Ages.* Ed. Joseph P. Strayer. Vol. 4. New York: Scribners. 385-92.

——. 1985. "Eddic Poetry." *Old Norse-Icelandic Literature: A Critical Guide.* Ed. Carol J. Clover and John Lindow. Islandica 45. Ithaca: Cornell UP. 67-156.

——. 1996. "Romancing the Rune: Aspects of Literacy in Early Scandinavian Orality." *Atti: Accademia Peloritana dei Pericolanti.* Classe di lettere, filosofia e belle arti. Vol. 70, anno accademico 265 [1994]. Messina. 109-40.

——. 1997. "The Prosimetrum of Icelandic Saga and Some Relatives." In Harris and Reichl 1997, 131-63.

Harris, Joseph, and Karl Reichl, eds. 1997. *Prosimetrum: Crosscultural Perspectives on Narrative in Prose and Verse.* Cambridge: Brewer.

(Lyrichord Stereo LLST 7335); and the dramatic recitation of the eddic poem *Þrymskviða* by Benjamin Bagby of the early music group Sequentia (cf. Bagby 1995).

Helgason, Hallgrímur. 1975. "Upphaf íslenzkrar tónmenntasögu." *Saga Íslands* 2. Ed. Sigurður Líndal. Reykjavik: Hið íslenzka bókmenntafélag. 285-88.

——. 1980. *Das Heldenlied auf Island. Seine Vorgeschichte, Struktur und Vortragsform. Ein Beitrag zur älteren Musikgeschichte Islands.* Musikethnologische Sammelbände 4. Graz: Akademische Druck u. Verlagsanstalt.

Helgason, Jón. 1972. "Eddasång." *Gardar: Årsbok för Samfundet Sverige-Island i Lund-Malmö* 3: 15-49.

Heusler, Andreas. 1941. *Die altgermanische Dichtung.* 2nd rev. ed. Potsdam: Athenaion.

Hofmann, Dietrich. 1963. "Die Frage des musikalischen Vortrags der altgermanischen Stabreimdichtung in philologischer Sicht." *Zeitschrift für deutsches Altertum* 92: 83-121.

Hofmann, Dietrich, and Ewald Jammers. 1965. "Zur Frage des Vortrags der altgermanischen Stabreimdichtung." *Zeitschrift für deutsches Altertum* 94: 185-95.

Hughes, Shaun F. D. 1980. "Report on *Rímur* 1980." *Journal of English and Germanic Philology* 79: 477-98.

Jammers, Ewald. 1964. "Der Vortrag des altgermanischen Stabreimverses in musikwissenschaftlicher Sicht." *Zeitschrift für deutsches Altertum* 93: 1-13.

Jónsson, Finnur. 1907-8. "Das Harfenspiel des Nordens in der alten Zeit." *Sammelbände der internationalen Musikgesellschaft* 11: 530-37.

Lönnroth, Lars. 1971. "Hjálmar's Death-Song and the Delivery of Eddic Poetry." *Speculum* 46: 1-20.

Laborde, Jean Benjamin. 1780. *Essai sur la musique ancienne et moderne.* Paris.

Lord, Albert Bates. 1993. "Oral Poetry." *The New Princeton Encyclopedia of Poetry and Poetics.* Ed. Alex Preminger and T. V. F. Brogan. Princeton, NJ: Princeron UP. 863-66.

Nagy, Gregory. 1990. *Pindar's Homer: The Lyric Possession of an Epic Past.* Baltimore: Johns Hopkins UP.

Nielsen, Svend. 1982. *Stability in Musical Improvisation: A Repertoire of Icelandic Epic Songs (rímur).* Acta Ethnomusicologica Danica 3. Copenhagen: Forlaget Kragen.

Ólafsson, Jón (frá Svefneyjum). 1786. *Om Nordens gamle Digtkonst. Dens Grundregler, Versarter, Sprog og Foredragsmaade.* Copenhagen.

Ong, Walter. 1982. *Orality and Literacy: The Technologizing of the Word.* London: Methuen.

Reichl, Karl, and Joseph Harris. 1997. "Introduction." In Harris and Reichl 1997, 1-16.

Thorsteinsson [Þorsteinsson], Bjarni. 1934. "Folkelig Sang og Musik paa Island." *Musik og musikinstrumenter.* Ed. Otto Andersson. Nordisk kultur 25. Stockholm: Bonniers. 139-51.

14   REFLECTIONS ON THE MUSIC OF MEDIEVAL NARRATIVE POETRY

John Stevens

In this short paper I shall confine myself to Europe, mainly in the twelfth and thirteenth centuries. I shall sketch the north European scene in some of its teeming variety and try to give an idea of the many ways in which music and narrative were combined in the early Middle Ages.[1]

By the nature of the case the only evidence is *written*, in words or in notation. My reflections concern hence the extent to which written musical evidence can be used to reconstruct a picture of narrative singing in medieval Europe, particularly northern Europe in the period ca. 1100 to 1400. The basic questions to be answered are: How were epics and other long narrative poems performed? And what was the relationship between words and music in them? Comparative material provided by students of oral epics and ethnomusicologists might help to give an answer to these questions, but the questions remain nevertheless puzzling.

There is, of course, a large corpus of evidence other than notated music — the evidence of "literary" and non-literary texts which describe or refer to musical-social occasions. Some of them are tantalizing. One would give a great deal to have been present in the streets of Paris when "the voice of the minstrel sitting on the Petit Pont tells how the mighty soldiers of long ago, such as Roland, Oliver and the rest, were slain in battle, then the people standing around them are moved to pity and periodically burst into tears."[2] But this can, alas, never be! This whole textual side of the enquiry, which demands critical judgment and experience, has been explored at length by Christopher Page in his book *Voices and Instruments of the Middle Ages* (1987). It is full of fascinating material from romances, chronicles, sermons, treatises and other medieval sources, which, through Page's penetrating analysis, throw an interesting light on medieval performance practice.[3] But such evidence can of its nature never provide the music itself. It is the musical rather than textual evidence I want to turn to now.

---

[1] For a fuller presentation and discussion of medieval narrative melody, see chapters six and seven in my study of words and music in the Middle Ages (Stevens 1986, 199-267).

[2] From a thirteenth-century sermon as quoted and translated in Page 1989, 177.

[3] See in particular Appendix 2 in Page 1987 (pp. 151ff.), providing a "selective typology of musical references in French narrative fiction to 1300."

Notation and Layout

Practically all the pieces we have (fragments and whole melodies) are notated on a stave. On the face of it, this seems to imply that we know the pitches of the melody. Matters are, however, more complex. As we know from the transcription and notation problems encountered by ethnomusicologists, the rendition of a performed song in writing poses a number of methodological and practical problems. This applies also to medieval music; pitches and scales were variable, especially in monophony. Furthermore, when music of the kind we are looking for was written down, one has to ask for what purpose it was written down: Were the composers/scribes using known material, bringing it up to date perhaps? Or were they inventing it in the taste of the time? At any rate, we must conclude that the surviving evidence belongs to the world of art-music and is not on a par with ethnomusicological transcription.

In the thirteenth century, monophonic notations are mainly of an early quadratic/square type, based on the neumatic notations of previous centuries. This form of notation is almost entirely non-mensural; it is only occasionally (partially) mensural. This means that the melodies written down do not give us longs and shorts; that is, we do not know the rhythms intended.[4] Apart from the problems of notation — which give melodic outlines of only dubious precision and practically no certain rhythm — there are other problems in the transmission of musical material. There is little information on the instruments used; there is almost no indication of nuance, dynamics and style in general.[5] The textual underlay, on the other hand, is in most sources good; it is based on a syllabic style, i.e. one note or note-group per syllable.

Although there are a number of sources available for the study of narrative melodies, not a single one of them is what one would like above all to have — an epic poem with its music. Some of the musical evidence may well seem far-fetched and its relevance uncertain. However, it is all we have.

Types of Narrative Melody

The most obvious feature of narrative melody in the Middle Ages is that it consists of several distinct formal types. This may be the most important aspect of which we can be sure.

---

[4]For a survey of medieval non-mensural notation, see the sections III.1 and III.2 of the article "Notation" in Sadie 1980, 13: 344-62 [by David Hiley]. I have discussed problems of the interpretation of non-mensural notation in Stevens 1986, esp. 435-59.

[5]On the instruments, see Page 1987.

(1) The Recitation-Tone

This type of melody is best illustrated from the repertory of ecclesiastical, i.e. liturgical chant. From the earliest days of the Church, prayers and lessons were intoned to very simple formulas; psalms, to formulas only slightly more complicated. A reading-tone for a prophetic *lectio* from Isaiah can serve as an example: see Ex. 1. Principal features of this melody are its closeness to speech and inflexions of the voice and its infinite extensibility. There is no reason why such a melody should not continue for ever. It also stylizes a common intonation of European speech, the upward cadence of a question, the falling voice at the end of the sentence.

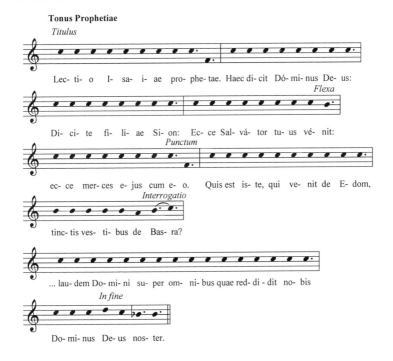

Ex. 1

I have often thought that certain religious poems, especially those in alliterative metres, such as even Langland's *Piers Plowman* from four-teenth-century England, might have been sung to the best known of all recitative chants, the psalm-tones. However, I must say that there is no firm evidence whatsoever that chant was ever so used in medieval England. We do, however, have evidence that the Old High German *Evan-*

gelienbuch (Gospel-book) by Otfrid of Weißenburg (completed between 863 and 871) was sung to the lesson-tones of the monastery of Weißenburg.[6]

(2) The Laisse-Type Melody

A *laisse* is a stanza of indeterminate length, held together by assonance or a single rhyme, and by a single melody or small group of melodies. It is the French *chanson de geste* stanza *par excellence* — for instance in the *Chanson de Roland*. But poems in *laisses* are not confined to heroic epic; the style is appropriate to sacred narrative too. Valuable information on the music of the *chanson de geste* comes from the medieval theoretician Johannes de Grocheio. In his treatise *De musica* (ca. 1300), he defines the *chanson de geste* in the following way:

> Cantum vero gestualem dicimus, in quo gesta heroum et antiquorum patrum opera recitantur, sicuti vita et martyria sanctorum et proelia et adversitates, quas antiqui viri pro fide et veritate passi sunt, sicuti vita beati *Stephani* protomartyris et historia regis *Karoli*.

> We call a song a *chanson de geste* in which the deeds of heroes and the achievements of our forefathers are recounted, like the life and sufferings of the saints and the conflicts and adversities which men of old endured for the faith and for the truth — the life of St. Stephen the first martyr for example, and the story of Charlemagne.[7]

He further says that the number of lines in a *laisse* of a *chanson de geste* is not fixed but variable and that each line should be sung to the same melody (*idem etiam cantus debet in omnibus <versiculis> reiterari*).[8]

There is some fragmentary musical evidence for Grocheio's single-line performance principle. One is a single-line *chanson de geste* melody quoted in *Robin et Marion*, a pastoral play from c. 1282 by Adam de la Halle: see Ex. 2.[9] A second example comes from a short narrative poem on the Battle of Annezin, a single *laisse* assonancing in *in*; at the end of

---

[6]On Otfrid's *Evangelienbuch*, see Kartschoke 1975, 271-339; on the musical performance of his work, see *ibid.*, 331ff.; Stephan 1956; Bertau and Stephan 1956/57; Jammers 1957; Jammers 1959; Bertau 1965; see also my discussion in Stevens 1986, 212-14.

[7]The text is from the critical edition by Rohloff (1972, 130); the translation is my own. For a corrected text and new English translation of key-passages from this treatise, see Page 1993 (this passage is found on pp. 22/23).

[8]Rohloff 1972, 132.

[9]On the music of the *chansons de geste*, see esp. Gennrich 1923; Gérold 1932, 79-90; Chailley 1948 and 1955; van der Veen 1957; Stevens 1986, 222ff. For my transcription of this melody and its source, see Stevens 1986, 224.

this poem we find the melody here transcribed as Ex. 3.[10] Complete poems in standard epic *laisses* with melodies attached are unfortunately non-existent. The rest of the evidence I shall bring is circumstantial. But it all tends to suggest (what certain texts alone also do) that the single melody could be interspersed or rounded off with one, or two, others.

Aud-di-gier, dist Raim-ber-ge, bou-se vous di.

Ex. 2

in   in   in   in   in   in   in

Ex. 3

A *laisse*-type melody is found in the delightful romantic tale *Aucassin et Nicolette* (late twelfth/early thirteenth century; it is a narrative in a mixture of prose and verse, appropriately called *chantefable* (or *cantefable*). The verse passages are sung, as illustrated by short-line *laisse* transcribed as Ex. 4.[11] The sophistication of the narrative borders on parody — in this case of the "arming of the hero." The refrain-line at the end *A la bataille!* is very much a *chanson de geste* (not a romance) feature. The arrangement of the underlay to the tripartite melody provided is not certain but my transcription AB AB...C is supported by other *laisse*-like songs.[12]

---

[10]Transcribed and further discussed in Stevens 1986, 224.
[11]See Stevens 1986, 226. On this *chantefable* and the mixture of prose and verse, as well as song and narrative verse, in Old French, see Butterfield 1997.
[12]For more examples, see the literature quoted in note 10 (and Stevens 1986, 227ff.).

Ex. 4

(3) The Lai-Type Melody

This is more "musical" again than the *laisse*. The form is closely related to that of the sequence (AA BB CC etc.) in which a new metrical form and a new melody is customarily invented for each strophe, but is freer. This so-called "lyrical" *lai* is to be distinguished from the octosyllabic, presumed spoken, *recited*, narrative *lais* of Marie de France and her contemporaries around 1200.[13] But it can itself tell a story and makes use in any case of what may be characterized as narrative-music idioms. On the basis of *lais* such as *Dolorum solatium, Samson dux* and *Omnis caro*, I would say that the *lai* when presenting a story prefers the dramatized narration. Not the dramatization of the speaker/singer himself but monologue or dialogue in a simple frame.

The "lyrical," i.e. in effect *musical, lai* as it survives with French and with Latin texts in northern Europe (as well as the German *leich*) is an elaborate *art-music* construct. It is the most ambitious of all medieval monophonic song-forms. One is struck by its manifestation of elaborate pattern, its contrived numbers, its "net," "mesh," of ever-changing, yet closely related syllabic melodies, its "aural geometry." But "net" and "mesh" are static images, whereas the *lai* is nothing if not dynamic. It owes its dynamic energy to the narrative element, the "narrative melody," as in the following examples. The first of these is taken from one of the northern French *trouvère chansonniers* of the later thirteenth century (MS. Paris, BN f. fr. 12615): see Ex. 5. This is the first strophe of the *Lai de Notre-Dame* by Ernoul le Vieux (or le Gastinois); it is composed of twenty-six short lines of six or eight syllables.[14] It has only three melodies — AB...BB...C —; many more melodies, however, are used in the course of this long piece. As can be seen, the melodies are of restricted range and stable in their tonality.

---

[13]For the lyrical *lai*, see the article "Lai" in Sadie 1980, 10: 364-76 [by David Fallows].
[14]Text and melody are edited in Jeanroy, Brandin and Aubry 1901, 33-37 (text); 106-13 (music).

Ex. 5

A second example — see Ex. 6 — comes from the *Canticum diluvii*, a widely known Anglo-Latin *lai* of the late thirteenth century. Its subject is the story of Noah's Flood, in the form of a dramatic monologue (in part) by God.[15] The extract given is from God's commands to Noah, telling

[15]It is anonymously transmitted in four manuscripts of English provenance: the Dublin Troper (MS. Cambridge, University Library Add. 710), MS. Paris, Bibliothèque Nationale fr. 25408, MS. Cambridge, Gonville and Caius 240, and MS. London, British Library Cotton Titus A.xx. See Stevens 1986, 144-55, where this Latin *lai* is compared to another important Latin *lai*, "Samson, dux fortissime"; on the latter, see now Stevens 1992.

him to get into the Ark quickly because He is about to flood the earth: in
the Ark Noah will find peace and salvation (stanza 10). Noah does what
he is told (stanza 11), and the rain comes (stanza 12). Stanzas 10 and 11
show a narrative melody characterized by a small melodic range and very
little variation. The melody for stanza 12 is more sweeping: one has the
impression that there is some melodic response here to the dramatic
situation in the enlarged range.

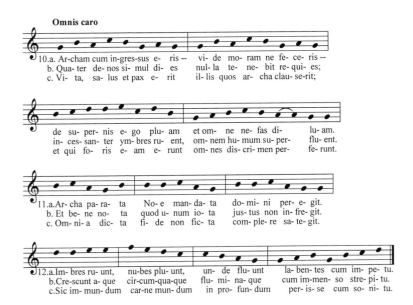

Ex. 6

(4) Strophic Melody

A fourth type is a story-song in which the same or nearly the same music
is repeated from stanza to stanza. This is the most frequently encountered
type of narrative melody in the Middle High German epic; most of the
melodies of the English and Scottish folk-ballad are also strophic.
Strophic song is at the other end of the scale from the recitation of chant.
An example is the *lai Voir Disant*: see Ex. 7.[16] It is unfortunate and quite
misleading that simple strophic narrative songs like *Voir Disant* are
named as *lais* in their medieval sources — the huge fourteenth-century

[16]The music of this *lai* is transmitted in two manuscripts (with different melodies), Vienna,
Österreichische Nationalbibliothek, Cod. 2542, and Paris, Bibliothèque Nationale, fr. 776;
for an edition of the text, see Fotitch and Steiner 1974, 78-84; of the music (from the Vienna
MS.), see *ibid.*, 160-61.

French prose romances. These four-line strophic songs are inserted into the prose narrative at relevant points. Formally they have nothing whatsoever in common with the *lai* proper, the "Paradestück des Minnesangs" (the showpiece of the [Middle High German] love lyric), as Wilhelm Scherer called it.[17] But *Voir Disant*, like other Arthurian romance songs, is long. It comes from the prose *Tristan* and in it Tristan complains against King Mark, "old, miserable and wicked." The music does not in itself in the least reflect the violent feelings expressed. It is rather "tuneful" in a very restricted range and in a popular mode of the period as regards scale and pitch-set as well as style. It should be noted, however, that this piece uses melodic idioms which are common in the *lai* proper (triadic formations on G, *ouvert* and *clos* form) and that it has the monorhymes associated with narrative.

Lai Voir Disant

---

[17]Quoted in Stäblein 1975, 95.

Ex. 7

In one of the manuscripts of the *Jüngere Titurel* of ca. 1270, a later expanded version of Wolfram von Eschenbach's fragmentary *Titurel* (ca.1170–ca.1220), the corrector has written out the so-called "Titurelstrophe" with its musical notes in the manuscript: see Ex. 8.[18] In this stanza a woman laments the pain her (presumed absent) lover is causing her.

---

[18]On this work, see de Boor 1967, 52-64. This voluminous verse epic, which has been attributed to Albrecht von Scharfenberg, is composed of over 6000 so-called Titurel stanzas and is transmitted in over 60 manuscripts. Of these, MS. Vienna, Österreichische Nationalbibliothek, Cod. 2675, from the beginning of the fourteenth century, contains the melody of the Titurel stanza; see the facsimile in Bertau and Stephan 1956/57, Plate 1 (facing p. 259) and their discussion *ibid.*, 262ff.; Stevens 1986, 216.

suf-czen trau- ren wai-   nen   wil ich han um ie- sen wer- den

rec- ken.

Ex. 8

I quoted Grocheio, the fourteenth-century theorist, earlier as linking
saints' lives together with *chansons de geste* as the two representatives of
heroic narrative. An Englishman, Thomas de Chobham, sometime around
1300, did the same. He speaks of three classes of entertainers (*histriones*)
— only a few from class 3 are up to any good: they are "the jongleurs
who sing the deeds of princes and the lives of the saints."[19] How then
were these sung? It was Jacques Chailley who first suggested that the
liturgy might provide the answer. My next example is an Epistle for the
Mass of St. Stephen's Day into which glosses in French verse
(monorhymed) have been interpolated: see Ex. 9. Chailley's transcription
comes from a Chartres manuscript (destroyed in the War). The French
opens with a very unliturgical, minstrel-like, address to the congregation:
"Seignors, oiez communement . . . ." The melody is rather *lai*-like in its
melodic phrasing, which is repeated throughout.

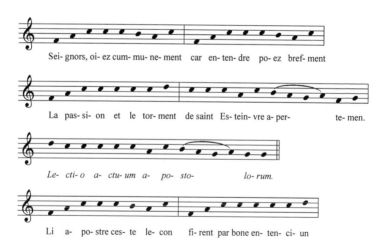

Sei- gnors, oi- ez cum- mu- ne- ment car en- ten- dre po- ez bref- ment

La pas- si- on et le tor- ment de saint Es- tein- vre a- per-   te- men.

Le- cti- o a- ctu- um a- po- sto-   lo- rum.

Li   a- po- stre ces- te le- con   fi- rent par bone en- ten- ci- un

[19]"Sunt autem alii qui dicuntur ioculatores qui cantant gesta principium et vitas sanctorum..."
(Broomfield 1968, 292).

de saint Es- tein- vre le   ba- run.

In   di- e-   bus   il- lis -

Em- prez le jor que Deus fu nez   et   por nous en- (ter- re) po- sez

fu saint Es- tein- vre la-   pi- de.

Ste- pha- nus ple- nus gra- ci- e etc.

Ex. 9

Finally, in some of the Latin church plays (in this case not properly to be called "liturgical dramas") we find long narrative structures serving dramatic purposes quite *un*dramatically.[20] My example comes from one of the Fleury St. Nicholas plays, *Tres Filie*. It tells the story of how St. Nicholas provides the three daughters of a poor man with a dowry (he hurls gifts of money through the window) and thus saves them from prostitution. From line 15 onwards the tune transcribed in Ex. 10 is used for the rest of the play (till line 168).[21] In this case the connection with known narrative types is two-fold: strophic, repeated about thirty times; and *laisse*-like, in its economical use of material which is almost stichic — not to mention its formal flexibility: it can be shortened if required.

---

[20]See further Stevens 1986, 255ff.
[21]For an edition and discussion of this Fleury play of St. Nicholas, see Young 1933, 2: 316-24; my transcription, with further notes, is found in Stevens 1986, 257.

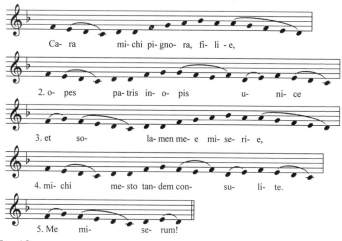

Ca- ra   mi- chi pi- gno- ra, fi- li - e,

2. o- pes   pa- tris in- o- pis   u-   ni- ce

3. et   so-   la- men me- e mi- se- ri- e,

4. mi- chi   me- sto tan- dem con-   su-   li- te.

5. Me   mi-   se- rum!

Ex. 10

Conclusion

My thoughts as I bring this paper to an end are of a kind that three days ago I could scarcely have conceived, unless purely intellectually. I have tried to give a condensed account of the genres of early medieval narrative music as they may be inferred from scanty surviving fragments and analogous material. To my knowledge no new evidence has turned up and no new hypotheses have been proposed over the last fifteen years. All the more illuminating, paradoxically, has been for me the experience of this symposium, the experience of hearing, and often seeing in action, the narrative musics of so many different cultures. In every case the gap between what has been performed and what could conceivably be transmitted by even the most sophisticated notation is unimaginably huge. The written record is a barren thing. No amount of new evidence of this kind could possibly provide the enlarged imaginative understanding of medieval European narrative song which we long to have. This may sound like a counsel of despair. But fortunately we can take consolation, and illumination, as I have, from what we can still glimpse in the rich mirror-images of living oral art worldwide.

References

Bertau, Karl. 1965. "Epenrezitation im deutschen Mittelalter." *Études Germaniques* 20: 1-17.

Bertau, Karl H., and Rudolf Stephan. 1956/57. "Zum sanglichen Vortrag mhd. strophischer Epen." *Zeitschrift für deutsches Altertum und deutsche Literatur* 87: 253-70.

Broomfield, F., ed. 1968. *Thomae de Chobham Summa Confessorum.* Analecta Mediaevalia Namurcensia 25. Louvain: Nauwelaerts.

Butterfield, Ardis. 1997. "*Aucassin et Nicolette* and Mixed Forms in Medieval French." *Prosimetrum: Crosscultural Perspectives on Narrative in Prose and Verse.* Ed. Joseph Harris and Karl Reichl. Cambridge: Brewer. 67-98.

Chailley, Jacques. 1948. "Études musicales sur al chanson de geste et ses origines." *Revue de musicologie* 17: 1-27.

——. 1955. "Autour de la chanson de geste." *Acta Musicologica* 27: 1-12.

de Boor, Helmut. 1967. *Die deutsche Literatur im späten Mittelalter: Zerfall und Neubeginn. Erster Teil: 1250-1350.* Geschichte der deutschen Literatur 3.1. 3rd ed. München: Beck.

Fotitch, Tatiana, and Ruth Steiner, eds. 1974. *Les lais du roman de Tristan en prose d'après le manuscrit de Vienne 2542.* Münchener Romanistische Arbeiten 38. München: Fink.

Gennrich, Friedrich. 1923. *Der musikalische Vortrag der altfranzösischen Chansons de geste: Eine literarhistorisch-musikwissenschaftliche Studie.* Halle an der Saale: Niemeyer.

Gérold, Théodore. 1932. *La Musique au moyen âge.* Les Classiques français du moyen âge 73. Paris: Champion.

Jammers, Ewald. 1957. "Das mittelalterliche deutsche Epos und die Musik." *Heidelberger Jahrbücher* 1: 31-90.

——. 1959. "Der musikalische Vortrag des altdeutschen Epos." *Deutschunterricht* 11: 98-116.

Jeanroy, Alfred, Louis Brandin and Pierre Aubry, eds. 1901. *Lais et descorts français du XIIIe siècle. Texte et musique.* Paris. [Rpt. Geneva: Slatkine, 1975.]

Kartschoke, Dieter. 1975. *Bibeldichtung: Studien zur Geschichte der epischen Bibelparaphrase von Juvencus bis Otfrid von Weißenburg.* München: Fink.

Page, Christopher. 1987. *Voices and Instruments of the Middle Ages: Instrumental Practice and Songs in France 1100–1300.* London: Dent.

——. 1989. *The Owl and the Nightingale: Musical Life and Ideas in France 1100–1300.* Berkeley: U of California P.

——. 1993. "Johannes de Grocheio on Secular Music: A Corrected Text and a New Translation." *Plainsong and Medieval Music* 2.1 (*Aspects of Medieval Song: Essays in Honour of John Stevens*): 17-41.

Rohloff, Ernst, ed. and trans. 1972. *Die Quellenhandschriften zum Musiktraktat des Johannes de Grocheio: Im Faksimile herausgegeben nebst Übertragung des Textes und Übersetzung ins Deutsche, dazu Bericht, Literaturschau, Tabellen und Indices.* Leipzig: VEB Deutscher Verlag für Musik.

Sadie, Stanley, ed. 1980. *The New Grove Dictionary of Music and Musicians.* 20 vols. London: Macmillan.

Stäblein, Bruno. 1975. *Das Schriftbild der einstimmigen Musik.* Musikgeschichte in Bildern 3.4. Leipzig: VEB Deutscher Verlag für Musik.

Stephan, Rudolf. 1956. "Über sangbare Dichtung in althochdeutscher Zeit." *Bericht über den Internationalen musikwissenschaftlichen Kongreß Hamburg 1956.* Ed. Walter Gerstenberg, Heinrich Husman and Harald Heckmann. Gesellschaft für Musikforschung. Kassel: Bärenreiter. 225-29.

Stevens, John. 1986. *Words and Music in the Middle Ages: Song, Narrative, Dance and Drama, 1050–1350.* Cambridge: Cambridge UP.

——. 1992. "*Samson dux fortissime*: An International Latin Song." *Plainsong and Medieval Music* 1: 1-40.

Van der Veen, J. 1957. "Les aspects musicaux des chansons de geste." *Neophilologus* 41: 82-100.

Young, Karl. 1933. *The Drama of the Medieval Church.* 2 vols. Oxford: Clarendon.